REPUBLIC OF

JIM WOLFREYS

Republic of Islamophobia

The Rise of Respectable Racism in France

HURST & COMPANY, LONDON

First published in the United Kingdom in 2018 by
C. Hurst & Co. (Publishers) Ltd.,
41 Great Russell Street, London, WC1B 3PL

Printed in the United Kingdom by Bell and Bain Ltd, Glasgow

A Cataloguing-in-Publication data record for this book
is available from the British Library.

ISBN: 9781849046886

This book is printed using paper from registered sustainable
and managed sources.

www.hurstpublishers.com

CONTENTS

ACKNOWLEDGEMENTS

I am very grateful to the editorial team at Hurst for inviting me to write this book and for their professionalism, patience and encouragement throughout the process. Particular thanks to Lara Weisweiller-Wu, who was a meticulous editor, and to Alison Alexanian, Alasdair Craig, Jon de Peyer and Daisy Leitch. My department at King's College London gave me valuable research leave and a travel grant. Edouard Morena provided detailed help with the manuscript, as did Megan Trudell, whose influence was indelible. Houria Bouteldja, Yasser Louati, Fania Noël, Ndella Paye and Omar Slaouti were very generous with their time and their insights, as were Denis, Meriem, Vanina and especially Selma. Thanks also to Sebastian Budgen, Hannah Dee, Stathis Kouvelakis, Yuri Prasad and James Wood. Throughout, I have benefited enormously from the tireless work of a number of engaged, French-based writers, notably Saïd Bouamama, Christine Delphy, Abdellali Hajjat, Marwan Mohammed and Pierre Tevanian, whose collective *Les Mots Sont Importants*, founded with Sylvie Tissot, has been a constantly useful resource. The book is dedicated to the memory of Julie Waterson.

INTRODUCTION

Emmanuel Macron's emphatic victory over Marine Le Pen's Front National (FN) in the 2017 presidential election, under the banner of the centre-right En Marche! movement, demonstrated two things. Firstly, that a majority of voters were not prepared to see an openly Islamophobic party with fascist roots take over the highest office of state; and, secondly, that over 10 million people were. This book examines the dynamic that has put Islamophobia at the heart of France's political agenda, tracing its origins and touchstones through an assessment of the relationships between the 'war on terror', authoritarian neoliberalism, republican secularism, inequality and anti-racism.

Across Europe, anti-Muslim prejudice has been reinforced by the global 'war on terror', its stigmatisation of Islam and demands for vigilance, monitoring and increased security.[1] In France Islamophobia has been fostered by a divided political elite that has used republican secularism, or *laïcité*, as a tool for putting Muslims under scrutiny and questioning their allegiance to the values of the Republic.[2] This has helped render the FN compatible with the mainstream, paving the way for its resurgence over the past decade. In an era of intense and rising inequality, the construction of moral panics, insecurity and scapegoats has found traction among social groups anxious about losing status and looking for someone to blame. Here the radicalisation of secularism, historically associated with progressive forces against reaction, has helped both divide and neutralise anti-racist groupings and institutions, hampering attempts to confront the rise of anti-Muslim sentiment. Away from the political field, however, and the vast array of hypotheses proffered about the 'true' nature of *laïcité*,[3] France nevertheless remains a multicultural society, if one in profound denial about it.[4] In this respect, the Islamophobic spiral described here, while marked by specific historical and contingent features, is neither unique nor irrevocable: the myths, premises and constructions it draws upon can be challenged, refuted and reversed.

The French 'war on terror'

In country after country the construction of a global Arab/Muslim threat has given rise to the identification of an 'enemy within' at home.[5] The French 'war on terror' predates 9/11. Its origins go back to the Republic's colonial mission, whose tropes and reflexes were revived in the early 1990s as the Algerian civil war spilled over into France, leading to an intensification of state security provisions and, as Paul Silverstein notes, 'the interpellation ... of Franco-Maghrebis as "Muslims", a hailing that has been abetted by the larger public drama around the hijab'.[6] As we shall see in Chapter One, the global escalation of anti-Arab/Muslim racism following the Gulf War, 9/11 and the invasions of Afghanistan and Iraq dovetailed in France with an increasingly persistent narrative dating back to the 1980s around the integration of immigrants and their descendants. This reached fever pitch with the various headscarf affairs that began in 1989 and produced legislation in 2004 and 2010 restricting what Muslims could wear.[7]

A shift in attitudes towards citizenship has taken place in twenty-first century France. As Vincent Martigny points out, debates about diversity and difference that had surfaced in the 1980s and 1990s have given way to a more accusatory stance that questions the 'authenticity' of certain categories of people when it comes to being truly French, notably those with an immigrant background, and Muslims in particular. This shift has been accelerated by a focus on incidents and episodes that have taken on the status of moral panic. The booing of the *Marseillaise* at a football match between France and Algeria the month after 9/11, for example, became a symbolic reference point that still endures today, signalling the threat to national identity posed by young people living in the *banlieues* (working-class neighbourhoods on the urban outskirts, also known as *quartiers populaires*). Subsequent episodes, notably around the hijab and the terrorist attacks of 2015–16, have reinforced this narrative and ensured, as Martigny notes, that the political field became dominated by a narrowly nationalistic approach. The paradox here is that French society as a whole was moving towards a recognition and awareness of difference, not reflected in political commentary. Here the FN's ability to exploit equivocation and assert a clearly defined position is a reminder that political actors do not simply reflect society, but attempt to assert an explanatory framework in order to seize the initiative and offer leadership.[8]

Internationally, post-9/11 preparations for war on Iraq saw the intensification of a 'clash of civilisations' narrative targeting Muslims. This depicted Islam as a block, impervious to progressive values, and fostered a climate of suspicion that saw Bin Laden's networks as the symptom of a wider problem.[9] Even before 9/11, Muslims in the post-Cold War era represented a new 'enemy within' seeking to impose sharia law on Western society. As an article in *The New York Times* put it in the mid-1990s, 'The Red menace is gone. But here's Islam'.[10] This was a sentiment that the Israeli government lost no time in turning to its advantage. 'After the fall of Communism,' argued the then

Israeli prime minister Shimon Peres, 'fundamentalism has become the greatest danger of our time.'[11] Israel and its allies could now depict opposition to settler colonialism as a manifestation of a new anti-semitism. One of Macron's first acts as president was to claim that anti-Zionism was today's form of a 'reinvented' anti-semitism.[12]

The neo-reactionaries

Domestically, these arguments have been taken up by a number of high-profile intellectuals and political actors and relayed by an enthusiastic media.[13] In a notorious 2006 article in *Le Figaro*, Robert Redeker attacked Islam as a religion based on a book of hatred and violence and warned that the West was under the kind of 'ideological surveillance' it had previously been subjected to by Communism. Islam, he went on, presents itself as 'the voice of the planet's poor'. Yesterday that voice came from Moscow, 'today it comes from Mecca'.[14] Despite Redeker's fears, there were plenty of voices on hand to denigrate France's poor, particularly those living in the *quartiers populaires*, or *banlieues*. Depicted as 'lost territories of the Republic',[15] these areas are routinely castigated as lawless zones inhabited by migrants (and their descendants) who come from North Africa bearing psychological baggage: pathological anti-semitism and the kind of licentiousness and misogyny that has traditionally characterised depictions of the savage 'other' in the colonial imagination.[16]

This kind of invective has not been the preserve of the right and the FN. Indeed, it has become the hallmark of an influential intellectual current known as 'neo-republicanism', an important impetus in the reactionary drift of mainstream debate largely driven by figures once associated with the left. Redeker, for example, was on the editorial board of both *Les Temps modernes* (co-founded by Sartre) and *Marianne* magazine. Individuals associated with neo-republicanism have managed to dignify essentially backward notions with the illusion that they belong within a progressive republican framework. This is partly because of their background as disillusioned Maoists or, in the case of Régis Debray, former Guevarists. Their trajectory is similar to that followed by former leftists like Bernard-Henri Lévy and André Glucksmann, who became known in the late 1970s as the 'new philosophers', united by melodramatic anti-totalitarianism and a craving for media attention.[17]

'Neo-republicanism', as Chabal argues, has shifted the 'transformative narrative' of French republicanism, characteristically associated with the left, onto right-wing terrain. Once a language of protest 'that demands change, or exhorts the state to be more faithful to republican values', it is now embraced across the political spectrum, not least by the Front National.[18] The 'neo-republicans', or 'neo-reactionaries' to use Daniel Lindenberg's term,[19] have made their influence felt most directly in making racism respectable in French society, a reality that Chabal largely overlooks.[20] Their strident, intolerant, vehemently Islamophobic take on republicanism has also played a part in opening the door of mainstream respectability to Marine Le Pen's Front National.

Two of the leading lights in this neo-reactionary constellation are well-to-do billionaire feminist Élisabeth Badinter and veteran media darling Alain Finkielkraut. In 1989 they helped launch an open letter to then Education Minister Lionel Jospin that likened permitting students to wear the headscarf in class to capitulation to Hitler.[21] 'We should not be afraid,' Badinter declared in 2016, 'of being cast as Islamophobes'.[22] Finkielkraut came to the defence of both Redeker's Islamophobic outpourings, noted above,[23] and the backward ramblings of the Italian journalist Oriana Fallacci, whose denigrations of Muslims (who breed 'like rats') were racist in the extreme.[24] Finkielkraut himself made a trenchant intervention during the 2005 *banlieue* uprising, which he described as an 'anti-republican pogrom' led by Muslims.[25] His other bugbears have included the '*banlieue* accent' ('no longer totally French'),[26] and the national football team, widely celebrated as a team of '*black-blanc-beur*' (black-white-Arab) players, but dismissed by Finkielkraut as 'black-black-black ... the laughing stock of Europe'.[27]

Ostensibly philosophers, the pair have been given a quasi-permanent media platform, which they have ruthlessly exploited to inject anti-Muslim prejudice into public debate. In this sense they are intellectuals for the shock-jock age, promoting a refined, republican version of the pop-culture Islamophobia peddled by more vulgar commentators elsewhere: a Left Bank Ann Coulter and the Glenn Beck of the Académie Française. Finkielkraut and Badinter's diatribes have been seconded by a range of other prominent anti-Muslim voices, from the 'progressive' gay rights activist and journalist Caroline Fourest to the reactionary sovereigntist Eric Zemmour, whose book, *Le Suicide Français*, became one of the best-selling examples of a developing genre in France, the catastrophe essay: lurid but ultimately dismal inventories of national decline.[28]

These currents have helped create a climate where, as we shall see, Islamophobia has flourished as a form of prejudice that emphasises culture rather than race, but transmits a message about race all the same. It is a climate where it has become acceptable for a president (Nicolas Sarkozy) repeatedly to castigate *banlieue* youth as *racaille* (rabble or scum) and to pontificate as head of state about Africans living lives shaped by the seasons rather than by history or modernity. A climate where Brice Hortefeux, then interior minister in a mainstream right government, was filmed referring to a young Arab activist at the party's summer university as a 'prototype', telling him, 'We should always have one. When there's one it's okay. It's when there's a lot of them that there are problems.'[29] A climate where a

Socialist interior minister, Manuel Valls, could declare that Roma people were not interested in integrating but instead created problems with local communities. Their role, he continued, was 'to go back to Bulgaria and Romania'. Their camps should be dismantled and they should be taken to the border.[30] A climate where a black justice minister, Christiane Taubira, architect of the gay marriage reform, has been compared by an FN electoral candidate to a monkey and greeted by children attending an anti-gay marriage protest in Angers with cries of 'A banana for the monkey!'[31] A climate where the newly-elected face of 'progressive' European liberalism, President Macron, can blithely offer up essentialist stereotypes about Africa's 'civilisational problems' being linked to high birthrates rather than the legacy of imperial conquest.[32]

Neoliberalism and Islamophobia

After more than a decade of protracted debate (since the first 'headscarf affair' in 1989) about Islam's role in French society, the mainstream right's decision to make republican secularism, or *laïcité*, the centrepiece of its legislative programme after Jacques Chirac's 2002 presidential election victory further eased the convergence of international and domestic trajectories of Islamophobia. The spiral has proven difficult to halt, let alone reverse.[33] This dynamic has been intensified by a chronic crisis of political representation, as parties attempt to shore up support for a faltering neoliberal project via scapegoating and stigmatisation.

Macron's victory was heralded internationally by liberal commentators as a ray of hope for the beleaguered pro-EU, market-friendly centre ground of mainstream politics.[34] But he is above all the telegenic symptom of a profound crisis of political representation. At the heart of this crisis is the break-up of the traditional social base of France's principal political formations, as the consequences of their affiliation to a neoliberal agenda play out. For the Socialist Party, it has meant implementing policies that drive against the interests of their working-class voters, a state of affairs that appeared to reach a terminal phase with the Hollande presidency (2012–17). Until that point, efforts to introduce 'flexibility' into the world of work had impacted mostly at the margins, affecting youth labour, the unemployed and part-time and temporary workers. With the Macron and El Khomri Laws, the Hollande administration took its programme of deregulation to the heart of the labour market, sparking a wave of protests, a heavy-handed police clampdown and an Occupy-style protest in the form of the *Nuit debout* (Up All Night) assemblies at the Place de la République in central Paris. The electoral cycle that ended in 2017 confirmed what had been true for some time, that the number one electoral choice for working-class voters was abstention. For most of the Hollande presidency their second choice was the FN. This development had sparked a debate within the Socialist Party, with some arguing that workers were effectively a lost cause and should be abandoned to the FN in order to focus on cultivating a more progressive, educated and socially mobile electorate.

This was part of a wider predicament for politicians across the spectrum, and not just in France. While the majority of political elites were won to a neoliberal economic outlook, propelled in most European countries by the dynamic of EU integration, electoral support for the project was fragile outside a hard core concentrated among one 'social liberal' section of the centre-left and part of the moderate right. These groups identified with the European project and neoliberalism but constituted a minority of voters: around a quarter of the electorate according to Amable and Palombarini. If neoliberal reform was to gain wider support and become the dominant project among voters (and wider society) then two alternative paths presented themselves: an emphasis on culturally progressive issues to win votes to the left, or a tougher line on social issues like immigration and national identity. Both options would depend on meeting basic economic expectations and delivering falling unemployment and increased purchasing power.[35]

The problem was not just that neoliberals were an electoral minority. They were also dispersed among parties. One survey of the 2015 regional election results estimated that an economically liberal outlook was shared by around half of mainstream right voters, a third of FN voters and under a fifth of left-wing voters.[36] So a major obstacle to the construction of a coherent and stable neoliberal bloc has been the left/right divide in French politics, a divide that has also hampered the emergence of other 'new' forces like the FN—hence both Macron's and Le Pen's persistent appeals to go beyond left and right. In contrast with the enthusiasm that greeted the victory of Macron's project among liberal voices in Britain, his government was elected in June 2017 by just 15 per cent of registered voters. Nearly half of the 8 million people who voted for him in the first round of the presidential election did so by default, to block another candidate.[37]

The right, too, has experienced long-term problems in reconciling the social basis of its electorate with its policy choices. Its traditional electorate is torn between those who want full-scale deregulation and market competition introduced throughout the economy and those who seek greater social protection. The result has been a stop-start approach to pro-market reform, which has often found itself blocked in practice by strikes and street protests. The difficulty of retaining existing electoral alliances, and of forming new ones, means that greater emphasis has been placed on themes that offer the possibility of extending electoral bases into new social groups. This, as Amable and Palombarini argue, explains why issues like immigration, national identity or *laïcité* have become such major preoccupations in French political life, overshadowing questions like taxation, social protection or the right to work.[38] Indeed, so inflated had the significance of *laïcité* become by 2003 that the Stasi Commission, which laid the basis for the 2004 ban on the hijab in schools, went so far as to claim, with an airy disregard for historical accuracy, that 'The French Republic was built around *laïcité*, which constituted one of its 'founding values'.[39]

A spiral has developed over the past three decades, with Islamophobia at its core, as political elites have attempted to compensate for a lack of positive affiliation to their core economic project by resorting to negative themes based on the scapegoating of immigrants, Roma people and Muslims. This spiral is discussed in Chapter Two. Some have argued that such an agenda cannot simply be understood as something foisted on a passive population from above.[40] Clearly the relationship between public opinion and elite agendas is more complex. As Amable and Palombarini argue, political action has to take existing expectations into account but over time also contributes to shaping these expectations, notably by influencing perceptions of what can or should be achieved by political actors. These constraints, once established, are then integrated by individuals and social groups into their political outlook.[41]

The politics of republican secularism

In some ways the 2017 presidential campaign offered small indications that the tide may have begun to turn against the kind of vulgar chauvinism that was a feature of the Sarkozy (2007–12) and, in a slightly more muted form, Hollande (2012–17) administrations. As we shall see in Chapter One, for a decade, between 2002 and 2012, Nicolas Sarkozy did more than any other politician to normalise racism in public debate. His attempt to win a third presidential nomination from his party, Les Républicains, saw this vulgar chauvinism escalate into an almost comical pastiche of republican nationalism. At one campaign meeting he declared that school students who didn't want meat at lunchtime (meaning Muslims who wouldn't eat pork) should not expect alternative dishes, insisting that they would instead have to order a double portion of chips. 'That's the Republic!' he thundered, preposterously.[42] In the contest for the nomination, Sarkozy was defeated by François Fillon, a hardline neoliberal social conservative who had prepared his campaign message in advance with a book, *Vaincre le totalitarisme islamique* (Defeating Islamic Totalitarianism).[43] Fillon benefited from a scurrilous campaign, which began on the far right, against his principal rival, veteran technocrat and Mayor of Bordeaux Alain Juppé, who was accused of planning to build Europe's biggest mosque in the city, and denigrated on social media as 'Ali Juppé'.[44] As things turned out, Fillon's campaign was completely overshadowed by the corruption scandal that engulfed him and his wife, rendering all other issues inaudible.[45]

Sarkozy's defeat was paralleled by that of the man who had taken up his mantle as most strident government advocate of the smack of an authoritarian hand when defending the Republic from its enemies. Socialist Manuel Valls had been interior minister and then prime minister under François Hollande. He suffered a humiliating defeat in the Socialist Party primary at the hands of a left-wing candidate, Benoît Hamon, who not only broke with the neoliberal authoritarianism that had gripped the Socialist Party under Hollande but also defied the Islamophobic drift that had destroyed the last vestiges of the party's anti-racist credentials. Asked what he thought of the nickname that his stance had earned him—'Bilal Hamon'—he replied that he took it as a compliment. His campaign was ultimately destroyed by the disintegration of the party in the face of the Macron surge as a wave of leading Socialists jumped ship to join the En Marche!

bandwagon. He just about managed enough votes to take him over the 5 per cent threshold ensuring state reimbursement of his campaign expenditure.

Hamon was overshadowed in any case by Jean-Luc Mélenchon, who persuaded a significant section of the left to campaign for a radical anti-austerity programme under the banner of the *Tricolore* flag and the *Marseillaise*. Mélenchon's message, standing in the name of La France Insoumise (Insubordinate France or France Unbowed), contrasted sharply with his 2012 platform in one important respect. The centrepiece of that campaign had been a speech in Marseille, where Mélenchon presented a stirring defence of France's long history of immigration, stressing in particular the role of North Africa in shaping the French nation. Despite his own support for legislation banning the wearing of the hijab in schools and the niqab in public, his 2012 campaign persistently castigated the far right for its stigmatisation of Muslims, comparing it with interwar anti-semitism. Interviewed during that year's parliamentary election campaign in the northern constituency of Hénin-Beaumont, where he had chosen to stand against Marine Le Pen, he was emphatic about his reasons for doing so:

> There were those among us who hesitated about standing, who said, 'You're going to narrow down our message.' I said, 'No, it's you who are reducing the meaning of the FN to a moral question.' The FN question is a social question, it's an ideological question. Either they win authority over the masses or we do. And the question will be: is it the banker or the immigrant who's responsible for the crisis? That's what's at stake here, in this place—and in the wider world.[46]

By 2017 Mélenchon's anti-racist message had been diluted. Where before he had praised immigration, now he denounced the practice of firms 'posting' workers from other parts of the European Union, undercutting the conditions of French workers. Where before he had castigated Le Pen's anti-Muslim rhetoric, his attempts to counter it were now more muted. In the first televised presidential candidates' debate he reminded everyone of his support for legislation restricting what Muslims could wear in public, thereby blunting his criticism of Le Pen's demand for a ban on publicly wearing the hijab. 'You can't police what people wear in the street,' he argued. 'But we already do in schools!' Le Pen replied. Where before he had addressed a left-wing audience, emphasising questions of class, he now addressed 'the people'.

The political scientist Laurent Bouvet argued in the wake of the 2012 campaign that the dynamic of Mélenchon's rise in the polls that year was broken by the Marseille speech. People suffering from 'cultural insecurity', those left behind by globalisation and multiculturalism, had turned as a result from Mélenchon to Le Pen.[47] For Bouvet, the defence of minority identities, whether ethnic, sexual or religious, was isolating white, heterosexual Catholics, making it harder for them to assert their own identity. 'Cultural insecurity' was a manifestation of the way they were being overshadowed by other claims and dominated. In 2017, Bouvet has noted approvingly, Mélenchon ran a 'patriotic campaign, directed at the French and not the left.'[48]

Bouvet's arguments were the expression of a rightward drift on the mainstream left. He was part of the Socialist Party's Gauche Populaire (Popular Left) current, warning that the party was abandoning the white working class. He was also a member of the Printemps Républicain (Republican Spring) movement, formed in 2015 by self-styled left-wingers claiming to defend the Republic from both the FN and 'political Islamism'. The movement's manifesto lamented the fact that republican secularism, or *laïcité*, had until a few years previously been a given, obvious to all, 'like the air that we breathe'. Now it had to be defended if it was to remain the 'cement' of the republican social contract. At the movement's official launch in March 2016, the kind of cement it was envisaging became clear. The Socialist mayor of the 20th arrondissement in north-eastern Paris, Frédérique Calandra, was enthusiastically received by the audience for defending the 'right to blaspheme', opposing the so-called 'Anglo-Saxon' model of multiculturalism and dismissing labels based on identity and the notion of an 'intersectionality' of struggles. 'Don't be afraid of the word Islamophobe,' she went on, 'because we are the bulwark against extremists'.[49] But if the Printemps Républicain viewed secularism as a 'permanent and living activity', its understanding of what it actually was appeared hazy.[50] 'As a practising Muslim,' declared Socialist Party official Amine El Khatmi, 'I keep the practising of my faith to the private sphere. In the public and political sphere, I only recognise the Republic.'[51]

In contemporary France this distortion of the 1905 Law of Separation between Church and State has become a commonplace way of defining *laïcité*. The original law guaranteed freedom of conscience. Today the republican secular tradition is invoked to call for bans on the hijab in public space, on the grounds that religious affiliation is something to be expressed in the privacy of the home rather than in society at large. As Chapter Three outlines, this is part of a deliberate attempt to shift the meaning of *laïcité* from a relatively open form of secularism to an exclusionary and often downright reactionary form of intolerance that unites hardline secular republicans across the political spectrum.

Opponents of this drift, like the historian of *laïcité* Jean Baubérot, point out that the 1905 Law of Separation and its pledge to defend freedom of conscience offers evidence that France's secular tradition is much more understanding, generous and tolerant than its narrow contemporary variant. But one of the elusive aspects of republican secularism is its presentation of an image of coherence and unity that is nevertheless shot through with tensions and contradiction. Of course, people claiming to uphold French values by bringing republican vigilance to bear on children's school dinner menus should be told that they've got secularism wrong. However, as Mayanthi Fernando points out, the history of secularism in France did not begin in 1905. *Laïcité* is also the history of republican state formation, of conflict and compromise with different groups, a history bound up with the mythology inherent in the creation of any national 'narrative'.[52] It is a tradition that involves both the separation and the interweaving of religion and politics.[53]

In the days evoked by the Printemps Républicain, when *laïcité* apparently came as second nature to all, the Republic organised separate Berber, Arab and Jewish legal systems in colonial Algeria. Today, no fewer than eight separate legal frameworks organise relations between state and religion in France.[54] Catholic festivals are celebrated with school holidays, but Muslim and Jewish ones are not. Secularism is not uniform but, in Fernando's words, 'fragmentary and unsettled', enhancing rather than diminishing its power, and that of the state, 'through a continual process of reiteration, rearticulation and regeneration'. Since the imperatives and norms of republican secularism are not a given, 'the secular formation called France must continually reconstitute itself as a cohesive entity, redrawing its boundaries and regulating its subjects.'[55] *Laïcité*, then, is as much about the overlapping of religion and politics as about their separation, 'about active state management rather than neutrality, and about the production and regulation of religious subjects rather than simply the guarantee of their freedom'. The ban on the hijab, like the state's creation of religious and cultural institutions for Muslims, does not represent a fundamental break with France's secular tradition, rather it is 'part of an array of disciplinary techniques aimed at cultivating secular religious subjects'.[56]

Inequality and anti-racism

What is at stake here is not just a matter of how to interpret secularism, or the relationship between universalism and particularism. The rise of Islamophobic reaction in contemporary France is about much deeper issues that cannot be resolved through words alone. This still-unfolding situation concerns more than just a debate over the historical management of public space in France. It is also about racism, colonialism and inequality, the generation of social insecurities, and the mobilisation of these fears behind authoritarian solutions. It is about how all of the above have converged to target French Muslims, disproportionately concentrated among the poorest section of the population.

France, as we shall see in Chapter Four, is a country of mounting inequality. Between 2000 and 2010, the average annual income for the poorest 10 per cent of the population rose by €400, or 5.3 per cent. Over the same period, the richest 10 per cent saw their annual income rise by 18.9 per cent, or €8,950. Disparities of wealth and income accelerated after the 2008 financial crash as the poorest 10 per cent collectively lost €520 million, while the wealth of the richest 10 per cent grew by €14 billion.[57] By 2010, the wealth of the richest 20 per cent was seven times greater than that of the poorest 20 per cent. This gap, as Savidan explains, is reduced by the impact of a redistributive social policy and by the welfare state, with the public sector playing a particularly important role in this process.[58] Deregulation and privatisation have made this safety net more fragile. Losing a job in France means that individuals then go through one of the longest periods of unemployment in any developed nation. Their previous status will have little bearing on the precarious and degraded forms of employment they are ultimately likely to find, with all the resulting financial and psychological consequences.[59] In 2006, 48 per cent of the population thought that they could one day become homeless. By 2008 this number had risen to 60 per cent.[60]

Awareness of inequality is growing. In 2013, 87 per cent of the population thought that inequality had risen over the previous five years, and 83 per cent believed that it would continue to do so in years to come.[61] At the same time, however, more people view social security as a problem, contributing to national debt, than as a solution.[62] The shift in such views, with less positive opinions recorded about the role of benefit payments, is paradoxical, but understandable. One of the consequences of neoliberal reform and austerity has been to erode faith in governmental solutions, weakening, by extension, a belief in collective solutions. This individualisation is part of the context for the rise in Islamophobia. Rising poverty and inequality have created a propensity for scapegoating that was not there before. Racist ideas may well have been widespread, as latent views or individual prejudices, but the construction of a political climate that condones and even encourages their expression creates a new situation. Political elites, then, do not simply reflect 'popular imagination' but 'participate in its construction', shaping rather than merely following opinion.[63]

This book argues that Islamophobia has been forged as a political and social reality by political actors, backed up by a chorus of neo-reactionaries and facilitated by an increasingly sensation-driven media. It is the product of political battles at certain key moments that have had an impact over time, in a context ruled by the 'war on terror', austerity and rising social inequality. At the same time, France has also seen some of the most emphatic rebuttals of neoliberal reform, and the birth of a social movement around the slogan '*Tous Ensemble*' (All Together). The fact that this movement has yet to converge with a developing current of political anti-racism is one of the preoccupations of Chapter Five. This book cannot resolve that question, but seeks instead to provide a resource for those who can.

1

STATE OF EMERGENCY

Something was out of kilter. Fifty world leaders had gathered on 11 January 2015 to commemorate the journalists killed in the *Charlie Hebdo* offices on 7 January and the police officer and shoppers murdered at a kosher supermarket over the following two days. 'I'm on my way to Paris to march with the French people,' David Cameron had tweeted that morning.[1] The leaders, like the unprecedented numbers that marched to express revulsion at the attacks, pledged unqualified allegiance to freedom of expression: 'I am Charlie'. But the heads of state did not march with the French people at all, instead linking arms for a brief 500-metre stroll in isolation from the rest of the crowd for the benefit of the media.[2] Their solidarity, however well intentioned, was symbolic, at one remove.

Curious dislocations like this were to permeate a year that had begun with the horror of the January murders and ended with the carnage at the Bataclan concert hall and surrounding streets on 13 November. When President François Hollande spoke in the aftermath of the November murders, he vowed that the forces of fanaticism and obscurantism would be defeated by the strength of the Republic: 'Those who fell on 13 November embodied our values. Our duty, now more than ever, is to breathe life into them.'[3] The state of emergency drew on legislation passed during the Algerian War in 1955. Police were given powers to search property and place individuals under house arrest without having to seek judicial authorisation. They were also able to prohibit public demonstrations and outlaw associations. Amnesty International noted the paradox inherent in measures that sought 'to suspend human rights in order to defend them.'[4] In the Rhône region the local prefect outlawed a climate change demonstration planned for the weekend of 28 November. 'All public events whose function is to protest or demonstrate are banned,' he declared. 'Sporting, recreational or cultural events', however, were not covered by the ban.[5] As some were quick to point out, the terrorists themselves had targeted precisely the latter kind of events, yet the authorities were clamping down on organic farmers and environmental activists.[6] What was going on?

The prominent and influential sociologist Emmanuel Todd saw the 11 January march as evidence not so much of dislocation but as the expression of a chasm opening up in French society. Although there was an obvious contradiction between the defence of a supposedly anarchist paper by crowds showing spontaneous support for the state and the police, something more fundamental was at play. According to Todd, 11 January represented the assertion of a sense of moral superiority by a dominant middle-class social group. The beneficiaries of globalisation were defending their privileges against the excluded, 'indigenous workers and the children of immigrants'. As such the mobilisation represented a moment of collective hysteria, underpinned by a radical form of rejection. In a country where mass unemployment hits youth of North African backgrounds particularly hard, and where discrimination disproportionately affects Muslims, the trumpeting of the right to blaspheme against a 'minority religion' was symptomatic of a repressed violence on the part of the demonstrators, the assertion of a form of domination: 'Millions of people came out on the streets to define, as a priority of their society, the right to pour scorn on the religion of the weak'.[7] Although Todd's analysis lacked nuance and suffered from a peculiar sociological determinism—reading current events through the static prism of historic affiliation to the Catholic Church ('zombie Catholicism')—his identification of a reactionary undercurrent in the 'Je Suis Charlie' phenomenon was both courageous and accurate. In the aftermath of the 2015 attacks, two powerful tendencies already at play in French society—authoritarianism and Islamophobia—were to escalate.

For many Muslims it was becoming uncomfortably clear what was going on. They were being made subject to greater scrutiny and suspicion. Three mosques were closed, an unprecedented move. The vice-president of the MEDEF employers' association, Geoffroy Roux de Bézieux, announced that his members had been advised 'to denounce to the police anyone on their payroll showing signs of radicalisation.' He confirmed that the question of imposing secular regulations in the workplace, in line with those in force for public servants, had been raised following the attacks.[8] In the Loiret region, south-west of Paris, the education authority issued a circular instructing head teachers to report any cases of parents wearing 'manifestly religious' clothing.[9] The authority was anxious that matters liable 'to threaten the values of the Republic' be reported. These included 'infringements of the principle of *laïcité*', or republican secularism. In theory this notion related to the state's neutral role in ensuring individual freedom of conscience and religious expression, by keeping matters of government separate from religious affairs. Increasingly it was being used as a means of policing the activities of France's Muslim population. In this instance, Loiret schools were explicitly requested to denounce any parent threatening this principle, notably via clothing that denoted a religious affiliation.

In keeping with the pattern of France's Islamophobic spiral, underway for nearly three decades but now accelerating alarmingly, there were calls for more such measures. As news broke of the November 2015 attacks, Lionnel Luca, a deputy for the mainstream right formation Les Républicains tweeted, 'Tonight Paris is Beirut! ... We'll pay a heavy price for our cowardice in the face of communitarianism!'[10] The veteran sovereigntist nationalist Philippe de Villiers took up the same theme: 'Immense drama in Paris, this is where leniency and the mosquetisation of France have led us'.[11] Others were more measured. 'For me,' declared former prime minister Alain Juppé, '*laïcité* means the freedom for all French people to practice the religion of their choice, including Muslims.' There was a catch, however. French Muslims could enjoy this freedom on condition that they 'clearly state that they have nothing to do with fanaticism, this barbarism, and that they subscribe fully to the values of the Republic.'[12]

The enemy within

In the febrile atmosphere that followed the November 2015 murders, government figures declared the atrocity an act of war. But who was the enemy? President François Hollande sent a dozen planes to Syria, dropping bombs on the Islamic State stronghold of Raqqa. Attention also focused on internal threats, real and imagined. Hollande announced proposals to tighten border controls, fast-track the deportation of foreigners suspected of posing a security threat, bar people from the country, boost police numbers, review the use of lethal force, and strip French citizenship from anyone with dual nationality convicted of terrorism. In attempting to maintain control, the government was playing a high-risk game, accelerating a drift towards authoritarianism.

Amnesty International again expressed concern at the way the situation was developing:

> Time and again we have seen emergency measures extended and codified until they become part and parcel of the ordinary law, chipping steadily away at human rights. In the long run, the pernicious ideology underpinning the Paris attacks can only be defeated by upholding the foundational values of the French Republic.[13]

These foundations, as we shall see, were shifting. In 2015 the prevailing view on how to respond to the situation opened up by the January attacks was expressed by Nathalie Saint-Cricq, political editor of a major national television station, *France 2*:

> It's precisely those who are not 'Charlie' that must be identified, those who, in certain educational establishments, have refused to observe the minute's silence, those who 'sound off' on social media and those who do not see how this fight is theirs. Well, they're the ones we need to identify, treat, integrate or reintegrate into the national community. And there, schools and politicians have a heavy responsibility.[14]

Muslims, in other words, could not be fully trusted. Did they really want to integrate? On 21 January 2015 President Hollande announced a major mobilisation of schools in defence of republican values.[15] Any student contesting these values would be reported to the head of the establishment who would then contact the parents and, if necessary, dispense sanctions. 'Every time ... a word is spoken calling into question a fundamental value of the school system and the Republic there will be a reaction,' he pledged.[16] 'Citizens' reserves' would be established, recruited from civil society, ready to intervene in schools. Pupils and parents would be obliged to sign up to a 'Secular Charter' and celebrate a 'Secular Day' on 9 December every year, the anniversary of the 1905 separation of church and state.

Meanwhile, a poster appeared on the government's 'Stop Jihadism' website directing citizens towards tell-tale signs of 'radicalisation', advising them to be on alert for changes in life-style—no longer listening to music (a distraction from the jihadists' mission); shunning old, 'impure', friends; changing eating habits (the illustration showed a baguette with a cross through it); or wearing different clothes (public attention was drawn in particular to girls who began covering up their bodies).[17] Ayméric Chauprade of the Front National, an advisor to Marine Le Pen and member of the European Parliament, took it upon himself to raise the stakes: 'We're told that a majority of Muslims are peaceful, certainly. But so were a majority of Germans before 1933 and national socialism.'[18] Marine Le Pen was quick to distance herself from such remarks. After all, her members had no need to engage in rhetorical excesses. As if to prove the point, Eric Ciotti, a deputy of the centre-right UMP (Union pour un movement populaire or Union for a Popular Movement), promptly tabled a bill that would withdraw child benefit from parents found to lack respect for 'the values of the Republic'.[19]

In the Paris suburb of Villiers-sur-Marne, the UMP mayor withdrew the Oscar-nominated film *Timbuktu* by the Mauritanian director Abderrahamane Sissako from the local cinema, on the grounds that it 'incited terrorism', seemingly having missed all of its previous showings in over 1,500 cinemas across France.[20] Within a week of the January attacks, over sixty Islamophobic incidents had been recorded.[21] Pigs' heads, firebombs and grenades were thrown into mosques, which were also targeted with gunfire. Muslim-owned businesses were bombed and there were reports of threats, racist graffiti and intimidation.[22] Lassana Bathily—a Malian national who saved a dozen customers from the anti-semitic attack on the Hyper Cacher supermarket—was granted fast-tracked French citizenship as recompense, along with a medal, at a ceremony attended by the prime minister and the interior minister. This did little to counter the daily insinuations that most Muslims fell short of such 'deserving' status. On escaping from the supermarket Bathily himself had been arrested and questioned by police on suspicion of being a terrorist.[23]

France's penal code defines 'apology for terrorism' as 'directly inciting or publicly defending terrorism'. By the end of January 2015 over 250 people had been accused of this offence. They included an eight-year-old boy who had announced at a school in Nice that he was 'with the terrorists', later confessing, when subjected to a police interview, that he didn't know what 'terrorism' meant.[24] In Nantes, a fourteen-year-old girl was put under investigation for 'apology for terrorism' after she told ticket inspectors on a tram, 'in a threatening tone', that she and her companions were the Kouachi sisters and were going to get out their Kalashnikovs.[25] In the same town, a sixteen-year-old was put under investigation after he put up a drawing on Facebook appearing to mock the *Charlie Hebdo* victims.[26] In Poitiers, a philosophy teacher was suspended from his post after complaints from parents. He had ventured opinions comparing Western imperialism to terrorism, drawing a parallel between French soldiers engaged in foreign interventions and terrorists. He too was later put under investigation for several weeks, accused of 'apology for terrorism' and remanded in custody for eight hours before the case was dropped.[27]

After the November 2015 attacks the spiral intensified again. In the southern French town of Béziers, Robert Ménard, the independent mayor with close ties to the FN, drew up a six-point charter for the imams of his town, making them promise not to establish links with extremists, put out calls for prayers in the street or preach in any language other than French.[28] He then issued an appeal for volunteers to help patrol the streets. 'Are you a former police officer, former gendarme, former soldier, former firefighter? Join the Béziers guard,' announced the posters displayed around the town. Unarmed, the foot patrol would be active for the duration of the state of emergency, guarding public buildings and schools and reporting suspicious activities.[29]

If Ménard's initiatives drew derision, other authoritarian proposals found wider support. Members of Les Républicains (as the UMP is now known) proved particularly imaginative in this respect. The deputy for Nice, Eric Ciotti (again), wanted to deprive those under house arrest of their mobile phones and internet access. Valérie Pécresse, head of the mainstream right's Paris list in the 2015 regional elections, called for the deportation of any foreigners on the intelligence services' notorious 'Fiche S', a list of around 11,000 people which included terrorism suspects along with political activists. 'The mere suspicion of radicalisation should, in the context of the state of emergency, lead to their exclusion,' she argued. 'They are foreigners,' she went on, adding, erroneously, 'they don't have a right to stay on French territory.'[30]

Her colleague Laurent Wauquiez was also concerned about the suspects listed on the 'Fiche S'. His solution? Set up anti-terrorist detention centres to house them all.[31] Proposed the day after the attacks and reiterated in the National Assembly, the idea provoked a certain amount of consternation. To those concerned about the threat posed to civil liberties by interning anyone who happened to find themselves on a list drawn up by the intelligence services, he offered the dubious reassurance that, 'It won't be Guantanamo, because we won't use torture.'[32] Three weeks later the Socialist prime minister, Manuel Valls, asked the Constitutional Council to consider the proposal.[33] As the historian Olivier Le Cour Grandmaison remarked, 'Last January the president and his ministers were commemorating "the spirit of Charlie", now eleven months later they're the spirit of the police.'[34] 'From now on,' wrote Matthieu Verrier in *La Voix du Nord*, 'it's about punishment, strengthening the state, not the spirit of 11 January.'[35]

Political responses to the attacks can be seen as an escalation of tendencies already at play in French society, as multiple narratives targeting Muslims came together. Islamophobia is not specific to France, indeed its manifestation shares elements common to many countries since the advent of the 'war on terror' and the targeting of Muslim populations as an 'enemy within'. As Arun Kundnani has shown, since 9/11 governments have drawn on an explanatory framework linking the origins of terror with an ideology rooted in a foreign culture, be it Islamist extremism or simply Islam. Like the Cold War notion of totalitarianism this framework establishes a causal relationship between belief in an ideology and acts of political violence. However crude, this link serves an important political function, obscuring the social and political factors that motivate terrorists, thereby absolving Western states of responsibility for generating violent conflict. Instead, explanations for the existence of such conflict are reduced to 'the content of an alien ideology'.[36]

In France, this explanatory framework draws inspiration not so much from the Cold War as from the country's colonial past. Since the turn of the century it has been given a powerful cutting edge by the development of a 'new secularism' discussed in the next chapter, that allows political actors to target Muslims by invoking the historic legacy of France's tradition of *laïcité*. The hardening of this legacy into a narrow, intolerant means of policing cultural practices associated with Islam has been pivotal to a process of racialising social relations in France. A number of mutually reinforcing dynamics are in play here as the trajectory of domestic political competition chimes with a wider geopolitical narrative. The stigmatisation of Muslim culture as some kind of barrier to integration and social mobility dovetails with the suspicion cast on Muslims as potential terrorists by the myth that a 'clash of civilisations' underpins the 'war on terror'. Each trope identifies Muslims as representatives of their religion rather than individuals in their own right. This essentialisation facilitates a kind of social discipline, casting doubt upon the desirability of their presence in France and invoking a need for suspicion and vigilance. Identification with Islam, in other words, marks individuals out as a potential 'foreign' threat, incapable of advancing, held back by a religion that breeds riots, terrorism and the subjugation of women. The problem, as mainstream parties are finding out to their cost, is that this kind of politics has no end point. Immigration? Law and order? Islamism? State of emergency? Burkini? Once set in motion, such issues, as we shall see, can develop or be constructed into moral panics with their own momentum, difficult to control, bolstering the impression that only the authoritarian outsider can provide solutions. It is no surprise that the Front National has achieved its highest ever scores in this climate, winning around a quarter of the total poll in the first round of every national election held between 2014 and the 2017 presidential contest, when Marine Le Pen won 21 per cent of the first-round vote.

In the early 1990s the FN had campaigned on a 46-point immigration plan, which included proposals to review cases of citizenship awarded since 1974 (when mass primary migration was ended), extend provisions to remove citizenship and call into question dual nationality. There was widespread alarm. Comparisons were made with the collaborationist Vichy regime during the Nazi occupation (1940–4). In 2010, Hollande's predecessor as president, Nicolas Sarkozy, had proposed stripping French citizenship from anyone of foreign origin who threatened the life of a police officer or gendarme. At the time, Hollande condemned the prospect as 'intolerable'. 'It's not France,' complained fellow Socialist Manuel Valls.[37] As his colleague Pascal Cherki pointed out, the precedent for such measures was indeed the Vichy regime, which had stripped Jews born in Algeria of their French citizenship.[38] 'How to defeat jihadism without repudiating ourselves?' asked one editorial.[39]

By 2016 a Socialist administration was proposing to dilute the historic perception that all citizens, whatever their origins, were equal before the law, with a measure that effectively made those with a foreign relative less equal than others. The state had already acquired the right to strip nationality from terrorists who had acquired French citizenship. Now, the government proposed its extension to those born in France. Former minister François Lamy underlined what was at stake: 'As a measure against terrorism it's ineffective so its value is only symbolic, and the symbol behind it is to call into question the *droit du sol*' (*jus soli*, citizenship rights based on birthplace rather than on parental citizenship—ties of soil rather than blood).[40] This proposal, and the accompanying discussions, offered an indication of how far public debate on migration, racism and citizenship had degenerated. Although eventually dropped when the government failed to secure enough backing for it, the proposal therefore also symbolised further concessions to the Front National. These, as we shall discover, are never cost-free. FN leader Marine Le Pen was fully aware of this, greeting the proposal with unabashed enthusiasm: 'When you see, in the space of a few hours, a President of the Republic take up the Front National's measures, there's an astonishing aspect to this, a homage to the FN.'[41] Indications of the dislocation between the government and the wider population, meanwhile, grew more evident. In July 2016, another attack saw eighty-six people murdered by a lorry driver who ploughed his vehicle into Bastille Day crowds in Nice. At a service in the city to commemorate the victims, Prime Minister Manuel Valls was openly booed and heckled by the crowd. By the end of the year Hollande, wretchedly facing up to his status as the most unpopular president since records began, announced his decision not to run for a second term, confessing in the process his regret at having proposed stripping dual nationals of their citizenship.

The Islamophobic spiral

Symbolic confrontations over *laïcité*, as Jeremy Ahearne notes, have produced 'an escalating pressure for demonstrable "restrictions"', locking politicians into 'a self-reinforcing process of bid and overbid'. This pattern had already been established with the 2004 ban on the hijab in schools. It signalled that Muslim culture was to be subjected to regulation and restriction, opening a space within which zealotry and racism could find expression. The repercussions of the law were to be felt for years to come. Competition between politicians over who could pose as 'the staunchest defender of an apparently beleaguered national principle' is ongoing.[42] Thomas Deltombe has traced the development and escalation of Islamophobia in France, examining the way it has been played out in the media. He shows how an 'imaginary Islam' was constructed, a 'community' of people uniformly ascribed the status of Muslim, whatever their actual relationship to Islam, and then counterposed to a notion of 'French' identity to which it was supposed to conform. The three stages of this process, from reactions to the Iranian revolution of 1979 to the Rushdie and headscarf affairs a decade later and the post-2001 'war on terror' era, reveal the mutually reinforcing dynamics of the construction of Islam as the primary international threat to the West following the end of the Cold War and the focus on perceived domestic threats to French values, notably *laïcité*, posed by Islam. Security and identity issues were merged into a single 'Islamist' threat, establishing a continuum that placed teenage girls who wore the hijab on the same spectrum as Islamist groups like the FIS (Islamic Salvation Front) party in Algeria or Al-Qaida.

A lurid and sensationalised vision of Islam was routinely depicted in the media, persistently linking Muslims to fanaticism, creating and reinforcing the notion that Islam posed an intransigent threat to Western values. When the Rushdie Affair broke, for example, it was presented by one national news network in the following terms:

> Good evening. This time, all of Islam is aflame. A little book written by Salman Rushdie, a British man of Indian origin, has been sufficient to

comprehend the gap that separates two worlds: on the one hand the Western world, our world, on the other hand the world of Islam, a billion people led by a strict religion.[43]

The Affair marked the point when the notion of a 'Muslim community' began to emerge, as attempts to construct and dramatise the 'Muslim problem' took hold in media representations of Islam. The construction of this threat was not the work of the media alone. In the following chapters we examine the role of political actors and public intellectuals in shaping and inflating it, and of economic and social factors in breeding an environment conducive to its reception. More suggestive elements have also played their part. Pierre Tevanian has identified the insidious role played by the use of opinion polls, illustrating how they do not simply record or reflect opinion but contribute to its production. He takes the example of an IFOP survey carried out for *Le Figaro*, which asked respondents if they thought 'the presence of a Muslim community in France' was 'a threat to the identity of our country' or 'a factor of cultural enrichment for our country' or 'neither one nor the other'. The question sets up an opposition between the 'presence of a Muslim community' and 'our country', the implication being that a distinct entity that is 'not ours' has been imported from elsewhere, producing either negative or positive results or neither. In reality, as Tevanian points out, Islam can produce a thousand reactions besides these binary alternatives on the part of Muslims and non-Muslims alike, including non-racist responses. The question as posed, by contrast, carries a latent or subliminal question: 'Do you know that Islam is a threat?'

The subsequent result, in this case the revelation that 43 per cent of the population consider Islam a threat, further bolsters the impression that there is substance to the idea. As Tevanian outlines, the constant repetition of the notion that Muslims pose a problem, often legitimised with reference to the 'groundswell' of opinion apparently confirmed by such polls, engenders suspicion and transforms subjectivity. This ultimately has an impact upon real-life interactions with Muslims. Opinions are not static, then, and nor is measurement of their emergence a neutral process:

> the expression of an opinion is not a simple and strictly individual phenomenon, but on the contrary an interaction, involving in a largely unconscious way, power relations, strategies of distinction and self-projection, questions of image, confidence and legitimacy.[44]

Although discriminatory measures are often presented in terms of the need to understand and act upon 'legitimate concerns' about immigration or 'communitarianism', politicians and the media neither simply reflect nor directly control opinion. It is mediated through the frameworks of different institutions, parties, associations, community groups and myriad other formal and informal networks. Its production is therefore complex and its development is not necessarily linear. An opinion's dominance can be reversed, challenged, stalled, entrenched, accelerated, overturned or escalated depending on particular contexts or interventions. But when discrimination becomes part of the fabric of the way institutions function, then its effects and justifications become harder to dismantle.

A defining aspect of French politics over the past decade has been the embedding of prejudice in the way state actors operate. As outlined in Chapter Four, a domestic social climate increasingly shaped by pessimism, uncertainty and insecurity, proved fertile ground for those seeking to identify scapegoats. Such efforts found an echo in much the same way as the 'clash of civilisations' narrative was able to exploit fears generated by the 'war on terror'. One of the central arguments of this book concerns the way in which the celebrated values and traditions of the French Republic have failed to prevent growing inequality and discrimination. Worse still, these values have been marshalled to justify stigmatisation of Muslim citizens. Politicians of all parties have played a part in the mutation of *laïcité* into a tool that hampers diversity in public space, based on increasingly arbitrary distinctions about how particular symbols or practices are perceived. Those wanting to escalate the debate have found that the possibilities for doing so are endless.

For months prior to the enactment of the 2010 law banning the covering of the face in public, the wearing of the niqab (full-face veil) and the burqa (full-body veil) 'on national territory' was identified as a significant threat, despite intelligence service findings indicating it to be an 'ultra-minority' practice. One report put the number of burqa wearers nationwide at 387.[45] The purpose of the law, and the protracted debate that led up to it, was not to facilitate social diversity but to stage an emblematic confrontation between republican secular values and an imagined threat from the arcane cultural practices of Muslims. As Ahearne notes, the symbolic value of the veil debate bore no relationship to the role actually it played in public life, which was negligible. What was required was not a real threat but 'a negative emblem around which a self-consciously lay republican coalition could coalesce'.[46] Open season was declared on the niqab. Radical left politician Jean-Luc Mélenchon called it an 'obscene garment'[47] and figures from across the spectrum lined up to argue that Muslim women must remove these 'muzzles', 'walking coffins', 'Mickey Mouse masks'.[48]

During the same year, praying in the street, the consequence of overcrowded mosques and a lack of suitable alternatives for prayer, also became an object of public scrutiny. Marine Le Pen said it made her feel as if she was living under an occupation. Within a year, Interior Minister Claude Guéant had outlawed the practice. An opinion poll in 2011 underlined the extent to which perceptions of cultural practices associated with Muslims were being magnified beyond reality. Respondents were asked how many streets in France were affected by the practice of praying outside on Fridays. The Conseil Français du Culte Musulman (French Council of the Muslim Faith) put the figure at under ten. Not even Marine Le Pen had ever suggested that there were more than ten or fifteen affected streets. Those surveyed gave an average figure of 185. When asked about the number of minarets, the average estimate was 191, with the actual number closer to twenty.[49]

The inflation of relatively insignificant acts into potential threats to 'republican values' has become intrinsic to the process of scrutinising cultural practices associated with Muslims, to the extent that even the most mundane of episodes possess the latent potential to develop into national scandals. In the 2012 presidential election campaign, both leading candidates, François Hollande and Nicolas Sarkozy, had devoted time in their speeches and interviews, and even the televised presidential debate, to the decision of a municipal swimming pool in Lille to allow a group of obese women (some of them Muslims) to be allocated a separate aqua gym class. The two candidates were extremely concerned at this apparent violation of secular principles, with Sarkozy identifying the swimming pool timetable as a threat to the Republic itself. Those advocating differences between men and women or non-compliance with the principle of equality had 'no place on the territory of the Republic'.[50] That the president of one of the world's leading economic powers felt compelled to set such store by the defence of mixed aqua gym classes in municipal swimming pools underlined the extent to which things were getting wildly out of perspective.

The episode also served as a reminder of the particular trajectory of French politics' authoritarian neoliberal drift: narrowing rather than expanding the terrain upon which state actors chose to assert their leadership. Never before, for example, had national political figures devoted quite so much attention to relatively obscure questions of diet. In autumn 2012 the conservative politician, Jean-François Copé, made the question of 'anti-white racism' a feature of his successful campaign for leadership of the UMP.[51] Addressing an audience in the south of France, he spoke up for his compatriots, for the families 'suffering in silence' with 'heads bowed', sometimes forced to move to a different area. He also brought to light a hitherto unremarked dimension of Islam's role in French society. Children, he revealed, were having their *pains au chocolat* snatched out of their hands at the school gates by Muslim 'thugs' who told them it was forbidden to eat during Ramadan. With no effective national challenge to such petty bigotry, the poisonous climate spread. Insulting acts that would once have invited scorn or ridicule began to be tolerated, even welcomed. Pork was imposed on school canteen menus.[52] Far-right activists, the self-styled '*identitaires*', began organising cocktail parties serving red wine and dried sausage ('*Apéros saucission-pinard*'). This crude anti-Muslim prejudice eventually found its way into the National Assembly, via the 'Popular Right' grouping of deputies within the mainstream right UMP party.

In 2012, Marine Le Pen announced her intention, should she become president, to ban halal meat from school canteens. The fact that virtually no school had ever adopted a policy of serving halal meat did not prevent Nicolas Sarkozy's prime minister, François Fillon, from warning that 'communitarianism' was putting the Republic itself in danger, musing that perhaps religions ought to show greater awareness of health issues and update their traditions in line with advances in science and technology.[53] Interior Minister Claude Guéant revealed that his opposition to granting immigrants the right to vote in local elections was motivated by fears that, if elected to local office, foreigners would make halal meat compulsory in school canteens or run swimming pools without taking into account the principles of 'diversity'.[54] In November 2013, when a court ruled that Muslim inmates at a Grenoble prison could be served halal meals, on the grounds that secularism meant that everyone should have the right to practice their religion, the Socialist government intervened to contest the decision, which was overturned the following July. Interior Minister Manuel Valls warned of the need to be vigilant, in a time of economic crisis, about anything that called into question 'our own identity' or gave the impression that 'fundamental principles' were being undermined. Secularism, he was at pains to stress, was one such principle.[55]

State institutions were also called upon to adjudicate trivial matters of apparel and uniform. Once the 2004 law had banned from schools any symbols or garments 'immediately recognisable for their religious affiliation', some took it upon themselves to provide students with an interpretation of what their clothes might denote. In spring 2013 a fifteen-year-old school student became the subject of a decision by the Council of State, France's supreme court, to expel her from college.[56] The reason? She had been wearing a long skirt over her trousers and a black headband between one and three inches wide that covered about a third of her hair. Her college's disciplinary panel believed the combination constituted a religious symbol and made her study in a separate room away from her classmates. She was not allowed to speak to her fellow students or take part in recreation. The parliamentary deputy for the area concerned raised the matter in the Assembly, arguing that a 'latent war' was taking place, waged by Muslim 'ideologues' who claimed to be fighting Islamophobia but were instead simply trying to impose their values on French society. Of course, if the outfit's meaning was subject to interpretation, then it is reasonable to question whether it could really be considered 'conspicuous'. As one Socialist deputy, Christophe Caresche, argued in the wake of the affair, the recurring debate over the hijab was less a sign of the rise of 'communitarianism' than a consequence of a narrowing of views around the question of identity in French society. This hardening of attitudes was producing an 'obsessive desire' to render invisible any sign of affiliation to Islam.[57]

After a decade and a half of such 'affairs', voices like Caresche's had become marginalised among mainstream parties. *Laïcité*, or republican secularism, is the principle of state neutrality, supposedly allowing for the expression of religious freedom in public space. Its implementation in schools was initially concerned with those working in public education in the late nineteenth century, as part of the Third Republic's efforts to shift control of education from the Catholic Church to the state. Today it has become increasingly directed towards school students and Muslim women. In the late nineteenth and early twentieth centuries, secularism was the cutting edge of anti-clericalism, deployed to break the hold of the Catholic Church and the influence of aristocratic elites over young minds. In the early twentieth century, the Socialist Paul Lafargue disparaged it as a way of getting 'workers to eat priests rather than eat capitalists'.[58] A century later, however, in the 'disenchanted' Republic of post-1980s France, secularism is being deployed to police the attire of high school students from the poorest sections of French society. If this is meant to incite people to eat anything, it certainly isn't priests.

State actors, meanwhile, have turned their attention to an apparently infinite array of trivial matters in order to uphold republican secularism. Their vigilance has meant that women wearing the hijab have found themselves barred from accompanying their children on school trips or working in nurseries. Interior Minister Manuel Valls personally intervened in March 2013 in the case of a nursery worker who had been sacked for wearing the hijab. Her dismissal was justified, he argued, because the headscarf remained 'an essential battle for the Republic'. And so it went on, with ever more surreal consequences. Members of the choir performing *La Traviata* at Paris' Bastille Opera in the autumn of 2014 refused to sing until a woman wearing a niqab, whom they had observed sitting in the front row during the first act, was escorted from the auditorium. On holiday from the Gulf and unaware of the law, she was ushered out during the interval.[59] The public-spirited chorists were themselves free to take part in the masked ball scene later in the opera thanks to the special dispensation written into the 2010 legislation that permitted theatrical performers to cover their faces.

States of exception

Tevanian makes a distinction between measures like the state of emergency, imposed on all for a limited duration, and an inverted state of exception imposed not in spatial or temporal but corporeal terms: the exceptional treatment meted out to those of the wrong colour or 'type', everywhere and at all times.[60] The convergence of security and identity issues following the 2015 attacks accentuated the state of exception already endured by Muslims in France. Pivotal to this convergence was the elevation of secularism to a central preoccupation of state actors, one requiring the permanent reinforcement of a security apparatus equal to the task of defending republican identity. The impact of this on Muslims had been noted in successive reports conducted for the National Consultative Commission on Human Rights (CNCDH). The CNCDH found Muslims to be the most stigmatised minority, subject to increasing mistrust.

Racist language, the reports noted, was becoming commonplace, feeding off the exploitation of issues like national identity, immigration and religion in political debate. Respondents were becoming more confident in expressing racist views. Anti-Muslim acts were also on the rise. Women were the primary victims, subject to 78 per cent of them, with those wearing the hijab the principal target of Islamophobic acts and discrimination—including a pregnant woman in the Parisian suburb of

Argenteuil who suffered a miscarriage following an attack in 2013.[61] Polarisation and distortion around questions of racism were underlined by a new phenomenon, the sense that 'the French' were the principal victims of racism, a view shared by 13 per cent of respondents in 2013. The CNCDH also noted the development of 'ethnocentric authoritarianism', drawing parallels with Adorno's studies of the phenomenon in 1950s America and linking rising ethnocentrism to 'a desire to impose the dominant norms of society on the other—"other" by their origin, religion, culture but also their sexual practices—by force if necessary.'[62]

Islam is France's second religion, although the number of French Muslims is often overestimated. The figure is most frequently put at 5 to 6 million, with more careful estimates ranging from 2.1 million to 4.2 million. In other words, it is generally assumed that France's 'Muslim population' equates precisely to the numbers of people of North African background living in France. 'Islam', then, frequently describes a diverse and huge population of individuals who happen to be Muslim as if it were a homogenous entity. Such essentialisation underpins the construction of the 'Muslim threat'. There is no more a fixed identity that can be labelled 'Islam' in France than there is a single entity that can be called 'French'. The history of immigration and citizenship in France shows that it is possible to exist in more than one culture, that identity is a fluid concept and that individuals engage in multiple relationships with society that can contradict, modify, reinforce or transform a sense of self.[63]

Reducing Muslims to an identity defined primarily by their religion and calling upon them to conform to 'norms' arbitrarily imposed by the 'host' nation impacts upon both perceptions of Islam and France itself. The republican model of citizenship, historically based on shared identification with a set of political values, is becoming more and more aligned with ethno-cultural notions of Frenchness, which emphasise differences based on religion, culture or 'tradition' that might threaten national identity. The persistent implication that there is something innate to Islam rendering Muslims incapable of assimilation gives credence to the notion that they represent an 'enemy within'. In 2012 Interior Minister Claude Guéant explicitly endorsed the notion of a 'clash of civilisations', announcing that he considered some to be superior to others. French civilisation, for example, respected women more than others—such as, by implication, Islam.[64]

In the wake of the 2005 uprising in the so-called *banlieues*, (literally 'suburbs', but very often specifically working-class suburban neighbourhoods), this narrative converged with longstanding colonial stigmatisation of the 'Arab male', discussed in Chapter Four. As the journalist Slimane Zeghidour pointed out at the time, such essentialisation revealed more about Western attitudes than about Islam:

> There's a kind of intellectual fundamentalism (among Westerners) that confines the Muslim to his origins. When they see him, they don't say he's perhaps a free thinker, an agnostic, a freemason, a communist, an atheist... No, it's a Muslim! Whatever he can do (play the piano, ride a motorbike, fly) is explained by Islam![65]

By the early twenty-first century, in a country with intensifying inequalities and stalling social mobility, the ability to portray working-class youth from the *banlieues* as prisoners not of poverty but of culture was a powerful political tool. If it could be established that they were held back by religion rather than inequality or oppression, then social relegation could be presented as their choice, their fault. As Arun Kundnani points out,

> Culture here plays the same role as race: a hidden force that underlies a whole people's behaviour; a single rule that can be applied everywhere to explain anything that Muslims do. According to the culturalists, Muslims live hermetically sealed within their homogenous culture,

> their lives entirely determined by it, whereas Westerners exist outside any specific culture in the universal space of modernity. In the West, people make culture, in Islam, culture makes people.[66]

The notion of a clash of civilisations did not emerge in France with the 'war on terror'. It had long been an integral part of the French colonial project, justified in terms of France's 'civilising mission'. Once the colonies had gone, 'postcolonial melancholia',[67] morbid resentment at the loss of empire, was to be embodied firstly by the Front National and then by a mainstream right eager to shake off its 'complexes'. FN founder Jean-Marie Le Pen had served France in the independence wars in both Algeria and Indochina, defeats that, by his own admission, determined his entire subsequent political engagement.[68] In the 1980s he emerged at the head of a party that had developed a strategy of projecting racial prejudice onto cultural issues, stressing that it was not racism that motivated its anti-immigration policies but recognition that Muslims could not be assimilated. This displacement has proven so effective that it is now embraced across the French political establishment. The emphasis on culture has the great advantage of producing the same outcomes as more overt discriminatory language but without unseemly allegations of racism clinging to those articulating it. The new racism is genteel and respectable, providing users with a sophisticated upgrade on the old while operating in a similar way.[69] Metonymy, for example, the use of objects to symbolise or embody race without having to spell out their meaning, is simply applied to a different set of things. 'Cultural tropes,' as Kundnani points out, 'such as wearing a hijab have come to serve as twenty-first-century racial signifiers, functioning in ways analogous to the more familiar racial markers of "color, hair and bone" that W. E. B. Du Bois identified.'[70]

Conclusion

Confronting Islamophobia in contemporary France is not straightforward. The very term is contested. In 2013 Manuel Valls brought his authority as interior minister to bear on the question. 'Behind the word "Islamophobia,"' he revealed, 'we must see what is hidden. Its origins show that it was fabricated by the Iranian fundamentalists in the late 1970s to shame women who refused to wear the veil.' The term, he went on, was simply 'a Trojan horse' used by Salafists 'to destabilise the republican pact'.[71] Such claims, frequently and energetically propagated by the feminist and gay rights campaigner Caroline Fourest and lazily repeated by media and politicians alike,[72] had one major shortcoming. They were completely false. Abdellali Hajjat and Marwan Mohammed have amply demonstrated the mendacious character of the narrative peddled by 'progressive' intellectuals such as Fourest and the growing breed of 'new reactionaries', whose role we discuss in the next chapter. The word 'Islamophobia' does not even exist in Persian, or Arabic. Its origins can instead be traced back to the language used by French colonial administrators in Africa at the beginning of the twentieth century, who cautioned against both Islamophobia and Islamophilia.[73]

For the authors of a 'counter-enquiry' drawn up more or less explicitly to undermine Hajjat and Mohammed's work, even if Islamophobia can be identified as a concern among certain layers of the population, 'the phenomenon remains marginal, and it's not by artificially inflating it that we will manage to eradicate it.' Kersimon and Moreau acknowledge that the story of the anti-feminist, fundamentalist origins of the term Islamophobia is nothing more than a 'fiction', although they do not pause to consider why prominent intellectuals and politicians should seek to discredit the naming of anti-Muslim prejudice with fake arguments. They fall back on another well-worn refrain, according to which the use of the term serves to inhibit anyone merely seeking in good faith to offer criticisms of Islam as a religion, rather than of Muslims themselves. Hence they identify a tendency 'to consider the slightest tension with regard to the Muslim religion, at best as an unconscious manifestation of xenophobia, at worst as a camouflaged form of racism'.[74] Kersimon and Moreau therefore dismiss 'Islamophobia' as a vacuous notion built around the paradigm of scapegoating, part of a multiculturalist outlook that tends to underestimate the social problems caused by the rise of Islamic fundamentalism and downplay fears of Islamic terrorism as a 'security fantasy'.

Islamophobia is an international phenomenon, but there are reasons why France's Muslim population has suffered such a powerful backlash. The renewed emphasis since the 2015 Paris attacks on inculcating respect for 'republican values' in schools, punishing those alleged to defy them, fast-tracking those accused of 'apology for terrorism' through the courts, and increasing surveillance and 'vigilance', is unlikely to prevent such atrocities from happening again. It will instead exacerbate a process that predates the attacks, a process of marginalisation that has seen France's Muslim population stigmatised, essentialised and racialised. The problem we are dealing with here goes beyond the embrace of bigotry by individual politicians or the suspension of human rights under the guise of defending them. The Islamophobic spiral detailed in this book is the product of a series of political processes that have dovetailed in contemporary France. These can be summarised as follows:

- the stigmatisation of Muslims as an 'enemy within' in the context of the 'war on terror', drawing on residual colonial tropes;
- the adoption of an authoritarian, neoliberal outlook by France's two major political currents (until their wipe-out in the 2017 presidential election), the post-Gaullist right and the Socialists;

- an increasingly intolerant and ethnocentric interpretation of republican secularism as a 'respectable' tool for stigmatising and disciplining France's Muslim population;
- growing social polarisation, structured by inequality, producing fear and insecurity and providing a context for scapegoating and racism;
- the incapacity of the established institutions of mainstream or 'moral' anti-racism to counter Islamophobia, and the inability of the radical left and wider anti-racist movement to mount an effective challenge to this drift.

The following chapters examine these factors, beginning with an assessment of the role of authoritarian neoliberalism in reshaping party competition, entrenching a 'respectable racism' in public debate, and uniting mainstream political actors around the shriveling parameters of an increasingly intolerant republican nationalism.

2

MAKING RACISM RESPECTABLE

5 May 2002. On a cold and wet spring evening Jacques Chirac greeted the enthusiastic crowd gathered to celebrate his presidential election victory over Front National leader Jean-Marie Le Pen. '[France] has refused to succumb to the temptation of intolerance and demagoguery,' he declared,[1] his notorious tirade a decade earlier about the 'noise and smell' of France's scrounging immigrant population merely a distant memory. Chirac took on this new role—republican bastion against racist adventurism—with the same cheery bonhomie that had characterised all the other incarnations he had adopted over his career. He was both the inheritor of the great Gaullist mantle of leadership over the French right and a pioneer of neoliberalism in France. For over three decades he had made himself busy either embracing or evading these legacies, his presence mutating from dynamic ambition into aloof ineffectiveness over the twelve years of his two terms in office. As president, he was criticised for failing to stand up to an increasingly assertive social movement and disparaged as the 'Resident' of the Republic.[2] Some of the sharpest attacks were to come from within the ranks of his own party,

notably from Nicolas Sarkozy, who embraced frank and unequivocal ambition with a zeal unmatched by any politician since Chirac himself. Soon after the latter's re-election, it was Sarkozy who became the dominant personality of the French right. Under his leadership, it was to embrace greater intolerance and demagoguery than anyone had thought possible on the night of Chirac's victory.[3]

This chapter looks at the way that authoritarianism and racism intensified and reinforced each other in French politics from 2002. This process has not been straightforward. Attempts to impose a neoliberal agenda have been persistently challenged over the past two decades by France's so-called social movement, a powerful combination of trade union militancy and grassroots activism that emerged in the mid-1990s. The movement defied the development of a cross-party policy consensus in the political mainstream around key economic and social issues. Below, we assess the causes and implications of this consensus: the erosion of longstanding ideological reference points and the narrow focus of political responses to chronic inequality around forms of scapegoating and discipline. Pivotal to this process in the decade that began with Chirac's 2002 victory was the figure of Sarkozy, pursuing with a compellingly kitsch and charismatic theatricality an agenda that sought not to undermine the FN but to displace it, that sought not to oppose the FN's politics but to absorb and transcend them. The embrace of racism by mainstream parties was justified by the need to 'respond' to public concerns about immigration and threats to national identity. As we discuss in Chapter Five, the process was bolstered by the complicity of the left as the latter prioritised fidelity to republican secularism over the defence of stigmatised minorities. In government from 2012 the Socialist Party adopted an increasingly authoritarian approach to resolving political and social questions, resulting in Prime Minister Manuel Valls' efforts to incorporate the state of emergency into the constitution and inaugurate a permanent state of exception.

A political elite in crisis

The isolation of the French political elite is part of a generalised problem. As Peter Mair puts it: 'The age of party democracy has passed. Although the parties themselves remain, they have become so disconnected from the wider society, and pursue a form of competition that is so lacking in meaning, that they no longer seem capable of sustaining democracy in its present form.'[4] During the 2017 electoral cycle, the two biggest parties—Les Républicains and the Socialists—failed to make the second round of the presidential election. In the parliamentary elections in June, over half the electorate did not vote in the first round, with nearly 60 per cent abstaining in the second. The Socialists lost around 90 per cent of their deputies, the party's worst ever performance; Les Républicains fared worse than during their 2012 defeat by François Hollande's Socialists, losing close to half their seats in the process. The most successful formation, the victorious President Emmanuel Macron's La République En Marche,[5] won around 75 per cent of seats in the National Assembly, but with a first-round mandate that amounted to less than 13.5 per cent of registered voters.[6]

Various factors mean that the crisis of party politics has been particularly acute in France. Historically, parties are weaker here than in other leading economies. The French right has no equivalent to the Conservative Party, a fixture of the British establishment for the past 150 years. In the modern era, the closest France came to having a dominant party of the right took the form of Gaullism, which emerged as a major force in the immediate post-war period. Since then it has gone through several revamps, adopting a neoliberal stance from the mid-1980s and changing its name in 2015 from the Union for a Popular Movement (UMP) to Les Républicains. Over the past decade, parts of the rival coalition of centre-right parties (formerly the UDF) have joined the Républicains, leaving behind the small Democratic

Movement (Mouvement démocrate) led by François Bayrou. The left, divided between Socialists and Communists for most of the twentieth century, returned to power under François Mitterrand in 1981 after twenty-three years of right-wing rule. The Communist Party, the largest political party in France in the immediate post-war period with a million members and close to a quarter of the electorate, was part of the 1981 government, leaving in 1984 following the turn to austerity. Today, unsure whether to throw in its lot with the radical left or operate as a satellite of the Socialist Party, it is increasingly irrelevant.

However, the long-term weakness of political parties and institutions in France does not explain their present predicament. Since the 1980s there has been a more or less continuous widening of the gulf between parties and population. Within two years of Mitterrand's 1981 victory the Socialists had adopted austerity measures as recession set in, ushering in three decades of structural unemployment that continues to run at levels of around 10 per cent. The Socialist Party subsequently devoted itself to a form of neoliberal managerialism that gradually eroded links with its activist base and severed connections with working-class areas. It adopted a cynical approach to anti-racism. Aware of a growing movement developing in the early 1980s among racialised youth eager to confront prejudice and discrimination, it established the SOS Racisme association, and put considerable resources into ensuring that it became the dominant national anti-racist organisation, propagating an integrationist republican message that stressed the capacity of immigrants and their descendants to 'become French'.

This emphasis was significant. Although bearing an ostensibly positive message—'there's nothing to fear from immigrants because they can be just like us'—the focus on integration implied a lack, a reproach directed at immigrants, whose position on the other side of a dividing line between 'national' and 'foreign' was constantly invoked. At stake when it comes to integration, as Abdelmalek Sayad argues, 'is the very legitimacy of the "immigrant" presence', a reflection of 'the generalised suspicion that attaches itself to any presence perceived as "foreign".' Ultimately, the demand that immigrants and their descendants integrate was an impossible one, its achievement always out of reach. The question became a moral injunction, a burden, turning a social problem into a depoliticised, individualised, technical question.[7]

The success of SOS Racisme meant that the Socialists were able to absorb and neutralise the black and Arab-led grassroots anti-racist currents that had begun to gain national prominence by the early 1980s, diverting their radicalism and anger towards the less threatening terrain of affiliation to the republican model of integration. At the same time, the Socialists failed to act on promises to extend rights for immigrants (like the right to vote in local elections), offered little or no opposition to racist right-wing policies and, with their fixation on 'integration', made a major contribution to fostering the notion of an immigrant 'problem'.

By the 1990s, the gulf between political elites and the rest of the population had widened. Over the course of the decade each major party achieved its lowest ever share of the vote. The two main political formations appeared to have lost their sense of purpose. Jacques Chirac, architect of the neoliberal turn undertaken by the French right in government between 1986 and 1988, found himself obliged to change tack in 1995 when challenged from within his own party by a rival presidential candidate, Édouard Balladur, running on a pro-market platform. Chirac chose to emphasise the need to heal France's 'social fracture', winning the election on the promise of 'A France For All'. The slogan then blew up in his face when his prime minister, the humourless technocrat Alain Juppé, introduced sweeping cuts to jobs and welfare on taking office. Millions mobilised in the biggest wave of strikes and demonstrations since 1968, forcing Juppé into a humiliating climbdown.

The emergence of the 'social movement' in the mid-1990s marked a sea change in French politics, challenging the orthodoxies of the 1980s. Neoliberalism and its imperatives—cutting welfare, fostering job insecurity and driving down wages—were powerfully contested by a series of revolts. These have continued intermittently ever since, via protests against homelessness, unemployment and racism and major mobilisations against labour and pension reform. Corruption scandals hit every major party during the 1990s, with Chirac himself heavily implicated, contributing to a sense of crisis that was further accentuated when Chirac blundered into calling early parliamentary elections in 1997, throwing away his parliamentary majority as the hapless Juppé lost out to the Socialist Lionel Jospin.

During Jospin's term as prime minister between 1997 and 2002, at the head of a 'plural left' coalition government with the Greens and the Communists, the Socialists articulated a vague aspiration to represent the aims of France's 'social movement'. Jospin's meek preference for 'a market economy without a market society' underscored his inability to contest the neoliberal dynamic driving policy.[8] Amid growing awareness of social inequality, the administration chose to deal with its consequences by emphasising a theme generally associated with the right: law and order. Interior Minister Jean-Pierre Chevènement, along with SOS Racisme founder Julien Dray, an enthusiastic convert to the security agenda, sought to present the latter as a republican issue, arguing that insecurity was a form of inequality. This shift, emphasising repression rather than education and bringing the Socialist Party into line with neoliberal authoritarianism, was justified in 'progressive' republican terms. Security was a left-wing concept, claimed Chevènement, because the Declaration of the Rights of Man put 'safety' on a par with liberty. The Jospin government's focus on 'urban violence', as Loïc Wacquant has underlined, was less about a surge in juvenile delinquency than a redefinition of the role of the state:

> A Keynesian state, vector of solidarity, whose role was to thwart the cycles and ravages of the market, to ensure collective 'well-being' and reduce inequalities, is succeeded by a Darwinist state which makes a fetish of competition and celebrates individual responsibility, whose flipside is collective irresponsibility, and which withdraws into its hypertrophied regal functions of maintaining order.[9]

This backfired spectacularly. Despite Jospin's attempts to promote Chevènement as the public face of austere republican discipline, the right and extreme right were always going to outflank the left on their natural terrain of law and order. The Socialists contributed not just to their own defeat, but also to an incipient climate of moral panic around the question of insecurity, the ramifications of which continue to reverberate today. In the cataclysmic first round of the 2002 elections, Jospin was pushed into third place by Jean-Marie Le Pen. The results sparked a remarkable wave of vehement and exuberant nationwide street protests, many involving school students. The demonstrators were outraged at the Le Pen score but unsure as to what solutions to offer beyond a reluctant vote for Chirac in the second round stand-off with Le Pen, their discomfort expressed in the caustic slogan 'Rather the crook than the fascist!'

The defeat of Le Pen was followed by the right's victory in the June parliamentary elections. Jospin's successor as prime minister, provincial party notable Jean-Pierre Raffarin, attempted to style himself as a man of the people representing 'the France from below'. The people themselves took to the streets in their millions in 2003 to oppose his pension reforms, a movement that outstripped even 1995 in scale. On four separate occasions more than 2 million people took part in nationwide demonstrations. Strike days were five or six times in excess of those recorded in

1995. Although eventually defeated, the mobilisations developed significant activist networks, forging links between trade unions, grassroots associations and radical left activists. 'It's not the street that governs,' Raffarin had famously declared during the 2003 conflict.[10] But the street had nevertheless asserted, as the conservative *L'Express* magazine put it, a capacity to 'counter-govern'.[11] In the spring of 2005, the social movement's ad hoc networks were to form the backbone of an extraordinary campaign to oppose the constitutional treaty for the European Union. This was put to the vote in a referendum and defeated, despite a concerted 'Yes' campaign by the two major parties. The radical left's assertion that the proposed constitution represented an intensification of market encroachment on the life and society of ordinary people became the dominant argument of the campaign, overshadowing the FN and sovereigntist racism.

In the wake of this defeat the establishment was further shaken as the biggest urban uprising in post-war European history spread across France's *banlieues* in the autumn of 2005. The uprising, as we shall see in Chapter Four, was met with an intensification of the twin dynamics of racism and authoritarianism on the part of government actors. It also revealed serious fault-lines in the relationship between the nascent radical left and France's most impoverished neighbourhoods. As Yasser Louati, president of the Collective Committee Against Islamophobia (Comité Collectif Contre l'Islamophobie, CCIF), put it, 'For three weeks they abandoned us'.[12]

Those seeking to stigmatise *banlieue* youth did not hold back. 'In the banlieues,' declared UMP parliamentary deputy Jacques Myard, 'we have racist, anti-French ghettos that will need to be brought into line, notably by fully-fledged disciplinary battalions'.[13] A week later, President Chirac announced that a law dating from the Algerian war was to be exhumed, permitting the creation of a temporary state of emergency in certain designated areas. Previously used only in Algiers during the war of independence and in the French overseas territory of New Caledonia, it was now to be applied to urban areas on mainland France itself. Once the uprising began to subside, it was announced that riot police would remain indefinitely in seventeen areas. 'We'll go into the most difficult places,' announced the head of the CRS riot police, adding, as if to complete the colonial parallel, 'We are going to reconquer these territories'.[14]

Efforts to assert the authority of the state had to compete with growing disaffection with its political representatives. The sociologist Emmanuel Todd, whose analysis of France's 'social fracture' had provided Chirac with a campaign slogan in 1995, was scathing in his assessment of the situation: 'In recent years, French political life has been nothing but a series of catastrophes. And each time the ruling class' lack of legitimacy becomes more flagrant'.[15] Within months a huge movement of trade unionists and students was proving the point. Mass demonstrations in the spring of 2006 against proposals to reform workplace legislation, making it easier for employers to lay off young workers, put the government on the defensive. When Chirac intervened to announce a climb-down, the manner of his doing so, declaring that the legislation would be ratified but employers urged not to act on it, was an excruciating public admission of impotence. The situation was now beginning to alarm international commentators. *The Economist* warned that the 'paralysis' caused by street protests was becoming a major source of instability for the whole of the European Union. What was required was a 'Madame Thatcher' prepared to 'take on vested interests',[16] a problem identified in 2002 by Francis Fukayama, media-friendly guru of the 'new world order':

> The United States and Great Britain had Ronald Reagan and Margaret Thatcher. Both broke the old order and laid the basis for new growth. The following generation saw the arrival of Bill Clinton and Tony Blair.

> Fundamentally, they applied the same economic and social recipes, under a left guise. Nothing of the sort has ever happened in France... France's handicap is that it has not yet found an actor or a party which will subject it to this cathartic exercise.[17]

By 2006, the prime candidate for this role was Nicolas Sarkozy.

The Sarkozy phenomenon

A lifelong career politician, Sarkozy's outspoken criticism of rivals, unashamed ambition and willingness to criticise aspects of the 'republican model' were to establish him as a plausible proponent of a 'clean break' or 'rupture' with past practice.[18] His political appeal relied on a carefully calculated hyperactivism and represented the culmination of a process underway since the 1980s. Intensified competition between the major parties, and voter disaffection with them, has seen the parliamentary majority change hands at every election since 1981 bar 2007. Greater emphasis on the highly personalised presidential election, the key contest in French politics, accelerated a shift in power away from ordinary activists and processes of collective decision-making to the party leadership. Sarkozy, despite his attention to the party machine, represented the apotheosis of this dynamic.

His hyper-presidentialism, however, was not simply an exercise in bombast and narcissism. He appeared to grasp better than any other mainstream figure the relationship between racist demagogy and authoritarianism that underpinned the electoral success of the FN. He understood that those voting for the Front were not simply drawn to racist ideas, but to a political figure capable of implementing them. Following Le Pen's poor showing in the second round of the 2002 presidential election, when he barely improved on his first round score, Sarkozy moved to position himself as the figure capable not just of making speeches about the dangers of immigration, but of acting upon them. It was a high-risk strategy, but Sarkozy did not hold back, responding to claims that he was seeking to win over FN voters by confirming that he was prepared to 'go and get them one by one'.[19] Sarkozysm was a symptom of the evolution of the French right as it embraced a neoliberal outlook reliant on a negative charge of scapegoating and discrimination. This dynamic, as we shall see, then took on a life of its own, creating a spiral that escaped control, engulfing Sarkozysm in the process.

In 2002 Chirac appointed Sarkozy to the post of interior minister, not prime minister as many commentators had anticipated. A series of law and order measures were immediately announced, targeting the *banlieues*. Legislation was passed to repress youth crime, equipping police with Flashball weapons, multiplying the use of tagging, reducing the age at which children could face legal sanctions from 13 to 10, and extending the period for which they could be held in custody from 10 to 24 hours. A new offence was introduced—showing contempt for a teacher—punishable by up to six months in prison. Sarkozy told an audience in Strasbourg that those who burned cars or injured firefighters were not youths but criminals, hooligans: 'We must take the war to them'.[20] He went on to introduce measures targeting prostitution, soliciting, procuring, squatting, 'aggressive' begging, Travellers, 'threatening or hostile gatherings' on estates and contempt for the French flag or the national anthem. Such legislation, critics argued, amounted to the criminalisation of poverty. It was part of a process of reviving the nineteenth-century concept of the 'dangerous classes',[21] exemplified by both Sarkozy's depiction of *banlieue* youth as a 'rabble' of lawless hoodlums and his offensive against France's Roma population, showcased by several high-profile raids and expulsions, ostensibly to combat the problem of mafia gangs and 'organised begging'.

After spells as finance minister and out of office—when he resumed the leadership of the UMP—Sarkozy returned to the post of interior minister in June 2005. In the race to gain the UMP nomination for the 2007 presidential election, he was pitted against Dominique de Villepin, embodiment of the elite against which Sarkozy revelled in defining himself. From the summer of 2005 to the election of 2007, Sarkozy took the limelight. No sooner had a confrontation broken out in a southern French town between racialised Arab and Roma youth than Sarkozy was on the spot, proclaiming, 'My job is to clear these hooligans out of France, and I'm going to go right ahead and do it!'[22] When a child was killed by a stray bullet in a *banlieue* north of Paris he promised to deal with the hooligans by cleaning out the area with a power hose. In October 2005—days before the *banlieue* uprising—he reiterated the message using even stronger language, featuring the word *racaille* (filthy rabble or scum), a particularly incendiary term in this context because of its racist connotations. In front of the television cameras, he declared to a local resident, 'You've had enough, huh? You've had enough of this *racaille*? Well, we're going to get rid of them for you!'[23]

Following his election as president in 2007, Sarkozy promised a break with the past, an end to the compromises that had seen successive governments thrown off course by protests against pension and social security reform. Vowing to 'liquidate the legacy of May 1968', he was seen by many as the 'neoliberal enforcer' whom conservative commentators had long identified as the missing link in French political life. Sarkozy's appeal was partly based on his self-consciously cultivated 'outsider' status. He did not belong to the conventional political elite. This manifested itself in his domineering, trenchant and frequently racially charged rhetoric and in his open infatuation with wealth, fame, glitz and glamour.

Having conquered the highest office of state, he indulged in an unprecedented display of unbridled narcissism. Much to the horror of party grandees like de Villepin, Sarkozy responded to his 2007 victory as if he had won a game show. During a special concert on election night at the Place de la Concorde in Paris, a nationwide television audience was treated to a self-indulgent parade of variety acts, the highpoint reached with former Playboy model and Eurovision contestant Jeane Manson's rendition of 'Oh Happy Day!' ('Oh Happy Day! When Nicolas Sarkozy was born...').[24] Sarkozy himself made a speech about how he would represent 'all of France and leave no one by the side of the road',[25] before heading off to the exclusive Fouquet's restaurant on the Champs-Élysées accompanied by various celebrities, a select band of political allies and a fairly large gathering of leading entrepreneurs. One study estimated that the value of the companies represented at Fouquet's rose by €7 billion in the months following Sarkozy's election.[26] The next day he travelled by private jet to the tax haven of Malta, where he holidayed on a yacht as the guest of a billionaire friend. Thus his reputation as 'the president of the rich' began to take hold right from the night of his election.[27] His subsequent decision to award himself a 140 per cent pay rise did little to help matters.[28]

Like the Berlusconi phenomenon in Italy, Sarkozysm was a response to the crisis of political representation. It was an attempt to short-circuit declining affiliation to parties by taking the 'presidentialisation' of politics one step further—marketing Sarkozy like a celebrity, ensuring that the national soap opera of his love life became the centrepiece of a deliberately constructed 'bling-bling presidency'. Sarkozy sought to dramatise his adopted persona, the 'president-entrepreneur', in order to embody 'energetic rupture'.[29] 'Since 2002,' he revealed, 'I've been engaged in a fundamental fight to master the public debate around ideas... Basically, I've adopted Gramsci's analysis: power is won through ideas. It's the first time anyone on the right has consciously taken on that battle'.[30] Sarkozy did not need to be reading Gramsci, however, to eventually discover that his 'outsider' status was not compatible with the role of president. This applied on a personal as well as a political level. Episodes that he may have imagined to be refreshingly irreverent were perceived as disrespectful of his office. Due to receive the title of Honorary Canon of the Basilica of St John Lateran at the Vatican a few months after his election, Sarkozy turned up late, with a stand-up comedian in his entourage, and proceeded to check his mobile phone for texts during an audience with the Pope.[31] In an exchange with a hostile member of the public on a walkabout at an agriculture exhibition in Paris, Sarkozy was caught on camera telling him, '*Casse–toi, alors, pauvre con*,' roughly translated as 'Sod off then, you twat'.[32]

Brustier and Huelin characterise Sarkozysm as a nascent combination of 'conservatism and contestation'.[33] His neoconservative bombast enabled him to present what was essentially an authoritarian neoliberal project as a form of insurgent rebellion against vested interests, yet he made no serious attempt to defend the free market or globalisation. Instead he combined an abstract, utopian emphasis on French culture with a focus, as one commentator noted, on 'what was not working in society, on what exasperated the electorate'.[34] Scapegoating and negative political campaigning therefore took precedence over advocacy of free-market discipline.[35] The persistent focus on national identity and 'insecurity', establishing and reinforcing a link between the two, as Florence Haegel has shown, was a major factor in the radicalisation of the mainstream right under Sarkozy.[36] Jean-Marie Le Pen had established his credentials as an authoritarian outsider figure by adopting a consistently hard line on immigration, decrying the failure of the 'soft right' to deal with the issue. The strategy was based on a fallacy, establishing a link between immigration and phenomena held to be emblematic of social decay like crime, anti-social behaviour and unemployment. Since immigration was not the cause of these problems, solutions would never be found by 'getting tough' on immigration. Their persistence was nevertheless attributed primarily to the establishment's failure to do so. This cycle eventually contributed to the exhaustion of the Sarkozy phenomenon, having entrenched racism as a fixture of public debate without undermining the FN. By 2012 polls showed that 51 per cent of the population, including 65 per cent of UMP supporters, believed the FN to be a 'normal party'.[37]

Sarkozy's ability to exert such swift, sweeping impact on a political formation like the UMP is a product of the volatile nature of the French right, historically composed of parties with a low level of institutionalisation, meaning that individual actors are relatively unconstrained by organisational norms and rules.[38] As we shall see below, the focus on threats to republican values—notably in the form of 'communitarian' impulses, Islam, the 'dangerous classes' of the *banlieues*—and the use of increasingly strident and intolerant language by politicians of both left and right is characteristic of the neoliberal polity, where political competition takes on a vigorous, at times ferocious, form but is underpinned by few significant differences over policy.

Racist authoritarianism provides a means of asserting political identity, by shifting the focus of the state's role from a social, productive or redistributive function to a penal one.[39] It also provides politicians with a means of asserting decisive leadership, an essential aspect of statecraft perceived to have less scope for expression in a neoliberal era. An important corollary of this process has been the bolstering of far-right populist and fascist organisations that simultaneously benefit from an outsider status, distinguishing them from disconnected political elites, and from the credibility granted them by those same elites' adoption of racist positions. The durability of such organisations may be seen as the direct product of the neoliberal reconfiguration of politics, which has deepened the gulf between parties and population. Mainstream parties have in turn attempted to bridge this gulf on the far right's terrain—creating scapegoats, entrenching racist attitudes and generating insecurities around law and order issues.

The development of French neoliberalism (1983–2002)

The apocryphal remark attributed to George Bush that 'The problem with the French is that they don't have a word for entrepreneur' was more than just a joke at his expense. It evoked widespread assumptions about the lack of pro-market reform in France. It has become commonplace to assert that France, with its 'bloated public sector', powerful trade unions, and lack of a 'neoliberal enforcer', lags behind other nations when it comes to economic transformation, a fate that could only be remedied through urgent compliance with free-market imperatives. This narrative has served as a permanent warning to parties and population alike that France must 'catch up' and embrace neoliberal orthodoxy with much greater urgency.

Since the 1980s, however, France has conformed to market imperatives via a series of measures that have transformed its economy. These include the privatisation of state-owned companies under governments of both left and right, the deregulation of the financial sector, central bank independence, and efforts to observe a European Union cap on budget deficits at 3 per cent of GDP. Acceptance by French elites of the neoliberal outlook that economic policy should be determined by the market has been described as a 'silent' revolution based on giving priority to integration with European and international economies. France was brought into line with market discipline via a 'neoliberalisation by default', based on the 'exclusion of alternatives'. Its origins lay in the Socialists' abandonment of progressive reform in favour of austerity in the early years of the Mitterrand presidency. Characteristics attributed to the British experience—positive identification with 'popular capitalism', the mobilisation of enthusiastic elite support and, to a lesser degree, public acceptance of market values—did not take hold in France. Neoliberal transformation therefore happened 'without much fanfare, behind the scenes, within the technocracy and the political elite... as a process of pragmatic normalization that was carried [out] in the name of modernity and progress'.[40]

The implications of this 'silent revolution' have been significant in terms of the role of the state (and public perceptions of it), the relationship between parties and their electorate (which continues to fragment) and parties' response to the lack of public affiliation with a programme of pro-market reform. The rise of 'respectable racism' in the twenty-first century, accelerating since the 2008 financial crash, should be seen in part as a product of this disjuncture: between an economic orthodoxy shared by mainstream parties, but not their electorates. For all the noise from British commentators about Macron's 2017 victory representing a new hope, as part of a French heritage of 'revolutionary political moments', a dynamic fusion of 'fresh capitalism' and moral concern for those most in need,[41] almost a third of Macron's first-round presidential vote came from people who chose him primarily to block other candidates. Four out of six Macron voters thus chose him 'by default', with significantly fewer people backing Macron by conviction than any other major candidate.

The French state has been reconfigured since 1983 by the pursuit of a neoliberal agenda by governments of left and right—its size has been transformed by privatisation and its influence by deregulation and internationalisation. This 'post-*dirigiste*', or post-interventionist, era has involved adapting an all-embracing state industrial policy to a new context. The state now acts less as a 'gatekeeper', directing or instructing companies, than as a facilitator. What emerged in the light of the 2008 financial crash, as Ben Clift argues, was a 'distinctively French version of the free market, infused with partiality, and reproducing market dominance for big French players, both domestically and internationally'. In other words, longstanding characteristics of the French economy's relationship to the state have survived in the new era, but in modified form. These include the interpenetration of private and public sector elites and state promotion of international champions as part of a process of 'selective liberalisation'. Following the banking crisis, for example, President Sarkozy made a number of speeches outlining the need for reconciliation between capitalism and morality and for an end to the bonus culture in banking. The state's bailout of BNP-Paribas nevertheless enabled the bank to take advantage of the weakness of British and German rivals and pursue a policy of combative expansion, establishing itself as the biggest bank in the Eurozone. The state, as Clift remarks, 'helped big financial players to help themselves'.[42]

Further influence has been handed over to market mechanisms in the allocation of resources but the state remains an important actor, playing a role in the labour market via the distribution of social benefits and, despite the absence of an overarching industrial policy, in stimulating the development of competitive markets via its control of public funding. Nevertheless, since 1983 there has been, as Peter Hall points out, 'a more pronounced market logic to the processes whereby public resources are distributed' and, in former public utilities, an erosion of public service values in favour of 'market logics that put more emphasis on the profitability of their operations.'[43] Outsourcing and subcontracting further diminish the notion of 'public service', often to the detriment of remote or impoverished communities.

Neoliberalism, then, has not made the French state irrelevant but has reshaped its role, subjecting it to a series of tensions. In theory the state has become 'one actor among many', but in fact it still brings its influence to bear in creating a favourable climate for business. It remains subject to conflicting pressures—

between deregulation and control, competition and oligopoly and, more broadly, market and society. Jamie Peck aptly sums up the dynamic at play, arguing that neoliberalism involves the 'remaking and redeployment of the state as the core agency that actively fabricates the subjectivities, social relations and collective representations suited to making the fiction of markets real and consequential.'[44] One of the effects of this dynamic has been the undermining of notions of collective solidarity as the 'fiction of markets' takes hold.

As Harvey notes, neoliberalism has become society's dominant ideological framework, 'incorporated into the common-sense way many of us interpret, live in, and understand the world'.[45] Yet little evidence exists, in France or anywhere, of widespread positive affiliation to neoliberalism's core values. A major report in the United States found that a large majority of people wanted society to 'move away from greed and excess toward a way of life more centred on values, community, and family'. At the same time, respondents did not believe that these views were shared by others and felt isolated because other people seemed 'increasingly atomised, selfish and irresponsible'.[46] Passive compliance in the face of neoliberalism may mean that it functions as an effective ideology, operating at the level of assumptions made more or less unconsciously, but this is a very different proposition from the politics embodied by Thatcher and Reagan in the 1980s, when rampant entrepreneurialism, share ownership and privatisation were not simply viewed as inevitable, but were embraced in sections of wider society as the embodiment of dynamic reform.

The focus on regulation rather than the management of production and distribution; the rise of non-majoritarian institutions such as courts, central banks or regulatory bodies which exercise public authority but are not run by elected officials; the increasing importance of the European Union and other transnational bodies; the growing significance of judicial or quasi-judicial means of problem-solving; and widespread acceptance of the modern state's regulatory rather than political or redistributive character, have all contributed to the replacement of party government by administrative government, or 'government by inertia'. As Peter Mair has argued, the enfeeblement of party democracy is the product of a mutual disengagement: of citizens from conventional politics on the one hand, and of political leaders from sites of collective engagement with state institutions on the other.[47] This is partly a consequence of the changing role of the state under neoliberalism. The enmeshing of state actors with other agencies and networks, both domestically and internationally, and the reconfiguring of state functions, makes it harder for state institutions and actors to embody, in Philip Cerny's words, 'the kind of communal solidarity or *Gemeinschaft* which gave the modern nation-state its deeper legitimacy, institutionalised power and social embeddedness'.[48]

This erosion of ideological conflict and policy choice between left and right in turn gives rise to 'opposition of form rather than of content', reinforcing the sense of mainstream politics as theatre and entrenching the divide between political representatives and the electorate. In France, where the state has traditionally played a more prominent role, the 'silent' adoption of a neoliberal orthodoxy by default has posed serious problems. Indeed, the neoliberal consensus has precipitated the erosion of the two dominant traditions of the post-war period, social democracy and Gaullism, culminating in the results of the 2017 electoral cycle. The blurring of longstanding distinctions between parties when it comes to policy objectives and motivations has not been a linear process—it is subject to tensions arising from the clash between market orthodoxy and the need to appeal to the residual values of an electorate still divided along partisan lines. Governments of left and right have overseen greater integration into a globalising economy, lower growth rates, long-term structural unemployment and rising inequality. In dealing with the social consequences of the policies driving such outcomes, both Socialists and Gaullists have become increasingly reliant on the rather narrow set of political tools provided by authoritarian neo-liberalism, supplemented by the comparatively rich legacy of France's republican tradition (see Chapter Three).

In the immediate post-war period, Gaullism sought national renewal and economic regeneration by integrating the legacy of wartime resistance into an ideology that aspired to national solidarity through state action.[49] By the twenty-first century, when its historic legacy had ceased to mean much in policy terms, the post-Gaullist right still drew on those values for justification. It deployed, as Peter Hall argues, 'a rhetoric of modernization, with its favorable Gaullist overtones of advancing France's place in the world, joined to an emphasis on republican values, redefined as support for "social solidarity" in the face of global markets.' Neoliberal measures tended to be presented without enthusiasm by the post-Gaullist right, 'as a necessary, if slightly distasteful, response to the imperatives of the global economy'.[50]

Faced with growing public perceptions of an irrevocable decline of the state, key political actors struggled to project the image of firm leadership critical to statecraft. Maintaining legitimacy and consent became more and more difficult. This, as we shall see, was partly due to the interplay between neo-liberalism and longstanding political traditions, but derived also from a more fundamental tension, between the values of community (family, church, nation and so on) and the destructive force of the market. Anthony Giddens, confectioner of Tony Blair's 'third way', describes the competing pressures at play as a 'self-contradictory' relationship between 'devotion to the free market' on the one hand, and to the 'traditional family and nation' on the other. The 'permanent revolution' of market forces means that the values of family and national identity cannot remain static. Instead,

Giddens argues, they are dissolved, fragmenting 'traditional structures of authority' and fracturing local communities. 'Neoliberalism neglects the social basis of markets themselves, which depend upon the very communal forms that market fundamentalism indifferently throws to the winds.'[51]

In attempting to address these tensions, the dominant French political figure of the early twenty-first century, Nicolas Sarkozy, in fact fostered a form of state racism that, for all the havoc it created, did nothing to resolve them.

State racism

Accepting the subordination of state to market, Sarkozy attempted to assert the state's regal functions when it came to law and order and national identity. His efforts to erect republican secularism as a fundamental part of France's heritage, recognising and asserting the primacy of Catholicism within that ostensibly neutral framework, foundered as the tension between neoliberalism's promotion of 'diversity' and the traditionalist elements at the core of his electorate led him into confused positions on the Republic's relationship to issues of diversity. As we discuss in the next chapter, Sarkozy was initially favourable to positive discrimination, the creation of an 'Islam of France' and gay marriage, but subsequently reversed his position on all these questions, before asserting in 2015, 'It's religion that adapts to the Republic, not the Republic that adapts to religion... This is the debate that must take place if we are to have an Islam of France that incorporates the values of the Republic. Those who join us must assimilate, adopt our way of life, our culture... Do we keep our shoes on when we visit a mosque abroad?'[52]

Fundamental to Sarkozy's presidency was a focus on 'national identity' and immigration. In May 2007 Sarkozy made Brice Hortefeux France's first minister of immigration and national identity. As a group of historians pointed out in a petition against the new office, the association of immigration with national identity was without precedent in the history of republican France. The ministry was to be given jurisdiction over political asylum and the policing of borders and was also tasked with 'promoting national identity.' 'This association [of the two issues],' warned the historians, 'can only reinforce prejudice towards immigrants.' National identity today, they argued, 'consists of a synthesis of pluralism and diversity of populations that should not be fixed within the boundaries of a ministry'.[53] The move signalled a further break with the traditional notion of integration, as a leading Socialist had warned during the 2007 presidential election campaign. 'What's shocking about this approach,' argued the Socialist former prime minister Laurent Fabius, 'is that by linking the two terms we're to choose between immigration and national identity, when the reality is that French national identity is built by integrating immigrants.'[54]

The government was undeterred. It organised a national debate on the question, with around 350 meetings held in town halls nationwide and a website set up inviting citizens to offer their thoughts on what it meant to be French, and on the contribution of immigration to national identity. There were 760,000 visits to the website and over 50,000 comments left, a fifth of them 'unpublishable'. Sarkozy eventually acknowledged that the creation of the national identity ministry had been a mistake, and that the national conversation it oversaw had led to 'tension and misunderstanding'.[55]

However, having established the terms of this unprecedented debate, the government then set about fixing quotas for the expulsion of undocumented migrants. Local state representatives in twenty regions were ordered to prioritise the issue in order to meet an annual target of 25,000 deportations. Joaquim Masanet, secretary of the police union UNSA, expressed his disquiet at the news. 'The principle of intercepting someone whose status is illegal and escorting them to the border doesn't bother me,' he said. 'Indeed, that is part of our job. But we don't want a quota to be set for human beings. It's ridiculous, especially in the country of the Rights of Man'.[56] The issue drew comparisons with the Vichy regime's acquiescence to Nazi demands for quotas of Jews to be rounded up and deported during the war, which led to the murder of 76,000 Jews. Such parallels, however exaggerated, did not trouble Hortefeux. Indeed, in November 2008 he organised a conference of European ministers on the question of the integration of immigrants. It was held in Vichy. Now was the time, argued Hortefeux, to 'put an end to the ostracism' that had weighed on the town for fifty years.[57]

This was all part of a longstanding desire of the French right to liberate itself from the 'complexes' of Vichy and colonialism, a major preoccupation of two of Sarkozy's closest advisors, the Gaullist Henri Guaino and Patrick Buisson, former editor of the far-right publication *Minute*. Accordingly, Sarkozy draped himself unashamedly in the colours of French colonialism with a speech in Dakar written by Guaino that detailed at length the 'problems' of Africa, notably the failure of the 'African' to 'enter into history'.[58] His advice to an audience of politicians, students and intellectuals was that if they really wanted to deal with the problem of starvation in Africa, then they should consider growing their own food.[59] The speech was part of an attempt by the right, discussed in Chapter Three, to shed its defensiveness over France's colonial record. It was steeped in such ignorance and racism that it was ultimately self-defeating: by anybody's standards Sarkozy was not the ideal exemplar of France's 'civilising mission' and his audience mostly greeted the speech with stupefaction and anger.

Rehabilitating the colonial legacy was a task that proved beyond Sarkozy, who was more at home expressing anger at the way republican institutions were disrespected by the 'dangerous classes'. In the other landmark speech of his presidency, he was in his element, matching crude bombast with a querulous, righteous indignation that he excelled at dramatising. Responding to disturbances in Grenoble in the summer of 2010, during which gunshots were fired at the police, he announced a series of draconian measures to deal with crime and delinquency. These problems were explicitly and repeatedly linked to 'the consequences of fifty years of insufficiently controlled immigration, which have ended in the failure of integration.' Declaring a 'national war on crime', he announced that anyone found guilty of shooting a police officer no longer deserved to remain a French citizen, insinuating a link between violent crime and immigration since only those with dual nationality could be deprived of French citizenship—it being illegal to render someone stateless. Those who attacked public servants should face thirty-year jail terms. Parents with delinquent children should be imprisoned. He revealed that he had instructed the interior minister to deal with the 'unauthorised squatting and camping' of Roma people: half of the country's 500 or so camps were to be dismantled within three months.[60]

Florence Haegel's study of the UMP found that in 2003, just after the party's formation, right-wing voters in France gravitated more towards the centre than their European counterparts. They identified less with economic liberalism but were also less strict when it came to moral issues and more tolerant where religious matters were concerned. The only question that placed these voters further to the right was immigration. Here lay the possibility for radicalisation. In her comparison of Chirac's and Sarkozy's speeches, Haegel found nothing to differentiate them on economic issues, but noted a much greater emphasis by Sarkozy on national identity and immigration, and in particular an attempt to link morality to religion. Sarkozy lay more stress than his predecessor on order (in its social, moral, educational and security aspects), delinquency and justice.[61]

The scapegoating of immigrants is based on the notion that they are somehow to blame for social problems like unemployment and crime or the scarcity of resources like decent housing. The mainstream's inability to stem the rise of the FN over the past thirty years is derived in part from a failure to counter this myth. The credibility given to it by Sarkozy meant that FN racism was further legitimised, but in the process he also exposed his own impotence: since immigrants are no more to blame for poor housing or unemployment than for inclement weather or wasp bites, no amount of 'tough' measures would ever be enough. The same went for law and order. As we shall see, despite the introduction of endless measures targeting 'insecurity', the mainstream's obsession with the issue bred rather than addressed fears. Ultimately, the real outsider will always be able to propose something more. And so it proved.

The resurgence of the Front National

After the Front's electoral breakthrough in the 1980s, journalists and academics attributed part of the organisation's success to the 'respectable' image that Jean-Marie Le Pen had fashioned for himself after years of haranguing audiences wearing an eye-patch. In a similar manner, much has been made of the role of Marine Le Pen, who replaced her father as FN leader in 2011. Attitudes towards her tend to be based on the notion, aided by an indulgent media, that she represents a 'softer' or 'gentler' image for the Front. In 2012 *The Guardian*'s French election blog carried a series of articles in precisely this vein. 'The Front National is different,' ran the quote in one headline: 'The knee-jerk racists are out'.[62] Yet candidate lists for the FN in the 2012 parliamentary and subsequent municipal, European and regional elections revealed a party whose representatives retained close links with the various currents of violent, negationist, Catholic fundamentalist and 'revolutionary nationalist' elements that form part of the FN's organisational culture, along with an emerging new current of '*identitaires*', reactionary nationalist activists who straddle the far right and radicalising mainstream, united by a racism that finds expression and legitimation in irreverent contempt for Muslims.[63]

Although Marine Le Pen has been shrewd enough to grasp that her father's anti-semitic provocations offer little or no benefit to the Front, her strategy represents a continuation of a process underway since 1972. Fundamental to the development of the Front has been the twin dynamic of seeking respectability while maintaining the party's outsider status. Both elements of this strategy carry risks, radicalisation threatening marginalisation and normalisation the danger of becoming a party 'like the others'. 'So today,' as Sylvain Crépon outlines, 'it is a double strategy of normalisation and radicalisation. All our studies show that in reality the FN cannot do without its demonisation.'[64]

During her breakthrough 2012 presidential campaign, Marine Le Pen employed the same bullish provocations as her father, attacking parties of both left and right for giving power over to the 'dictatorship of the banks—a gilded fascism which doesn't speak its name'[65] and declaring herself the only 'anti-system candidate', the candidate of 'the forgotten, the middle-classes, the popular classes'. In response to her unprecedented score in the first-round poll in 2012, she reappropriated a slogan from May 1968, '*Ce n'est qu'un début, continuons le combat*' ('This is just the beginning, let's keep up the fight').[66] Her decision, also in line with her father's stance, to support neither Sarkozy nor Hollande in the second round, underlined that the Front's outsider status was more important to it than the prospect of alliances of any kind with the mainstream right. Such alliances may yet take place, but they will be the result of the disorientation of the mainstream, and the reactionary radicalisation of sections of

Sarkozy's UMP (now Les Républicains), rather than any supposed 'moderation' on the part of the FN.

In 2002, when Jean-Marie Le Pen came second in the presidential election, a wave of anti-FN mobilisations dominated the entire fortnight between the two rounds, ensuring that his final vote share barely improved on his first-round score. The most significant change affecting the extreme right in the subsequent decade has been the accelerated integration of racism, demagogy and intolerance into mainstream rhetoric and policy. The FN's respectability derives from this, rather than its change of leader. The remodelling of the FN as a staunchly republican, secular party has been crucial to its process of so-called 'detoxification', cited by many as the central factor in its recent resurgence. What the FN has benefited from more than any superficial changes to its image, however, is the fact that over the past decade racism has become respectable in a way that the organisation could only have dreamed of at its formation in 1972. In stark contrast with the 2002 mobilisation against her father's candidacy, when Marine Le Pen finished second in the 2017 election there were virtually no demonstrations—those that did take place were tiny. An indication of the distance travelled was signalled by Macron's decision to participate in a televised debate with Le Pen, something that Chirac had refused to do with her father.

Following poor parliamentary election results in 1973, when it achieved only 0.5 per cent of the total poll, criticism was raised by hard-core fascist elements about the party's stress on immigration, since, it was argued, public opposition to immigrants had not yet crystallised into a political attitude. This meant that potential supporters were being alienated from the FN by the issue of racism.[67] By 2012, a leading member of the Socialist Party, Arnaud Montebourg, was talking about a 'consensus' between the Socialists, Sarkozy's UMP and the FN on the immigration question: all accepted that there was a need for a certain number of immigrants to France and for limits to be imposed beyond this minimum. Pointing out that more undocumented migrants had been regularised under Sarkozy than under the Socialist Jospin, Montebourg continued: 'When Sarkozy argues that immigration should be stopped, I don't judge him'.[68] Sarkozy went out of his way to insist that the FN was a fully legitimate part of French political life,[69] giving short shrift to anyone criticising the convergence between FN views and his own rhetoric: 'If Le Pen says the sun is yellow, should I say it's blue?'

As one of the leading archiects of the FN's 'detoxification', party vice-president Louis Aliot has explained, 'detoxification only concerns anti-semitism. When handing out leaflets in the street, the one glass ceiling I found was not immigration or Islam. Others are worse than us on these subjects. It's anti-semitism that prevents people from voting for us. Only that'.[70] The superficial nature of the strategy is underlined by polling conducted over a number of years by the National Consultative Commission on Human Rights (CNCDH). The hard core of the FN's electorate, those who felt closer to the party than to any other without necessarily being members, expressed alarming levels of anti-semitism, Islamophobia and ethnocentrism. For nearly half (45 per cent) of the Front's supporters, the phrase 'Dirty Arab' was not considered reprehensible. Neither, for 36 per cent of them, was the phrase 'Dirty Jew'. A significant proportion of the Front's supporters did not consider Muslims (73 per cent) or Jews (35 per cent) to be fully French and had a negative view of both Muslims (76 per cent) and Jews (38 per cent). Over half of FN supporters (53 per cent) expressed 'very strong' anti-semitism, 82 per cent considered themselves racist and 87 per cent expressed 'ethnocentrist' views. Indeed, between 2011 and 2014, when the press was full of articles about the strategy of 'moderation' being pursued by Marine Le Pen, the proportion of FN sympathisers considered 'very racist' remained constant at 87 per cent.[71] In contrast to the message some journalists lazily chose to transmit, knee-jerk racism remains a fundamental aspect of the culture of the FN.

The Islamophobic spiral that took hold in the Sarkozy era was partly a consequence of UMP efforts to emulate the FN. Yet, if the previous four decades had shown anything, it was that the FN possessed an endless capacity to trump such initiatives. In 2010 Marine Le Pen compared the sight of Muslims praying in the street to the Nazi occupation of France. Within a year, the government had banned prayers in the street. Following the ban on wearing the burqa and the niqab in public, Le Pen called for the hijab to be outlawed on public transport. And so it went on. In February 2012, Le Pen had whipped up a storm over the ludicrous claim that all meat being sold in the Paris region was halal produce but not labelled as such. By early March, Sarkozy was arguing that this was the number one preoccupation of the French.[72] Early in the 2012 presidential campaign, Sarkozy had called for immigration to be cut by half. 'There are too many foreigners on our territory,' he declared. 'The functioning of our system of integration is getting worse and worse because we can't find them a home, a job, a school'.[73] Such rhetoric continued throughout the campaign, intensifying between the two rounds, with Sarkozy labelling Hollande a 'communalist' candidate following unfounded claims from UMP deputies that 700 mosques had called on Muslims to vote for him.[74] By the time of the next presidential contest in 2017, of course, both Sarkozy's and Hollande's parties were completely overshadowed by Le Pen, who made it through to the second round while their careers lay in tatters.

The new reactionaries

The radicalisation of the right and the narrowing of political competition around the twin themes of insecurity and immigration took place within a wider climate of reaction. Since the 1990s, a stream of books and articles had contributed to a growing mood of intolerance. Essays lamenting France's decline were not uncommon—Nicolas Baverez's *La France qui tombe* became a best-seller in the early twenty-first century, calling, like others before him, for a more rigorous assertion of neoliberal orthodoxy. During the Sarkozy era, however, an openly retrogressive and bigoted intellectual current emerged in the form of the 'new reactionaries', spearheaded by the journalist Eric Zemmour, whose *Le Suicide français* was a runaway success in the mould already established by reactionary diatribes of the late nineteenth century—a provocative and polemical exercise in cultural pessimism. Zemmour flourished on ground already staked out since the 1970s by the Nouvelle Droite (New Right; see Chapter Three) and given new prominence and legitimacy by Sarkozy. The right needed to rid itself of its 'complexes'? Zemmour was on hand to argue that Marshall Pétain had 'saved' French Jews from the Holocaust,[75] apparently indifferent both to the historical evidence amassed and detailed over nearly half a century and the plight of those considered 'foreign' by Vichy (thousands were stripped of their French nationality before deportation to the camps). Sarkozy was waging a Gramscian struggle for hegemony? Zemmour was eager to join the fray: 'I'm in an ideological and cultural battle and I've turned the left's own weapons against it.'[76] He echoed Sarkozy's desire to destroy the legacy of May 1968, the highpoint of French decadence and permissiveness. His lurid assessment of contemporary France essentially amounted, as one commentator put it, to a 'condemnation of everything that has happened in the past fifty years', from birth control and abortion to gay rights, consumer capitalism and immigration.[77] Zemmour reserved particular ire for Muslims, who 'lived among themselves in the *banlieues*', forcing the French 'to leave them'. Muslims, a 'people within a people', were leading France 'to chaos and civil war.' Asked whether the answer was to deport five million Muslims from France, he replied: 'I know it's unrealistic, but history is surprising. Who would have said in 1940 that a million *pieds-noirs* [European-origin French Algerians], twenty years later, would leave Algeria to return to France?'[78]

Other figures linked to the neo-reactionary current include Renaud Camus, who details his concerns about immigrants 'from a different civilisation' and their capacity to integrate from the seclusion of his fourteenth-century castle in rural Gascony, where he lives in 'self-imposed isolation'.[79] Camus, who wrote for the gay press in the 1970s, is responsible for developing the outlandish theory of the '*grand remplacement*' (great replacement), according to which France's white Christian population is being replaced by non-European Muslim immigrants. In 2015, he joined Souveraineté, indépendance et libertés (SIEL), a small component of the FN satellite organisation Rassemblement Bleu Marine. Like Zemmour, Camus articulates a series of race-centred preoccupations that echo the longstanding obsessions of a pessimistic, right-wing chauvinism present in French political culture since the Revolution.

Over the past decade this current has been bolstered by the reactionary turn taken by various 'neo-republican' figures previously associated with the left. A number of former supporters and associates of republican nationalist Jean-Pierre Chevènement have found their way into the FN. These include the Front's former vice-president Florian Philippot; Chevènement's former chief advisor Bertrand Dutheil de la Rochère, who became the Front's advisor on 'the Republic and secularism'; and Paul-Marie Coûteaux, a former Chevènementist deputy in the European Parliament who played a leading role in Marine Le Pen's 2012 election campaign. Some, like the journalist Elisabeth Lévy, kept their distance from the Front while following a political trajectory that identified Islam as a greater threat than the far right. Her reaction to the furore created by Jean-Marie Le Pen's showing in the 2002 presidential race, for example, was to write an article for *Le Figaro* entitled 'Anti-fascism will not pass'.[80] Others once associated with the left, like academic Pierre-André Taguieff, philosopher Alain Finkielkraut and the feminist historian Élisabeth Badinter, contributed to legitimising various concepts that were to become central to the resurgence of reaction, from the development of 'new secularism' as an instrument for asserting intolerance (discussed in the next chapter) to identification with the spurious notion of 'anti-white racism'.

One of the principal achievements of these neo-republican figures was to legitimise an ethno-cultural drift in interpretations of secularism and reinforce authoritarian attitudes towards the imperatives of republican statecraft. In other words, Finkielkraut et al gave credibility to the FN's efforts to recast racist attitudes in a republican framework. In 1989, Finkielkraut and Badinter had put their names to a histrionic statement comparing the danger of allowing Muslim students to wear the hijab with the appeasement of Hitler. By 2011, Badinter was lamenting the fact that 'aside from Marine Le Pen, nobody defends secularism anymore,'[81] while Finkielkraut was expressing views that were indistinguishable from those of the Front National:

> France is confronted, like the rest of Western Europe, by a huge problem... immigration... it's a civilisational problem, because a certain section of today's immigrants, unlike yesterday's, do not feel bound by the norms, rules, values, traditions or ideals of the society welcoming them. But France, or at least a whole section of the French elite, is reacting strangely to this situation by becoming—and it's pathetic—apologists for *métissage* [cultural mixing or cross-breeding]. It's through *métissage* that we're going to solve the problem! So, values, ways of being, styles are somehow going to mix, and out of this mix a new happy civilisation will emerge... The elite is contributing to this phenomenon, aggravating and accelerating it further, by dissolving all that remains of identity in this strange, omnipresent, deceitful concept of... *métissage*![82]

Since 1989, Finkielkraut and a growing band of neo-republicans have played a major role in making racist attitudes respectable. In 2006 they leapt to the defence of a high school philosophy teacher and writer, Robert Redeker, a member of the editorial board of *Les Temps modernes*, who had received a death threat for writing an Islamophobic diatribe in *Le Figaro*.[83] Redeker argued that Islam was by its nature a barbaric religion, that the Koran educated 'every Muslim' in hate and 'incredible violence', and that Mohammed was 'a merciless warlord, a looter, a mass-murderer of Jews and a polygamist'. In contrast to this 'master of hate', Jesus was 'a master of love'.

Redeker believed Islam was playing an identical role to Communism during the Cold War, posing as the voice of the poor while using archaic violence and intimidation to assert its hegemonic and intolerant ideology against the 'free world' and the latter's values of generosity, open-mindedness, gentleness, women's liberation and democracy. Hate was exalted by Islam and violence inscribed as a sacred duty in the heart of every Muslim believer. How, precisely, was this assault being waged on the West? Redeker detailed all the ways in which Islam was 'imposing its rules'. First on the list was 'the opening of swimming pools with certain times reserved for women', followed by the banning of caricatures of Islam, the demand for particular dietary requirements for Muslim children at school mealtimes, the battle to defend the wearing of the headscarf in schools, and the accusations of 'Islamophobia' directed at 'free spirits'. To cap it all, thong bikinis had now been banned on the artificial beaches installed on the banks of the Seine in summer—for fear, no doubt, of Islamist protests.

A petition signed by Michel Onfray, a philosopher once associated with the left, offered 'unconditional support' to Redeker.[84] Anything less would be 'a concession to barbarism'. It was also signed by Pierre-André Taguieff, an academic once associated with anti-racism, and a number of other 'progressive republicans' who, as Aurélien Mondon notes, were now contributing to the 'spread and mainstreaming of reactionary and racist attitudes within the public arena' by making clear 'their complete and unquestionable defence of a racist philosopher at the expense of the Muslim population'.[85]

France since 2002

French society experienced a series of convulsions between 21 April 2002, when Jean-Marie Le Pen won 4.8 million votes, and 22 April 2012, when 6.4 million people voted for Marine Le Pen. Throughout the decade, powerful mobilisations challenged the neoliberal consensus shared by governments of left and right. A wave of protests defined the two weeks separating the first and second rounds of the 2002 presidential election. But after this, there were few effective challenges to the racist drift that took hold of society during the Sarkozy era. The neoliberal consensus was matched by a consensus around republican secularism, as if the decline of the state in one field was to be compensated by its reinvigoration in another. The deployment of secularism as a means of policing and isolating France's Muslim population was part of a wider reconfiguration of French politics. The strategy chosen to confront the FN's emergence in 2002 as a genuine threat to the dominance of social democracy and Gaullism—asserting the authority of the Republic—proved high-risk. On the one hand, the imposition of the state's authority in social terms—policing headscarves, bandanas and skirts—created a spiral, discussed in the next chapter, that saw secularism increasingly aligned with ethno-cultural notions of citizenship. On the other hand, the state's acquiescence to neoliberal economic imperatives merely underlined its impotence when it came to stemming widening inequalities. This in turn produced a redoubling of efforts to assert state mastery of the relatively trivial, as republican imperatives were imposed on swimming pools, street prayers and school dinners. This republican inferiority complex was perfectly embodied by the agitated hyperactivity of its diminutive president, Nicolas Sarkozy, bestriding the world stage in two-inch stacked heels.

A study by the Fondation Jean-Jaurès (a political foundation close to the Socialist Party) underlines Sarkozy's success—before the strategy unravelled—in both radicalising the mainstream right's electorate and winning over sections of the FN vote. Polls conducted in the run-up to the 2007 presidential election showed that almost half of the FN's 2002 electorate had more faith in Sarkozy than in Jean-Marie Le Pen when it came to questions of law and order. In the election itself, over a third of those who had voted for Le Pen in 2002 backed Sarkozy.[86] But there were other areas where there was an apparent convergence of outlook between the UMP and the FN. Fourquet and Gariazzo identify a shift in the presentation of economic issues, with the emergence of themes like 'purchasing power' and 'scrounging'. Rather than emphasising remote, often hard to grasp, macroeconomic issues such as unemployment, growth or inflation, these terms offered a more affective impression that chimed with subjective perceptions of decline without establishing any clear link to economic policy. They put the focus on individual effort and responsibility rather than shortcomings in the welfare system, obscuring the role of government actors in overseeing neoliberal economic priorities. The replacement of relatively neutral terms like unemployment or inflation with references to benefit cheats and welfare scroungers highlighted issues like benefit fraud, scrounging and immigration, feeding into a blame culture. With UMP deputies like Laurent Wauquiez labelling handouts 'a cancer' in French society, such rhetoric both accelerated the radicalisation of the UMP and helped 'normalise' the FN, framing issues like migration in terms of their economic cost, as products of a dependency culture.

Ultimately, Sarkozy was unable to straddle his promises of 'rupture' on immigration and law and order policy with the neoliberal management of the economy. As Fourquet and Gariazzo put it, the priorities adopted by Sarkozy in 2007 'enabled Marine Le Pen to become audible in 2012'.[87] The resurgence of the FN was partly a result of disappointment with Sarkozy. The image he managed to fashion as a public figure close to the people and contemptuous of elites was broken by 2012. A survey of Sarkozy's electorate in 2012 recorded individual reactions to his term of office. 'We were expecting a better life,' said one working-class voter, 'we told ourselves that soon everyone would be able to buy a house and go on holiday.'[88] The disenchantment of FN supporters was particularly rapid. Their confidence in Sarkozy on law and order issues plummeted from 88 per cent in August 2007 to 31 per cent a year later. By 2009, 72 per cent of FN voters saw Sarkozy's decision to launch the debate on national identity as a ruse to shore up support ahead of the following year's regional elections.[89]

One reason for this abandonment of faith in Sarkozy was the global financial crisis of 2008, which accelerated an already pervasive sense of national decline. This manifested itself in fears about France's standing in the world relative to its global competitors, but was also expressed in perceptions that power relations between 'native' French people and immigrants were threatened by the risk that instability and inequality on the other side of the Mediterranean would be imported to France in the wake of the 2011 Arab Spring. Here, attitudes towards Islam revealed not so much fear of the 'Islamification' of French society, but the crystallisation of a series of concerns about a loss of cultural identity and France's ability to maintain control of its territory and destiny. In 2010, over half the UMP electorate expressed agreement with Marine Le Pen's comparison of Muslims praying in the street with the wartime occupation.[90]

Le Pen, daughter of a millionaire, was therefore able to take up the mantle adopted by Sarkozy in 2007—that of the politician who understands ordinary people's concerns. In particular, she was able to seize upon the mantra propagated throughout neoliberal Europe, that people had rights but also responsibilities, and make it her own.[91] When an extraordinary backlash against gay marriage took to the streets in 2013 (the self-styled 'French Spring'), some were quick to point to a convergence of the FN and UMP electorates. But the radicalisation of the UMP was not uniform. The non-religious section of its electorate remained broadly supportive of gay marriage, as did one in two of its younger voters, with its Catholic base and most of its older supporters vehemently opposed.[92] There are also divergences within the UMP/Les Républicains electorate on economic issues. A majority of those from poorer backgrounds want more state intervention in the economy, as do most FN voters. But among wealthier sections of the party's electorate, only a third share this view.[93]

Regardless of this complexity, the UMP was undoubtedly radicalised during the Sarkozy presidency. In 2006, 62 per cent of UMP voters expressed the view that there were 'too many immigrants' in France. By 2013, this figure had risen by a quarter, to 87 per cent. In 2006, 38 per cent of UMP supporters claimed to feel unsafe everywhere, yet by 2013 nearly double that number, 73 per cent, felt this way—despite an entire parliament's worth of draconian law and order measures. Such radicalisation was more than matched by the shifting outlook of FN voters, 86 per cent of whom believed there to be too many immigrants in 2006, rising to 96 per cent in 2013. When it came to law and order, 54 per cent of FN voters did not feel secure anywhere in 2006, with 89 per cent expressing this view by 2013.[94] Furthermore, as we have seen, anti-semitism among the hard core of the FN electorate has increased under Marine Le Pen's leadership.[95] Thus, despite the apparent 'detoxification' of the FN, the organisation had radicalised alarmingly since 2006.

This radicalisation of both the FN and the UMP was not so much an alignment of the two electorates, but a mutual shift to the right. This shift has validated longstanding, albeit evolved, features of the French far right's ideology, including a sense of national decline that requires regeneration through strong leadership, and suspicion of an 'anti-France': untrustworthy and unruly elements loyal to a foreign power that demand constant vigilance and policing. As the crisis of French politics and society deepened, it gave rise to all kinds of morbid symptoms, as the centre of gravity moved dramatically to the right across the mainstream.

Nowhere was this more apparent than on the question of gay marriage, which exposed a number of longstanding shortcomings in the 'republican model' and its capacity to offer a sustained defence of minorities under attack. The backlash against gay marriage took the form of what Gaël Brustier describes as a 'conservative May 68':[96] an unprecedented, irreverent carnival of reaction that embraced multiple forms of bigotry. One of its primary targets was the black justice minister, Christiane Taubira. An FN municipal councillor was expelled from the party for comparing her with a monkey, while *Minute*, the publication once edited by Sarkozy's advisor Buisson, put a picture of Taubira on its front page with a headline playing on the expression '*avoir la banane*' (to be happy): 'Crafty as a monkey: Taubira gets her banana back'. Such abuse was the consequence of the way that racism had become normalised in French society since 2002. Pivotal to this shift, as we shall see in the next chapter, was the appropriation of republican secularism by the right, and its transformation into a means of asserting dominance over the most dominated in French society.

3

MORAL PANIC SECULARISM

The policemen approached the Muslim woman sleeping on the beach in Nice. They had come to enforce a directive imposing seaside attire that conformed to secular values. A number of women on Côte d'Azur beaches had already been fined or cautioned for infringing these regulations, introduced by thirty local mayors across the south of France in August 2016. In Cannes a woman wearing a headscarf, leggings and a top had been fined and instructed to leave the beach after refusing to undress. Bystanders had jeered and made racist remarks. In Nice, the officers had batons, tear gas and guns attached to their uniforms. The four men stood over the woman as she removed her long sleeved top.

The French Republic, inheritor of the Revolution so admired by Goethe and Wordsworth, victorious at Valmy and on the barricades of 1848, its values enshrined in the Declaration of the Rights of Man and Citizen and its legacy defended by the Popular Front and the martyrs of the Resistance, had become an international laughing stock. Its police forces were now scouring the shoreline in search of Muslim women they could instruct to undress, collecting a €38 fine from any who refused. Racist intolerance had found a new means to assert itself, seeking justifications in the language and customs of France's secular tradition, *laïcité* (from the Greek *laos*, of the people).[1] 'The Republic is invaded by reactionaries of every kind,' Émile Zola had warned at the height of the Dreyfus Affair, 'they worship it with a brutal and terrible love, they embrace it in order to stifle it.'[2] By 2016, the Republic's much vaunted 'secularism', so dear to the left and, increasingly, the right, had become, in the words of Shlomo Sand, 'the last refuge of the scoundrel'.[3] In this chapter we discuss how *laïcité* forms part of a contested national republican myth whose origins are bound up not just with progressive opposition to feudalism, monarchy and reaction, but also with colonialism, women's oppression and class inequality. Far from promoting 'living together', or social cohesion, *laïcité* has become a dangerous relic, an obstacle to recognising the changing, multicultural reality of French society—one that fixes and polices closed, imperial notions of identity in a nostalgic ideological straitjacket.

The burkini versus the Republic

David Lisnard, the mayor of Cannes, announced in August 2016 that he would be banning the wearing of the burkini on the town's beaches. 'I simply forbid a uniform that is the symbol of Islamic extremism,' he declared.[4] Sales of the garment, invented in 2004 by an Australian woman of Lebanese background, had topped 700,000 within a decade, almost half of them to non-Muslims, with Marks and Spencer among the outlets launching their own lines. 'I took away the traditional veil which did symbolise a Muslim woman,' remarked its designer, Aheda Zanetti, 'and replaced it with a hood type of top to blend in and integrate within Australian culture and lifestyle. It was also meant to be worn by all women no matter what race, religion, shape, colour and for whatever reason.'[5]

Drawing on the specialist lexicon honed during France's long-standing headscarf affair, Lisnard warned that any beachwear displaying 'ostentatious' affiliation to religious beliefs would not be tolerated. One of his officials claimed to perceive in the burkini an affiliation to Islamist terrorism. In any case, Lisnard was clear: his decision to ban the full-body swimsuit was in line with the French tradition of '*laïcité*'.[6] This, as *The Guardian* pointed out in its coverage of the issue, was 'a founding principle of the French Republic'.[7] Writing for the BBC, Agnès Poirier demonstrated how lack of critical distance from such crass initiatives could normalise discrimination just as effectively as outright racism. The burkini, she argued, challenged 'two fundamental French values and traditions: women's emancipation and a desire to live together as one nation.' 'The country that gave the bikini to the world, following on a long tradition of influential women,' she mused, randomly citing Madame du Châtelet, Coco Chanel and Simone de Beauvoir to support her case, 'is shocked to see that some French women accept what it sees as the diktat of religion and of men on them'.[8] It was left to *The New York Times* to note the obvious contradiction of a situation that involved 'imposing rules on what women can wear on the grounds that it's wrong for women to have to obey rules about what women can wear'.[9]

This was about more than a failure of logic, however. An editorial in *Le Monde* pointed out the absurdity of the furore, noting the proliferation of measures singling out or discriminating against Muslims. It nevertheless concluded that the affair was also partly a 'symptom of a Muslim community which, at least as far as its radical component is concerned, refuses to acknowledge the conspicuous, even ostentatious character of a garment like the burkini, only seeing proof of ostracism'.[10] 'Social diversity' in contemporary France had somehow become dependent on the capacity of Muslims to make themselves invisible. The notion of 'social diversity' or *mixité* has, like feminism, become a kind of appendage to *laïcité*, used to justify measures taken in its name when secular arguments alone prove wanting. For the then Socialist prime minister Manuel Valls (2014–16), the burkini was incompatible with French values and the Republic since it represented 'a political project for a counter-society based on the enslavement of women'.[11] The burkini was anything but 'an anodyne swimming costume', he argued, pointing out that it was a 'contraction of the bikini and the burqa' and concluding, with asinine bombast, 'It's a provocation, radical Islam is rising up and wants to impose itself in public space!'[12] Confronted by such problematic swimwear, there was only one solution: 'the Republic must defend itself.'[13] His arguments were backed up by Jean-Luc Mélenchon's Parti de Gauche, whose 'national secretary for anti-racism and *laïcité*', Benoît Schneckenburger, claimed the burkini to be the product of 'a Salafist religious offensive' that contradicted his party's feminist convictions.[14]

The degeneration of mainstream anti-racism in France, discussed in Chapter Five, was further underlined by Laurence Rossignol, appointed minister for women's rights in the Valls government in February 2016. Casting doubt on the wisdom of local bans on the burkini, she nevertheless offered no solidarity with the women being told what to wear by men holding municipal office. Denouncing fundamentalists who posed as 'victims', she declared the burkini to be 'a beach version of the burqa' whose purpose was to 'enclose, to hide women's bodies the better to control them'. The garment symbolised 'a profoundly archaic vision of the role of women in society and the relationship between men and women.' With no trace of irony, she added that 'The control of women's bodies and their sexuality has been a central issue in traditional societies. And to emancipate themselves women have had to break free from this control.'[15] Earlier in the year Rossignol had been interviewed about the proliferation of fashion garments designed for Muslims. She saw it as regressive, highlighting the 'growing hold of Salafist groups' over Muslim women. When it was pointed out that some women chose to wear the hijab of their own accord, she replied, 'There were also American Negroes [*nègres*] who were in favour of slavery.' She later apologised for her 'mistake' in using the word *nègre*, whose meaning in English is conveyed by both 'Negro' and 'nigger'. Rossignol had been a founder member of SOS Racisme.

What is laïcité?

At the core of the French republican notion of citizenship is the belief that shared values, rather than ties of blood or race, are fundamental to the relationship between individuals and the state. Identification with the Republic's 'universal' values takes precedence over particular, individual interests or affiliations based on gender, sexuality, ethnicity or religion. State institutions play a central role in disseminating these values, acting as 'pathways to integration'. Historically schools have been the most important institutions in this process; some argue that this partly explains contemporary concern over 'divergent and pluralistic appearances in the public schools'.[16] Defending the burkini ban in September 2016, Prime Minister Valls set out his vision of secular France as follows:

> The French nation is built on the conviction that for citizens to be free and equal, religion must be a private matter. Unlike other countries, France does not think of itself as a juxtaposition of communities, each following its own autonomous path. In other words: we don't conceive of identity as something ethnic. French identity is a commitment, a desire to share the same destiny.[17]

Ultimately, however, as Bowen argues,

> *Laïcité* remains one of those 'essentially contested concepts' that is politically useful precisely because it has no agreed-on definition. Or

rather, it is useful for political debates because its use conveys the double illusion that everyone knows what *laïcité* means and that this meaning has long been central to French republicanism.[18]

Sixteen-year-old students taking their *brevet* certificate in 2014 were asked to define the concept of *laïcité* and to give an example of its application in France. A study of a thousand answers revealed just how many had internalised the high-profile debates on the issue. A number of responses saw it as a means of defending the predominant culture: 'The principle of *laïcité* is to respect the Christian religion.' Others believed it to be a way of erasing other cultures: 'The principle of *laïcité* is that you shouldn't show your origins at schools or elsewhere'; '*Laïcité* is hiding your opinions, especially about religions in public places unless they are discreet. For example: the banning of the burqa'; or, perhaps most eloquently of all, '*Laïcité* is believing what I want but without showing it.'[19] Such views were unsurprising given the tone of debate, which had also infected school textbooks. One history textbook used in secondary schools teaches students that, 'In France, *laïcité* also requires the refusal of all religious expression in public space'.[20]

Laïcité is often presented as a given, a fixed and immutable aspect of the 'republican tradition', but its meaning at any time has been dependent on political battles and therefore subject to change, modification, compromise and distortion. The tendency, as Bowen points out, to present *laïcité* as 'an historical object' in its own right is characteristic of the myth-making surrounding the concept, as if it somehow 'represents the General Will and indicates the Common Good':

> The difficulty with this notion is that there is no 'it.' Not only has there never been agreement on the role religion should play in public life—some in France hold *laïcité* to guarantee freedom of public religious practice, while others think that it prevents such practice—there is no historical actor called '*laïcité*': only a series of debates, laws, and multiple efforts to assert claims over public space.[21]

Frequently understood as homogenous or 'indivisible', republican *laïcité* has always combined elements of openness and tolerance with exclusivity and divisiveness, as well as scope for exceptions. Secular legislation does not apply in five departments (regional administrative divisions), for example, and the state still provides subsidies for thousands of churches. School holidays continue to revolve around Christian festivals, reflecting the way French *laïcité* has absorbed and incorporated the nation's Catholic heritage. The imperial secular French state also deployed various methods of governance over its Muslim subjects, subsidising the building of the Paris mosque in 1926 and giving the colonised population of Algeria a legal status of, initially, 'indigenous Muslims' and then 'French Muslims of Algeria'.[22]

Contemporary advocates of legislation restricting religious expression in the public sphere routinely refer for justification to the 1905 Law of Separation of Church and State. On the one hand the law marked a rejection of Catholicism and its influence over the state, effectively ending France's role as 'the elder daughter of the Church'. On the other it sought neutrality of the state, and state actors, but freedom of expression for individuals and tolerance of their views. The 'new secularism' discussed below marks an apparent departure from this framework, engineering increased state suppression of individual expression.[23] Opponents of this drift have been at pains to point out that recent developments mark a departure from the concept's origins. Article One of the 1905 law declared: 'The Republic ensures freedom of conscience. It guarantees the free exercise of religion subject to the sole restrictions enacted hereafter in the interest of public order.'[24] During the law's parliamentary debate an amendment was tabled to prevent priests from wearing ecclesiastical robes (the *soutane*, or cassock) in public space, on the grounds that it constituted a provocation, that it infringed 'freedom and human dignity', that it amounted to proselytising attire—thus rendering the priest a 'prisoner' or 'slave'. Deputies overwhelmingly rejected such suggestions. 'The day after separation,' declared Aristide Briand, principal author of the law, 'the *soutane* becomes a garment like any other.'[25] The National Assembly instead adopted another amendment, which extended freedom of religious expression in public space. The deputy moving this amendment was unequivocal: 'Respect for freedom of conscience leads to the mutual respect of beliefs and not to the prohibition of external manifestations of religious worship in public.'[26] In other words, the 1905 law, so frequently cited today in support of the new secularism, meant more, not less, freedom of expression.[27] The Republic recognised 'no religion'. In other words, under the terms of the 1905 law, the Republic should attribute no special significance to the *soutane* or the hijab or the burkini. Bienvenu Martin, minister for arts and religion at the time, intervened in the parliamentary debate on separation to counter accusations that it was an atheist measure. The government's intention, he argued, was not to 'affirm a philosophical doctrine but simply to apply the principle of freedom of conscience and proclaim the neutrality of the state in religious affairs.' To recognise religions would be to give them official consecration and to constitute state intervention in how they were organised.[28]

Many Catholics nevertheless saw the law as an aggressive manifestation of anti-clericalism. Conflict between the Church and republicans was understandable. The Church had backed numerous attempts to restore the monarchy following the revolutionary upheavals of 1789–99 and retained its influence over the education system until the late nineteenth century. The Third Republic (1870–1940) broke this hold by banning priests from teaching in state schools. One legacy of this conflict is the strong current of anti-clericalism that remains a feature of French society today, particularly on the left. At the time, 'bourgeois anti-clericalism' was attacked by Marxist observers of developments in France, like Lenin and Luxemburg, as a way of distracting workers from social questions and class struggle. Marx himself, as Plenel stresses, believed 'what people do together [to be] more important than what they believe separately'.[29] Today, as Christine Delphy notes, many on the left are 'still living the anti-papist fight of a hundred years ago':

> Yet they make no protest about the fact that the state pays for the upkeep of 36,000 churches, among other official marks of indulgence for the Christian faith. Nor are very many seen rising up against the fact that political secularism is not applied in five departments of France, where priests, pastors and rabbis are paid by the state just as they were under Napoleon. Yet, at the same time as they want to make the state school a 'sanctuary', they never mention that almost half of all French children and teenagers are educated in religious-run (mostly Catholic) schools.[30]

Although the proportion of secondary school students taught in Catholic schools is nearer a fifth than half of the total, this is still a higher proportion than in countries like Britain or the United States, where 'communitarianism' is supposedly rife. The accusation that France is suffering from 'secular fundamentalism' is therefore incorrect: if this were the case then the state's preferential treatment of Catholic establishments and its alignment of school holidays with Catholic festivals would be more keenly contested. Put bluntly, France's problem is not *laïcité* but racism. *Laïcité* has simply become the most 'respectable' and therefore effective means for it to be expressed today. Since 1989, when the issue of *laïcité* came to the fore, measures aimed at upholding or preserving France's secular traditions at both national and local level have primarily been concerned with policing what Muslim women wear. It has become commonplace to refer to religion as something that must be confined to the 'private sphere' or to demand 'discretion' from Muslims whose headgear (or beachwear) is perceived by non-believers as too conspicuous an expression of religious affiliation. In practice, then, *laïcité* has come to mean 'obliging Muslims, and Muslims alone, to make themselves invisible'.[31] Along with *mixité*, the concept of '*vivre ensemble*'—living together, the pursuit of social cohesion—has become the justification for increasingly rigid secular regulations. Although this notion appears to pay lip service to the concept of diversity, in practice, as Delphy argues, it has come to mean 'living together without changing anyone's situation or status in society—you in your place, me in mine'.[32] The emergence of this concept as part of a 'tradition' is instructive. It did not feature in the 1905 Law of Separation (neither did the word *laïcité*) and the measures that rely on it for justification, notably those banning the burqa, the niqab and the burkini, directly contradicted not just the 1905 law, but also the Universal Declaration of Human Rights (1948), which asserts not only the 'right to freedom of thought, conscience and religion' but also specifies that this right includes the freedom, 'either alone or in community with others and *in public or private*, to manifest his religion or belief in teaching, practice, worship and observance.'[33]

Secular morality

The distinction between 'open' and 'closed' attitudes towards secularism is today often obscured by a tendency to present the principle as instinctive, rooted and intrinsic to France and the French people. In December 2003, President Jacques Chirac announced: 'The French being what they are, the wearing of the veil, whether we like it or not, is a kind of aggression which they find it difficult to accept'.[34] At the other end of the political spectrum, Jean-Luc Mélenchon has argued that 'our way of life, for us the French, is that we don't wear the veil to school.'[35] Republican nationalism has generally prided itself on affiliation to a 'colour-blind' political model of citizenship, rather than ethno-culturalist appeals to tradition and lineage based on the German *volkisch* model of citizenship. However, the lines between these two models are becoming increasingly blurred. The republican tradition to which most of the left still cleaves has been embraced by the far right as part of its national heritage, along with the emblematic figures of Clovis, the first king of the Franks, and Joan of Arc. As Béatrice Mabilon-Bonfils and Geneviève Zaïa argue, 'French *laïcité* is today caught between a right that is developing "uninhibited" notions of cultural hierarchy, and a left trapped by its reference to an emancipatory universalism necessarily based upon superiority of values.'[36]

In contemporary France, this 'new secularism' of supposed national culture holds sway. Since 2015, school students have been given fortnightly classes in 'secular morality'. The Socialist education minister responsible for the initiative outlined the rationale behind it in 2012:

> Secular morality means understanding what is right, distinguishing between good and bad, it's also about duties as much as rights, about virtues and, above all, values. My hope for French schools is the kind of teaching that will inculcate students with notions of universal morality, based on ideas of humanity and reason.

Evoking the threat of fundamentalism, he warned that, 'If the Republic does not say what its vision is of vice and virtue, good and bad, right and wrong, others will do it in its place'.[37] The aim of 'secular moralism' was to allow students to emancipate themselves, since *laïcité* was founded on respect for freedom of conscience. But in order for this freedom of choice to be given, students must be 'torn away from all the determinisms: familial, ethnic, social, intellectual, to be able to then make a choice'. Such messianic notions of the role of education in republican society indicate the overlap between the political and cultural aspects of *laïcité* that have historically been a feature of the concept, particularly as part of the nation-building project undertaken by the Third Republic from 1870. In other words, republican secularism is presented as a political framework for establishing a community of citizens, but also forms an integral part of a national myth, bound up with the construction of 'Frenchness' and its implicit sense of superiority.

As Suzanne Citron has demonstrated, this myth establishes a 'collective memory' of the nation based on a teleology that smacks of racialised nationalism: the Republic is the absolute expression of the public good, inheritor of a process of centralisation and homogenisation begun under kings like Clovis and Charlemagne and leading to the goal of 'France', the bearer of universal values to all of humanity. The multilingual and multicultural history of France is overshadowed by the myth that the Gauls were the ancestors of the French, by the establishment of French as the national language after the Revolution and by a dominant historical narrative developed under the Third Republic from 1870. Under the Third Republic the state played the central role in forging a sense of 'Frenchness', notably in breaking the affiliation of the peasantry with parochial identities and winning it to an identification with the nation, turning, as Eugen Weber has described, 'peasants into Frenchmen', a process of state-led inculcation that he compares with colonialism.[38]

Central to this was education. When 98 per cent of conscripts reported for duty in 1914 this was heralded as a victory for the republican schoolteacher. The peasant who, a few decades earlier, had understood his 'country' to be his locality and who used neither the national currency nor the national language, was now prepared to give his life for a thing called France. In contrast to the assumptions underpinning the ethno-centrist secularism that sees *laïcité* as a fixture of 'the French way of life' and integral to the national character, in reality the nation, as Citron explains, 'is not an essence that has emerged through the ages, and its narrative, transmitted by the republican school system, is not a sacred text, an untouchable taboo. The nation is a construction, an evolution, a dynamic, a series of interactions.'[39]

As we shall see, the Republic's 'universal' myth comprises notions of superiority, 'communitarianism' and colonialism. For Pierre Bourdieu, France was the embodiment *par excellence* of the West's 'false universalism', tacitly presenting its own particularity as a 'universal yardstick'.[40] This 'imperialism of the universal' does not stand outside time, but is shaped by particular contexts. In this respect, there is a significant difference between today's 'new secularism' and the deployment of *laïcité* in the late nineteenth and early twentieth centuries. The moral and civic education introduced by the education minister Jules Ferry in the late nineteenth century was part of an ambitious social project to build a nation, drawing on the extension of democratic rights and the optimistic individualism produced by industrialisation and the development of a national market and infrastructure. As Mabilon-Bonfils and Zaïa outline,

> today, on the contrary, the promotion of this 'morality' manifests itself as a remedy, an exasperated defence in the face of 'problems': of insecurity, of incivility, of authority, of 'communitarianism'... Emanating from the Enlightenment, this tradition gave itself a goal of building a community of citizens against all local particularisms, cultural differences. However, in societies marked by migration and the logic of globalisation, we believe that today what's required is not so much civilising weak minority groups as promoting their involvement in this society, in terms of recognition and access to resources.[41]

False universalism

The shortcomings of this republican morality today are particularly apparent when it comes to the invocation of women's rights to defend the superiority of French identity. 'I believe in national identity,' Sarkozy declared during the 2007 presidential campaign. 'France is not a race, France is not an ethnicity, France is a community of values, it's an ideal, it's an idea. Women in France are free like men, free to circulate, free to marry, free to divorce. The right to abortion, equality between men and women, that's also part of our identity'.[42] For former prime minister Valls, there are two fundamental and related principles that make France what it is: equality between men and women, and *laïcité*. 'We must be open-eyed about the growing influence of Salafism,' he warned in 2016, 'which implies that women are inferior and impure and must be sidelined.' France, by contrast, was fighting for the liberation of women, 'who must not live under the yoke of a chauvinist order... or be subject to any domination whatsoever.'[43]

Despite such celebrations of the status of women's liberation as a 'fundamental' French value and tradition, it is a comparatively recent and incomplete innovation. While universal male suffrage was first established relatively early in France, in 1848, and eventually consolidated following the formation of the Third Republic in 1870, female suffrage was not achieved until 1944, long after it had been granted to women in most of the rest of Europe. A persistent argument against granting women the vote was that they were too influenced by the Church and would therefore be a conservative brake on progress. It was not until 1965 that women won the right to open their own bank accounts and choose a profession without first seeking their husband's consent. 'Parental', as opposed to paternal, authority in the home was not established in law until 1970 and it took a further five years, and protracted campaigning, for abortion to be legalised, partly reflecting the fact that France's Catholic traditions still ran very deep.

For all the celebration of the nation's universal values and commitment to women's rights, misogyny remains deeply entrenched in France. Women earn around 80 per cent of what men earn, are under-represented among high earners and massively over-represented among low earners.[44] Domestic violence claims the life of one woman every three days.[45] It is estimated that 75,000 women are raped every year, a tenth of these cases reported to the police. When the Socialist former finance minister Dominique Strauss-Kahn was accused in 2011 of raping a chambermaid in a New York hotel, prominent left-wing advocates of republican orthodoxy displayed a remarkably libertarian attitude to the issue. Among those who rallied to the defence of 'DSK' were his colleague and fellow leading Socialist Jack Lang, who wondered why he had been taken into custody since 'nobody had died'.[46] The journalist and editor of the staunchly republican magazine *Marianne*, Jean-François Kahn, argued that it was not so much rape that had taken place as 'an imprudence', which he dismissed as 'the lifting up of a domestic's skirt'.[47] Alain Finkielkraut displayed a similar attitude in relation to another high-profile case when Roman Polanski was accused of illegal sexual relations with a thirteen-year-old girl. Polanski was not a paedophile, he declared, and his accuser was not a little girl or a child, but an adolescent who had taken her clothes off to pose for *Vogue homme*.[48]

'[W]hat universalism is it exactly that these defenders of French identity are so proud of?' asks Christine Delphy, 'What is this universalism they claim to be protecting against the dominated groups' supposed "communitarian" tendencies?' A false universalism, she argues, founded on inequality, requiring women 'to conform to the model of the dominant'.[49] Edwy Plenel talks of a 'French mental block', rooted in republican universalism and a model of integration based on the unequal relationships established during the colonial era. 'The Other,' he argues, 'was only recognised as such depending on the goodwill of the dominator'.[50] Cleaving to 'this abstract universal that only accepts the Jew, the black or the Arab on condition that they divest themselves of their history and their memory',[51] French elites today consequently refuse to accept France 'as it has become, as it lives and works, as it grows and expands', relying instead on 'the neo-colonial demand to assimilate that seeks to compel one section of our compatriots (of Islamic culture, Arab origin, black skin, etc.) to erase themselves and dissolve, in short, to whiten themselves. The requirement, in other words, to disappear in order to be accepted.'[52]

The universalist myth is sustained by other myths. The charge of communitarianism, for example, common currency in debates ranging from halal meat to gay rights, has become a metaphor used by 'respectable racism', with opposition to it presented as a cornerstone of republicanism, distinguishing France from the so-called 'Anglo-Saxon' (British and American) model, supposedly based on celebrating multiculturalism and condoning 'communitarianism'. Like the 'new secularism', the significance of 'communitarianism' has grown in parallel with the rise of racism in French society. The word itself did not appear in the French dictionary until 1997, its use rising exponentially following the 2005 *banlieue* uprising.[53] 'Real communitarianism,' as Delphy points out in response to accusations that this is the goal of gay liberation,

> means the coexistence of different rules for different parts of the population, described as communities. That's the case in Lebanon where [the unitarian] Druzes have a different civil law than the [Christian] Maronites, and in turn theirs is different than the Muslims. That is the case in Israel and in India (among other places), where 'personal status codes' regulate marriage, inheritance, etc. according to people's religious affiliation. As far as I'm aware, that's not what gay movements are asking for, here or anywhere else. In fact, they're demanding exactly the opposite: they want the common law to be applied to them equally, and the abrogation of the exceptions and exemptions that make them into a specific category. The present situation is the real communitarianism: not *theirs*, but the communitarianism of the society that discriminates against them. And they want an end to this situation.[54]

The first step towards a genuine universalism is the recognition of particular situations. Abstract universalism—'man always the same in all times and all places'[55]—cannot do this. Starting from the premise that all are in theory equal, it shuns the means to strive towards lived equality. The refusal to recognise particular needs and concerns means that France does not practice ethnic monitoring or affirmative action. When it came to legalising gay marriage, the reform was articulated in broad universal terms: 'marriage for all'. Faced with the unfurling of the 'French spring', an unprecedented outpouring of bigotry in opposition to the reform, proponents of the legislation were put on the defensive and unable to mount an effective riposte to the backlash. The demand for equal representation for women in politics was also advanced in universal terms, as a call for 'parity' rather than as affirmative action ('positive discrimination' in French), given the latter term's overtones of multiculturalism and communitarian drift.[56]

What is required in France today, argues Plenel, is the capacity 'to think at the same time the universal and the singular, solidarity and diversity, unity and plurality. And, as a result, to firmly reject the neo-colonial demand to assimilate'.[57]

Policing Muslims

One of the ironies of this refusal to recognise and accept difference is its counter-productive nature. Nowhere has this been more apparent than in the policing of Muslim women's dress in the public sphere. Here, the demand for invisibility has produced a retreat from the public to the private sphere. In *A Dying Colonialism*, Frantz Fanon detailed the mechanisms deployed by the French to bring about the disintegration of Algerian society: '"If we want to destroy the structure of Algerian society, its capacity for resistance, we must first of all conquer the women:

we must go and find them behind the veil where they hide themselves and in the houses where the men keep them out of sight'".[58] Algerian women, presented as 'humiliated, sequestered, cloistered', were to be saved by the colonial power from medieval and barbaric Algerian men: '"We want to make the Algerian ashamed of the fate that he metes out to women"'.[59] According to Fanon, the colonial mindset saw in Algerian resistance to such efforts the influence of a supposedly mystical or savage religion:

> The method of presenting the Algerian as a prey fought over with equal ferocity by Islam and France with its Western culture reveals the whole approach of the occupier, his philosophy and his policy... the occupier, smarting from his failures, presents in a simplified and pejorative way the system of values by means of which the colonised person resists his innumerable offensives. What is in fact the assertion of a distinct identity, concern with keeping intact a few shreds of national existence, is attributed to religious, magical fanatical behavior.[60]

Today, the echoes of such attitudes are unmistakable—and then, as now, the operation was entirely counter-productive: 'The tenacity of the occupier in his endeavor to unveil the women, to make of them an ally in the work of cultural destruction, had the effect of strengthening the traditional patterns of behavior.' During the war of independence (1954–62), many previously unveiled Algerian women reacted to the sight of French soldiers forcibly removing the hijab by taking to wearing it themselves, in defiance of the imposition of Western values as part of an alleged civilising mission.[61]

In 2002 President Chirac set up a commission headed by the then Ombudsman (Mediator) of the French Republic, Bernard Stasi, to frame legislation on the headscarf issue.[62] While the commission deliberated, a scandal unfolded at a school in Aubervilliers, northern Paris. Two girls were expelled for wearing the hijab following agitation around the issue by teachers at the school, led by Georges Vartanianz and Pierre-François Grond, who also happened to be national representatives of the far-left organisations Lutte ouvrière and the Ligue communiste révolutionnaire. In December 2003, after six months of deliberation, the Stasi Commission submitted its report, recommending that the hijab be banned in schools. A leading feminist, Gisèle Halimi, declared it a 'just and courageous' decision, condemning the 'veil' as a symbol of female inferiority: 'a veritable sexual apartheid'.[63] A month later, Stasi was interviewed about the commission's work. 'Islam,' he told his audience, 'only exists in under-developed countries, in countries where the rights of man are not respected, often in countries where Islam is the only religion, a dominant religion, and the least that can be said is that it does not respect others.'[64]

By September 2004, 'the wearing of signs or clothing by which students visibly manifest a religious affiliation' in primary and secondary schools had been outlawed. Following the commission's recommendations, turbans, kippahs and 'outsized' crucifixes would also fall under the ban.[65] As Jean Baubérot, the only member of the commission not to back the report (he abstained) has pointed out, the exclusion of young women from state schools and colleges has forced them into distance learning—thereby 'de-socialising' them—or into private education. A 'paradoxical' outcome, as Baubérot remarked, 'for a so-called secular law'.[66] Other proposals by the commission, such as the creation of school holidays for Yom Kippur and Eid, were ignored.

The United Nation's Committee on the Rights of the Child, meanwhile, expressed its concern that the ban on the hijab was not in the best interests of children and could undermine their right to education. This proved to be the case. In January 2005, an official report put the number of exclusions at forty-nine, with sixty children having left school as a result of the ban. Other estimates put the figures much higher, between 200 and 700, as a result of the 'silent exclusions' that took place prior to the beginning of term—girls who could not contemplate removing the hijab and did not want to endure the humiliation of being excluded.[67] Those who removed the headscarf in order to attend school faced another kind of humiliation, as some teachers interpreted the ban as a licence to pass comment on their new appearance: 'Soon we'll be able to find out if you're a blonde or a brunette', 'You're going to have cold ears', 'Ah, I didn't know you had hair!', and so on.[68] There was even a report of a local official contacting a mosque on the eve of the new term to ensure that fathers were encouraged to send their daughters to school without a hijab, thus facilitating compliance with a law whose ostensible purpose was to counter the communitarian tendencies allegedly fostered by mosques and authoritarian Muslim fathers.[69]

Such ironies reflected a wider failure, wilful or otherwise, to grasp the simple fact that symbols change according to context. There is a difference between wearing the hijab in Saudi Arabia or Iran, where the state decrees it compulsory in public, and wearing it in France, where it can be an act of conformity but also, in an Islamophobic environment, of defiance. 'We would never wear it in a country where it was obligatory,' argued the two students expelled for wearing the hijab in Aubervilliers.[70] As the accounts of young French Muslims discussed in the next chapter show, the repression of the hijab often became a reason in itself for them to begin wearing a headscarf, as a symbol of independence and an assertion of individual choice. By contrast, the 'universal' meaning of the hijab appears, as Delphy notes, to be discernable only to non-Muslim Western feminists.[71]

Whatever the pretext afforded by the outlawing of entirely hypothetical oversized crucifixes—and the collateral discrimination meted out to real Jews and Sikhs—the principal achievement of the 2004 law was to give formal state authority to the stigmatisation of Muslims. Islamophobes could now declare open season, which they did. The education minister at the time of its passing, Luc Ferry, announced that, 'as soon as anything becomes a religious sign, it will fall under this law,' raising the prospect of a future clampdown on beards or bandanas if it could be construed that they were being worn in a 'religious' way.[72] And this is exactly what happened. In 2011–12, some Muslim students wearing long skirts or dresses became the subject of disciplinary action and were told to wear something else or face exclusion, since skirts of such length could be construed—by others—as having a 'religious connotation', amounting to a 'provocation'.[73] Similar 'connotations' were imputed to bandanas, with students facing expulsion and long appeals processes for wearing them. One journalist declared in 2013 that the sight of Muslim men turning up to work with 'black beards' was 'unbearable'.[74] Some schools took it upon themselves to ban mothers who wore the hijab from accompanying their children on school trips, a move backed in 2011 by the then education minister, Luc Chatel, who declared that 'pupils' parents must respect the principles of neutrality and secularism.'[75]

Wearing the niqab in public was banned by legislation that came into force in 2011. Months of debate were devoted to denouncing the burqa and the niqab in a campaign led by the Communist André Gerin and the UMP's Éric Raoult. Despite their much-trumpeted concern to enact legislation in the interests of gender equality, their commission chose to allow only one Muslim woman to address them, and they made her take off her niqab before doing so.[76] Although the resulting legislation clearly targeted the niqab, it was framed in disingenuous universalist terms that implied belated concern about the threat posed to 'living together' by covering the face in all manner of ways. Motorcycle helmets, balaclavas and hoodies therefore also came under the remit of the law. Those contravening it were liable to pay a fine of €150 and attend a citizenship class to remind them of the republican values of secularism and gender equality.

Anyone making someone else cover their face 'because of their gender' could face a €30,000 fine and a year in prison. In cases concerning minors (under eighteens) being made to cover their face, the penalty could be doubled. This was justified in terms of government concern to fight 'this new form of the subjection of women, which the Republic cannot allow on its territory'.[77]

In 2011, having played a key role in waging this fight, Raoult was charged, and later acquitted, of domestic violence, remarking that 'telling your wife "you dress like a slut" isn't domestic violence'.[78] In 2014, charges of sexual harassment were brought against him after he sent over 15,000 unsolicited texts to a female colleague who accused him of sacking her when she refused his advances, which included observations about her 'triple-A-rated breasts'.[79] In his defence Raoult claimed, with characteristic macho bullishness, that the accusations were politically motivated and argued, with no trace of irony, that 'she had no hesitation in showing her body. I'm suspected of harassment but nobody suspects a girl of enticement'.[80]

Male advocates of legislation to regulate women's access to garments they find offensive have offered various interpretations of the sexual implications of the public display, or concealment, of the female body. Jean-Luc Mélenchon, for instance, writing in 2010, found the niqab not only 'degrading' but also 'obscene' since it reduced 'the status of those wearing it solely to that of potential sexual prey'. Where Raoult complained of the temptations of naked female flesh, Mélenchon objected to the way he felt the niqab, by concealing it, assumed all men to be sexual predators, since in his view it implied that the 'object of desire' should be hidden from the 'lust of all those who looked at her'. Criticising Jean-Marie Le Pen, whose view was that outlawing the niqab should be possible under existing legislation, Mélenchon argued that the secular character of the Republic must be reinforced through a new law. Women who wore the niqab were engaged in a spectacle of 'self-humiliation' that amounted to a 'breach of public order'. Veiled in this way, women were denying their own status 'as autonomous subjects'. They must therefore be instructed by the state to dress differently. Left-wing parliamentary deputies, he argued, should back the law but also press for it to go further: nobody should be permitted to request medical treatment by a doctor of the same sex, all municipal sporting activities should be mixed and separate swimming pool timetables should be outlawed.[81]

Once Gerin and Raoult's law was passed, women who wanted to wear the niqab, like those who wore other garments to cover their faces, were obliged do so in the privacy of their own home (dispensation was granted to allow women to wear the niqab in a car, provided it did not impair vision when driving). Here, the twisted logic of the new secularism becomes clear. As Stéphanie Hennette-Vauchez and Vincent Valentin argue, by intervening ostensibly to protect women from the violence, pressure or subjugation presumed to be behind the wearing of the hijab, or the full-face or full-body veil, the state makes delinquents of those who refuse to accept its authority. Muslim women and girls are offered the choice between accepting restrictions on their autonomy in public space or being confined to the home or forced to accept private schooling. This recalls the suspicion of women that characterised the misogyny of anti-clerical attitudes in the early twentieth century. Once vessels of the Catholic priest, women now posed problems as vessels of the imam: 'for the Republic to make "progress", women and religion must be relegated and confined to the private sphere'.[82]

The new secularism is making a mockery of the republican principles it claims to be upholding, notably the quest for equality, supposedly one of the purposes of free, compulsory, secular education. We have seen how the application of secular zealotry has driven young women from state to private schools. Many more will have felt humiliated or undermined as a consequence of such public assertions of intolerance. Others will have experienced the government's 2013 decision to display a 'secular charter' in all state schools as a hostile act. Some schools took it upon themselves to push their secular credentials to the limit. At least one institution put up a notice declaring that 'pupils must present themselves bare-headed on entering the establishment'.[83] The head teacher at a school in Bondy, north of Paris, sent a circular to parents notifying them that all children would be served with meat in the canteen. 'If for religious reasons you do not wish your child to eat meat,' she wrote, 'please make arrangements to see me as this is not acceptable. I remind you that your child is educated in a republican [state] school and that *laïcité*—one of the foundations of this Republic—must be respected in its entirety.'[84]

In this instance the head teacher later apologised for her 'bad transcription of the principle of *laïcité*',[85] but halal meat remains a moral panic waiting to happen. When the fast food chain Quick experimented with halal-only menus at eight of its 350 outlets in 2009, there was an outcry. One right-wing deputy complained that the lack of choice for non-Muslim customers was unacceptable. The government felt moved to comment, its spokesperson and education minister Luc Chatel declaring, 'I respect the traditions, including dietary ones, of every community but I think that French society, its history, its culture, is not a communitarian one'.[86] In February 2010 a local newspaper ran the headline: 'Judged too communitarian, Quick's halal hamburgers stir controversy'.[87] In the summer of 2016, shortly prior to the burkini furore, a mini-market on the outskirts of Paris was threatened with closure by the social housing association, presided over by the local right-wing mayor, that leased out the premises. The problem? Communitarianism. According to one of the housing association officials, 'This mini-market is communitarian because of what is not there—pork and alcohol—but also because of what is: meat that is 95 per cent halal, and prayer mats.'[88] An aide to the Les Républicains mayor Nicole Goueta explained the importance of combating 'the communitarianism of shops', pointing out that the mayor herself had visited the store asking that pork and alcohol be stocked.[89]

This is the spiral that has been created by the anti-Muslim edicts and laws of the past two decades. The sentiment expressed in the frequently cited 1905 Law of Separation—that 'respect for freedom of conscience leads to the mutual respect of beliefs and not to the prohibition of external manifestations of a cult in public'[90]—has been overshadowed by a desire to render invisible outward signs of affiliation to Islam. As Mabilon-Bonfils and Zaïa argue, 'To say "secular" today is thus another way of saying French'. Presented from its origins as a superior means of ensuring social cohesion, the 'secular' agenda has become a form of reactionary collective nostalgia that asserts the identity of the majority, 'maintaining a climate of suspicion and *feeding* the construction of a "Muslim problem"'.[91] *Laïcité*, they conclude, has become a form of moral panic.[92]

Secularism of the right

As we saw in the last chapter, Chirac's 2002 presidential victory prompted the right to lay claim to *laïcité*. Until this point secularism had never been a preoccupation of the mainstream right. As Ahearne explains, those around Chirac saw it as an opportunity to capitalise on the election victory by recasting *laïcité* as an expression of right-wing values. The architect of this manoeuvre, the UMP politician François Baroin, viewed it as a 'stock reference for French identity', a means of confronting the 'progress of individualism and multiculturalism' that posed a challenge to the 'principle of authority and the transmission of common values that allow the idea of the nation to endure as a living idea'. Should France simply 'resign itself to the growing development of particularities' or 'continue to promote a common culture based on the emancipation and autonomy of the citizen'? Embracing *laïcité* would be an opportunity to capitalise on the supposed nationalist republican revival behind Chirac's election. Baroin advocated a 're-politicisation' of *laïcité*, envisaging it becoming one of the right's values 'against a left that has broadly embraced multiculturalism and been unable to respond to the challenge of communitarianism'.[93]

The right's newfound muscular secularism was to bear fruit with the 2004 ban on the hijab in schools. This provided the most mercurial politician of the period, Nicolas Sarkozy, an opponent of the law, with a challenge, since his outsider's anti-elitism had partly been based on a critique of the republican legacy and an idiosyncratic attitude towards its secular traditions. His political prominence itself a symptom of the crisis of republicanism, Sarkozy's distinctive brand of Gallic neo-conservatism combined aspects of right-wing traditionalism, notably with regard to Catholicism, and an openness to notions like affirmative action, which had more in common with the neoliberal diversity agenda in Britain and the US than republican orthodoxy. However, as Ahearne observes, *laïcité* 'provides, in French contemporary contexts, a source of resonance and iconic projection that a politician as adept in symbolic manipulation as Sarkozy could not neglect.'[94]

As interior minister, Sarkozy set up the Conseil Français du Culte Musulman (French Council of the Muslim Faith, or CFCM), a clear example of state intervention in religious affairs and an overt attempt to create, as he reiterated ad nauseam, an 'Islam of France' as opposed to an 'Islam in France'. His efforts to court the Union of French Islamic Organisations (UOIF), which became the predominant influence within the CFCM, was also a break with the notion that religion pertained only to the 'private' sphere, but Sarkozy had no qualms about promoting religious orders or engaging in mediation with individuals on the basis of their religious affiliation. Moves to recognise religious organisations as legitimate mediating groups proved untenable in the atmosphere created by the 2004 hijab law and the accompanying debate, particularly given Sarkozy's own openly anti-Muslim interventions around the *banlieues* in 2005. His 'positive *laïcité*' instead took the form of emphasising France's Christian roots, arguing that the Catholic Church had been the victim of the anti-clerical Law of Separation and that secular schoolteachers would never be able to teach the difference between good and evil like priests.[95] Sarkozy nevertheless retained his 'iconoclastic' attitude towards republicanism after becoming president in 2007.[96] In December 2008, he made a speech in which he announced that the republican principle of equality had become a myth: 'How can we talk about a republic when your success at school and in professional life depends not on ... merit but largely on your social origin, the neighbourhood where you live, your name or the colour of your skin?'[97] His professed desire to combat discrimination followed the establishment in 2004 of the HALDE (High Authority for the Struggle Against Discrimination and for Equality), the creation in 2005 of a Ministry for Equal Opportunities and the appointment of Azouz Begag, the first ever cabinet minister of North African background, to the post. Sarkozy had also, as interior minister, appointed the first Muslim prefect (a local state representative). Following his 2007 election to the presidency, two women of Algerian heritage, Rachida Dati and Fadela Amara, as well as the Dakar-born Rama Yade, were appointed to François Fillon's government in the Ministries of Justice, Urban Affairs and Human Rights respectively. Early the following year, Sarkozy indicated that he wanted the principle of diversity to be inscribed in the preamble to the constitution. Although this did not happen, a commission set up to examine diversity issues did support the collection of data measuring the extent of inequality and discrimination—ethnic monitoring in all but name—a process identified as essential to combating discrimination, but previously shunned by a supposedly 'colour-blind' Republic.[98]

Rachida Dati lost her post in a reshuffle in 2009, with Rama Yade and Fadela Amara leaving theirs a year later. In 2011, following a row about the selection of candidates for the 2012 elections, Dati wrote an incandescent open letter to Prime Minister Fillon, accusing him of using the UMP elite's control of the party apparatus to block the advancement of women and ethnic minorities.[99] The post-Gaullist right's embrace of diversity was not, then, a straightforward process. In March 2011, Sarkozy lost his advisor on racial and religious diversity, Abderrahmane Dahmane, who claimed that the UMP, under the leadership of Jean-François Copé, was 'a plague on Muslims'. He went on to argue that the government's forthcoming debate on Islam had been taken over by party members who were 'very close to the FN',[100] labelling Copé a 'neo-Nazi' and urging France's Muslims to wear green stars in protest at 'runaway Islamophobia' and 'an ideology which consists of expatriating French citizens by the boatload'.[101]

The travails of these ministers were a small part of a much bigger problem. The government's Observatory on *Laïcité*, established in principle late in the Chirac presidency in 2007 and eventually set in motion under Hollande, declared in 2014 that

> France today is characterised by far greater cultural diversity than in the past. This is why it has never had as much need for *laïcité*. *Laïcité* guarantees that all its citizens, whatever their philosophical or religious convictions, can live together in freedom of conscience, the freedom to practise a religion or to practise none, equality of rights and duties, republican fraternity.[102]

Government attitudes to race and ethnicity in contemporary France turn on a tension between the social reality of a multicultural France deeply polarised by inequality, and widespread political refusal of this fact. Pivotal to this denial is France's undigested colonial past.

The colonial legacy

Since 2002, France has seen the most concerted attempt to revive its colonial heritage since the end of the Algerian war in 1962. In February 2005 a bill was introduced containing an article that required schools to teach children about the 'positive role of the French presence overseas, notably in North Africa'. Opposition to this measure, particularly from historians, forced its withdrawal from the bill in 2006. Following his election in 2007 Sarkozy gave a speech in Dakar that dramatically underlined the extent to which colonial arrogance and racism remained a powerful component of French political culture. Although he began the speech with an acknowledgement of colonialism's crimes—the pillaging of wealth, the exploitation and the way individuals were stripped of their freedom, land and personality—he made his intentions very clear: 'I have not come to talk to you about repentance.' Slavery was a crime against humanity, but it was time to go beyond pain and suffering. The coloniser may have taken, he went on, 'but he also gave'. 'He built bridges, roads, hospitals, dispensaries and schools. He turned virgin soil fertile. He gave his effort, his work, his know-how. I want to say it here, not all the colonialists were thieves or exploiters.'

What followed was to provoke an outraged reaction. Sarkozy's references to the havoc created by colonialism were dramatically undermined by the tone and content of the vision of Africa he proceeded to outline, dredging up nineteenth-century clichés about the continent that were patronising and simplistic. 'Who gave him the right,' asked the Cameroonian philosopher Achille Mbembe in an open letter to Sarkozy, 'to talk about Africa and

Africans in a manner of a master who has the habit of ill-treating his slave?'[103]

'The tragedy of Africa,' Sarkozy declared,

> is that the African has not fully entered into history. The African peasant, who for thousands of years has lived according to the seasons, whose ideal in life was to be in harmony with nature, knows only the eternal renewal of time, to the rhythm of an endless repetition of the same gestures and the same words. In this imaginary world, where everything starts over and over again, there is no place for human adventure or for the idea of progress... This man (the traditional African) never launches himself towards the future. It never occurs to him to escape this repetition and to invent his own destiny.

He then took it upon himself to outline, for the audience of teachers, researchers, students and journalists present, precisely what Africa's problems were. He did so at length:

> The problem facing Africa, and allow a friend of Africa to say it, is to be found here. Africa's challenge is to enter to a greater extent into history... Africa's problem is how to stop always repeating, always mulling over, how to liberate itself from the myth of the eternal return... Africa's problem is that it lives too much in the present, out of nostalgia for a lost childhood paradise... Africa's problem is not how to invent for itself a more or less mythical past to help it to support the present, but how to invent the future with suitable means. Africa's problem is not how to prepare itself for the return of misfortune, as if that is supposed to repeat itself indefinitely, but finding the will to give itself the means to combat misfortune, because Africa has a right to happiness like all the other continents of the world. Africa's problem is how to remain true to itself without remaining immobile.[104]

What Africa had to do, then, was 'to learn to view its accession to the universal not as a renunciation of what Africa is but as an accomplishment... to learn to feel heir to all that is universal in all human civilisations.'

Pointing out that some considered African culture to be backward, and Africans 'to be big children', he proceeded to offer a solution to famine, much as one might outline the problem to an infant, or to an imbecile: 'Do you want there to be no more famine in Africa, never again a single child who dies of hunger?' he asked. 'Then find a way to be self-sufficient in food production. Develop food. Africa must first produce food to feed itself.' As his sophisticated audience of intellectuals and professionals listened, Sarkozy reassured them that his nation was ready to offer a helping hand to overcome starvation and all the other problems Africa faced: 'If that is what you want, young people of Africa, then you hold in your hands the future of Africa and France will work with you to build this future'.[105]

Sarkozy's speech was not an aberration. Ever since May 1968, an influential current of opinion on the intersection of mainstream conservatism and the extreme right, the so-called Nouvelle Droite or New Right, had been working to rehabilitate aspects of French history that had become taboo, from colonialism to collaboration, in order to establish a right 'without inhibitions'. Sarkozy's speech was an example of this. François Fillon, his successful rival to be Les Républicains' presidential candidate in 2017, spoke during the primary campaign of the need for history to be taught in schools in a way that glorified France: 'No, France is not guilty for having wanted to share its culture with the peoples of Africa, Asia and North America,' he declared. 'No, France did not invent slavery! France is fifteen centuries of history, from the baptism of Clovis in Reims.' He was appalled by the fact that teachers had to 'teach children to understand that the past is a source of interrogations'. It was 'shameful' that children were being made to 'doubt our history'.[106]

Neo-colonial attitudes were not the sole preserve of the right. Under the Hollande presidency (2012–17), the neo-colonial attempt to build an 'Islam of France' begun under Sarkozy was revived. The name of Jean-Pierre Chevènement was put forward to head the Fondation de l'Islam de France. The primary role of the Foundation would, according to Chevènement, be to teach imams 'what French citizenship is'. When it came to the burkini furore, he advised Muslims to exercise 'discretion': 'Muslims, like all French citizens, must have complete freedom to practice their religion. But they must also understand that in public space, where the general interest is defined, all citizens must make the effort to resort to "natural reason".'[107] Chevènement's proposed appointment was subject to further controversy when he implied that in Saint-Denis, in the north of Paris, 'there were 135 nationalities but there's one that's almost disappeared'.[108] By implication, white French citizens were on the wane (Chevènement later claimed he was referring to the French working class). He then made things worse by boasting that he 'knew the Muslim world well', since he had been to Cairo and Algiers 'forty or fifty years ago'.[109] The establishment of such a foundation indicates the extent to which the 'new secularism' is both a distortion of the supposedly 'pure' values of the 1905 Law of Separation, and part of a long tradition of such distortion, an institutional manifestation of the suspicion and scrutiny Muslims were subjected to by the French state during the colonial era. This legacy has found new scope for expression today as the control and surveillance of Muslims becomes an entrenched political priority.[110]

Conclusion

François Fillon wanted a 'grand national narrative' to be developed on the model of Ernest Lavisse's textbooks for schools under the Third Republic. These had taught children about a France that brought democracy and freedom to the world, that didn't want slaves in the countries it had subjugated, a France that was 'good and generous to the people' living in them.[111] This is the France defended by Prime Minister Valls in 2016,

'France, country of the Enlightenment and country of liberties', where 'women are free'.[112] It is a France where a Moroccan woman married to a Frenchman with three children born in France can be refused citizenship because her 'radical religious practice' is considered 'incompatible with the essential values of the French community, notably the principle of gender equality'.[113] According to Valls, secularism cannot be construed as 'an instrument of discrimination and humiliation', since the ban on conspicuous religious symbols in schools 'concerns the kippah as much as the headscarf or the Catholic cross'.[114] The ban came after fifteen years of debate on the hijab and a commission established with a remit widely understood to be specifically about that garment. The kippah, the turban and 'large crucifixes' affected a smaller number of students, ultimately serving as an alibi for discrimination of Muslims.

The law's universalism was as fake as its feminism. The principal petition in favour of the ban explicitly targeted the hijab, 'symbol of women's oppression'. This, as we have seen, was President Chirac's own understanding of the measure. Feminist arguments were marshalled to ensure support for this unprecedented and controversial measure. But if, as Tevanian notes, the hijab is considered an affront to all women, so much so that the state must intervene to ban it, then why only remove it from schools? Why continue to allow women to wear it in the street?[115] The hijab was singled out as a unique symbol of oppression and its prohibition then articulated in law, not as a measure promoting women's emancipation but as part of a need to ban 'conspicuous' religious symbols. This fake universalism was the republican fig leaf obscuring the law's primary motivation: racial discrimination. A similar procedure underpinned the 2010 law that banned the niqab and the burqa. After months of debate lambasting these 'walking coffins', the law included items and practices that had rarely, if ever, elicited any public concern, like pedestrians wearing motorcycle helmets or ski masks. A law enacting President Sarkozy's decree that 'the burqa is not welcome in France'[116] was therefore couched not in terms of *laïcité* but *mixité*, social diversity. But just as the supposed craving for women's liberation that led to the 2004 law was not followed up by any policies targeting gang rapes, female genital mutilation or forced marriages, so the passion for 'living together' that apparently underpinned the 2010 law was not followed by any fall in social inequality, polarisation or segregation. 'Does the government really want social diversity?' asked Thomas Piketty as students went back to school in 2016, noting 'an absolutely extreme level of social segregation' in France's post-sixteen educational institutions.[117] The government's response? 'There cannot be an authoritarian imposition of social diversity.'[118]

The true function of secularism in neoliberal France now becomes clear: to displace economic, social and political questions onto the fields of ethnicity, culture and religion. In this way, as Saïd Bouamama argues, revolt against inequality can be disarmed via the construction of an 'enemy within'. Islamophobia provides the neoliberal project with a means of undermining social protest by 'displacing the boundaries that allow for an understanding of social reality':

> The right to free education, for example, is one of the social gains that the neo-liberal project seeks to reverse... It's therefore not surprising that school should be held up as the site of an essential battle against the 'new enemy', the 'headscarf' or 'communitarianism'. The term '*laïcité*' is here mobilised to mask the reality of social divisions, to unite what the neoliberal project divides and to divide what it unites.[119]

Fresh from a major social confrontation over pensions that saw teachers engage in one of the biggest waves of industrial action seen in contemporary France, the Raffarin government (2002–5) found unlikely allies in members of the far-left organisation Lutte ouvrière, whose presidential candidate Arlette Laguiller, as

Tevanian notes, marched on International Women's Day 2004 'against the veil' and 'for *laïcité*' alongside a minister in that same government, Nicole Guedj, and the Socialist Malek Boutih, under the banner of Fadela Amara's pro-ban Ni Putes Ni Soumises (Neither Sluts Nor Slaves).[120] The march was notable for the fact that the Collectif national des droits de femmes (National Women's Rights Collective) tried to stop women wearing the hijab from participating, as if, in Delphy's words, not only is the headscarf *the* symbol of women's submission' but 'the women who wear it ... are unworthy of fighting for women's rights'.[121] This 'sacred union' between the far left, the Socialists and the UMP on the question of the headscarf was not the only unholy alliance produced by the affair, as Tevanian underlines:

> We also saw a convergence, on the basis of their hostility towards the headscarf and their shared belief in the political virtues of prohibition, of the most secular parts of the left and the most clerical parts of the right, sincere activists for the Palestinian cause and unconditional supporters of Ariel Sharon, feminist groups and the most chauvinist elements of the political class, teachers just out of a long strike movement and the minister they had been confronting.[122]

The impact of division between and within progressive forces, caused not just by the affair itself but by the ongoing projection of *laïcité* as an essential element of French politics and society, would be felt for a long time to come. The wave of mobilisations that had swept France since December 1995, presenting a serious challenge to the establishment of neoliberal dominance in France, was interrupted. The anti-racist movement, divided between pro- and anti-ban elements, suffered irreparable damage and has been unable to organise a major national mobilisation for over a decade. When years of frustration at inequality and injustice in the *banlieues* exploded in the biggest urban uprising ever seen in Europe in 2005, the left was nowhere to be seen, leaving the youth of France's urban peripheries to confront the police alone.

Laïcité's impact, in dividing what neoliberalism united, could not have been starker.

Laïcité's implementation remained somewhat arbitrary. The chorus of politicians that had intervened in defence of women's rights during the debate over the 2004 and 2010 laws, and who would line up in condemnation of the burkini 'threat' in 2016, was remarkably silent when the issue of *mixité sociale*, or social diversity, came up in relation to access to the beach in 2015. In order to accommodate the holiday plans of King Salman bin Abdulaziz Al Saud and his 1,000-strong entourage, a stretch of Côte d'Azur coastline around the Saudi monarch's luxury villa near Cannes was sealed off. The public beach in front of the Château de l'Horizon was reserved for the sole use of the holiday party and a 300-metre exclusion zone imposed out to sea. The party built a lift to provide direct access from the grounds to the beach below. Although the authorities cited security concerns as the motivation for the segregation, many of those wanting to exercise their right to sunbathe, fish or swim in the public spaces around the villa saw things differently. For them, the much-trumpeted, 'inviolable' principle of *laïcité* appeared rather less sacrosanct when it came to playing host to the Saudi royal family. This impression was reinforced when reports emerged that the king had complained about the presence of a female police officer on the beach, a controversy that her superiors were anxious to keep quiet. As the business magazine *Forbes* noted, with unconscious irony given the judgements to be made by French mayors about over-dressing on beaches the following year:

> on the Cote d'Azur, the world capital of beach toplessness—and on a beach literally a few hundred yards from where Brigitte Bardot wore the world's first bikini—it was the French national gendarmerie's fully clothed and armed policewomen who became the problem.[123]

The Republic, cradle of universalism, resolute in deploying its might against teenagers who wanted to wear a bandana to school, or women who chose to cover their bodies on holiday, appeared less indivisible when it came to complying with the vacation requirements of an oil-rich monarch. The distinctions drawn were not really about how the 1905 Law of Separation ought to be interpreted. They were about something much more prosaic and fundamental: inequality. In the following chapter, we examine how this issue manifests itself in contemporary France, exploring the economic and social backdrop underpinning the rise of Islamophobia. Profound inequalities have provided the context for the hardening of republican orthodoxy and the emergence of Islam, or rather Muslims—with their immigrant past, hijabs, run-down housing estates and rioting—as the perfect scapegoats for a society increasingly disfigured by the ruthless communitarianism of the wealthy.

4

CONFRONTING INEQUALITY

Unequal France

The extent of inequality in France today is dramatically illustrated by Thomas Piketty's *Capital in the 21st Century* (2013). Around 10 per cent of people born in 1830s France, who were to inherit family fortunes later in the nineteenth century, eventually received inheritance sums greater than the lifetime income earned by the bottom 50 per cent of the population. In contrast, by the 1950s only 2 per cent of those born in 1910 were inheriting wealth on this scale; 'People,' as Piketty remarks, 'believed that the arbitrary inequalities of inherited wealth were a thing of the past.'[1] In contemporary France, however, Piketty estimates that as many as 12 per cent of those born in 1970 could inherit a greater total fortune than the lifetime income of the poorest 50 per cent.[2] By this measure, the scale of inequality in France today is greater than in Balzac's time. By 2016, nearly 5 million people were living in poverty (calculated on earnings under 50 per cent of median income), while the number of millionaires had reached 2 million. Surveys indicated that 38 per cent of the population had some experience of poverty, 66 per cent had a friend or family member in poverty, and 55 per cent believed their daily life to be threatened by it, up 10 per cent since the financial crisis hit.[3] Before 1990, poverty had been falling, but from the year 2000 it began to rise, and the gap between those at the top and those at the bottom widened. 'We can choose not to see this phenomenon,' noted the Observatory on Inequality, 'but then we must be ready to put up with the social tensions that it will produce.'[4]

According to the OECD (Organisation for Economic Co-operation and Development), income inequality in advanced economies has reached a 'tipping point'.[5] By 2015, it was at its highest level for fifty years: across the thirty-five OECD nations the earnings of the richest 10 per cent of the population stood at close to ten times that of the poorest 10 per cent, up from eight times more in the 1990s.[6] Although income inequality had remained relatively stable in France between the 1980s and the 2008 financial crash, from that point there was a sharp break with the long-term trend: inequality then increased more rapidly than almost anywhere else, in both absolute and relative terms. Over the period 1996–2011, the gap between rich and poor reached its highest levels in the three years that followed the 2008 crash.[7] By 2014, there were over a million more people living in poverty than in 2004 (9 million in total with an income at 60 per cent of median earnings); 80 per cent of this rise came in the four years following the 2008 crash.[8] Although poverty levels in France remained relatively low in European terms, at around 14 per cent, only two countries experienced a bigger rise in disposable income inequality between 2007 and 2011—and in terms of 'market income inequality', before taxes and benefits, only Spain, Ireland, Greece and Estonia experienced greater disparities than France.

In the years following the 2008 crash, income for the top 10 per cent rose in France at double the average rate for OECD countries, by an average of 2 per cent a year, and fell by 1 per cent for the bottom 10 per cent. Half of all net private household wealth found its way into the hands of the top 10 per cent and nearly a fifth into the hands of the top 1 per cent alone, leaving the bottom 10 per cent with less than 2 per cent of the pot.[9] In starker financial terms, between 2003 and 2013 the poorest 10 per cent lost on average €320 a year, while the richest 10 per cent made annual gains of €4,300. In other words, the income of the richest in society, already nine times higher than that of the least well-off, then increased proportionately by the equivalent of half the annual income of the poorest 10 per cent, every year for a decade.[10]

Between 2004 and 2007, the number of people earning over half a million euros a year rose by 70 per cent.[11] Along with rising salaries for the better off, the major source of rising income inequality was downward pressure on wages for the majority. The labour market underwent significant reorganisation during the period that followed the financial crash, coinciding with the Sarkozy presidency. This resulted in a significant expansion of non-standard labour: temporary or part-time work or self-employment, jobs which in France pay around 40 per cent less than standard jobs. Around a third of those in work are employed in this way, with jobs concentrated among women (63 per cent) and young people (46 per cent). In France only a fifth of people with non-standard jobs in 2008 had found full-time work by 2011, compared to 48 per cent in Britain. Those in full-time work also suffered. The huge inflation of earnings at the top meant that two thirds of full-time workers took home less than the average full-time wage.[12]

While disparities of wealth and income have widened, social mobility has stalled. In the mid-1950s, during the post-war boom, average salaries for managers were four times those of workers. Growth and inflation rates at the time meant that it would take a worker thirty years to earn the same amount as a manager. By the mid-1990s, a manager's salary was 2.6 times higher than the average worker's, but lower growth rates meant that it would take ten times longer for the latter to make good the difference: 300 years. Put more starkly, between 1945 and 1975, average net wages increased threefold—more than in the previous thirty decades. When the boom ended in the mid-1970s, it would take nearly seven years to achieve what would have been an annual pay rise during that period, the so-called 'thirty glorious years'.[13]

Since the 1990s, this lack of social mobility has contributed to a profound change in outlook among significant sections of the French population. For the first time since the war, belief in social progress could not be taken for granted. Parents no longer assumed that their children would have more opportunities than they did, and they were right. In contemporary France, 87 per cent of parents believe that poverty is a more likely prospect for their children than it has been for them. Six out of ten children share this fear. Most children believe it will difficult for them to find a job when they grow up.[14] For millions of working-class and middle-class people, the lived reality of life in precarious employment, with career or employment prospects blocked, contributes to cynicism or wariness about politicians' promises of rosy economic prospects for those who 'get up early'.[15] But the individual impact of economic decline goes much deeper than this, as Louis Chauvel underlines:

> the internalisation by the victims of a setback that seems personal, but which comes to a much greater extent from a collective debacle, can have pernicious psychological effects and dangerous political consequences. For the children of middle-class parents destined for subaltern social positions or exclusion from the productive sphere, the question is how to construct a positive social identity in a collective system offering prospects for the future.[16]

Workers in France had experienced significant upheaval since the 1980s, with restructuring, deindustrialisation, structural unemployment and a crisis of labour movement organisation (see Chapter Five). One corollary of all the narratives about the end of the working class, however, had been the notion that everyone was now middle class: upwardly mobile in a moderate, democratic, consumer society where only the 'excluded' lost out—the Republic of the centre.[17] Since the 1990s, accelerating since 2008, chronic recession and austerity have put paid to this notion, and with it the sense of optimism embodied by the aspirant middle class that emerged in the post-war boom. The political assault on the public sector and the generation of economic and social insecurity has uprooted many of the certainties that made middle-class life relatively comfortable. Instead, uncertainty about salaries, career prospects, redundancies and pensions breeds frustration and disquiet. Or, as Chauvel puts it, middle-class identity used to be bound up with hope and optimism about the future, not just individually, but for the whole of society. The middle classes' dream was supposed to extend to everyone, generating a sense of positive aspiration throughout society. Today, by contrast, anguish reigns, threating to become 'everyone's nightmare': the middle class 'no longer spreads confidence, but anxiety.'[18]

Racism and discrimination

One of the central arguments of this book is that a key political battle is being waged in contemporary France in order to focus this anxiety onto immigrants and their descendants—in other words, to blame the consequences of inequality on those who tend to suffer from it the most. At times this battle is articulated via open prejudice and scapegoating, as we have seen in earlier chapters. It also draws on more insidious means.

Inequality, for example, is accentuated by discrimination. This is not unique to France but discrimination is often harder to identify, and therefore to combat, than elsewhere. As Patrick Simon and Joan Stavo-Debauge point out, when there is general agreement on what discrimination is, then it should not be difficult to identify how it manifests itself in everyday situations—to deconstruct the mechanisms and rationales by which discrimination operates in order to locate prejudice and then work out a means of countering discriminatory acts. But things are not so straightforward, particularly when it comes to ethnic or racial discrimination. The discrediting of the notion of 'race' also makes identifying discrimination harder, since measures that discriminate on the basis of ethnicity are prohibited and overtly proclaimed racist acts are rare: 'In the vast majority of cases, discrimination is not directly perceived.'[19]

Lofty proclamations against racism, in other words, are not sufficient to combat discrimination. Simon summarises the 'French paradox' as follows:

> French society is one that has taken the gamble of rooting out racism by declaring it unacceptable in principle, combating and condemning its overt manifestation and believing that this strategy exonerates it from having to deal with the insidious expression of racism in the form of discrimination. Moreover, the political equation of universalism, based on a strategy of rendering minorities invisible, does not ensure them protection and access to equality, but instead disarms them from confronting the establishment of a racial and ethnic hierarchy that is hidden behind formal equality.[20]

Discriminatory practices are not simply events, but part of a pattern inscribed in power relations. They therefore have to be identified within apparently banal processes of selection, governed by conventions and procedures that are often inaccessible to the actors themselves, arising from indirect processes rather than direct acts. This is what makes awareness of discrimination and its pervasiveness difficult to pinpoint. A poll conducted in 2004, for example, found that 74 per cent of respondents believed an individual's career prospects could be handicapped by their origin or skin colour. Exactly the same proportion of respondents, 74 per cent, nevertheless did not believe that such practices occurred in their own workplace.[21] Identifying discrimination therefore involves scientific study and a comparative perspective; these require, crucially, access to relevant data.[22] It is precisely this—the merit of collecting data on discrimination—that has been the subject of fierce debate in France.

In the face of assertions that ethnic monitoring would run counter to the principle of a 'colour-blind' Republic, researchers have had to painstakingly point out the obvious drawback of this approach. In a society whose model of equality is based on 'being oblivious to difference' (the 'colour-blind' Republic), problems are posed when it becomes apparent that discrimination is not only persisting, but getting worse. This 'voluntarily theoretical approach' has, in other words, been unable to stem the spread of prejudices and stereotypes feeding discrimination. To make matters worse, the social impact of discrimination is accentuated by a model that actively prevents 'detection of the subtle distinctions based on perception of origins'. In contemporary French society, 'saturated with ethno-racial and, increasingly, religious references', all that is being offered by government actors is 'the incantatory affirmation of abstract equality.'[23]

It was not until 2008–9 that the relationship between a person's origins and skin colour and their experience of racism became the subject of a major study in France. The research, conducted over nearly ten years and involving 22,000 respondents, recorded the birthplace and nationality of over 8,000 migrants and a similar number of their descendants, and compared their responses with those of French nationals without foreign heritage. The findings, presented in a 2015 report, *Trajectory and Origins*,[24] identified evidence of an 'asymmetrical integration'. The children of immigrants obtained educational qualifications, found friends and partners who were not from migrant backgrounds and frequently put to one side their parents' language.[25] But their social integration was not matched by economic integration. They spent longer unemployed than the 'majority' population and felt discriminated against.[26] According to Patrick Simon, one of the coordinators of the study,

> Our work shows that there is no distance between the descendants of migrants and the national community. On the other hand, the evolution of French society and its institutions worries me. They are becoming closed in on themselves and it's this shutdown, experienced by the descendants of immigrants as an unbearable exclusion, that is blocking the process of integration today.[27] ... They are doing the work of integration. But when the dynamic should come from French society, obstacles appear.[28]

A diploma, the survey shows, has less value for the child of a migrant than for someone of so-called 'French stock'. 'Since it's more difficult for them to enter the world of work, they generally accept unskilled posts and then make less progress than colleagues who are not from an immigrant background,' points out another of the project's coordinators, Christelle Hamel. 'What is true in the search for a job also applies to housing and access to leisure.' Her conclusion is blunt and damning: 'The children of immigrants face discrimination everywhere.' Visible minorities, those of North African, Turkish and sub-Saharan backgrounds, suffer the most, regardless of the extent to which they have integrated socially.[29] 'The trajectories and practices of immigrants and their descendants,' the survey's coordinators argue, 'reveals a process of differentiation and singularisation, on the one hand, and of homogenisation and cohesion across French society on the other.'[30] The report vindicated longstanding criticisms of France's political establishment, and the way it had obscured the social and economic impact of discrimination. It detailed the way in which racial prejudice relegated migrants and their descendants to a status of precarity and insecurity, in particular when it came to housing and employment.

In the aftermath of the 2005 uprising in the *banlieues*, Stéphane Beaud and Olivier Masclet had described the 'wall of rejection' that confronted young people in these areas. They pointed to the impact of a decade in which homogenisation had been imposed on them as the opportunities available to young and qualified people of Maghrebian or African background dried up. The rise of unemployment among qualified youth fed the 'educational demoralisation' of young people and their families, who lived with the effects of discrimination in employment. If the sacrifices and efforts of their elder siblings had come to nothing, if years of higher education led only back to casual work, then what other conclusion could be drawn than that there was no place for them in the labour market?[31]

These were the kinds of setbacks that politicians attributed to cultural shortcomings on the part of racialised individuals. They were communitarian, segregating themselves away, polygamous, misogynistic, submissive, violent, unwilling to integrate. Yet the evidence, obscured from view for so long in the name of a 'colour-blind' Republic, demonstrated that the children of migrants, like their parents, were more likely to find themselves in run-down estates or on temporary contracts, in unskilled or part-time work or unemployed, whatever their qualifications. This was not because of their own failure to play a part in society—their social integration was manifest—but because of the obstacles put in their way by a society that had been unable to confront discrimination or inequality. Instead, politicians had cultivated a narrative that racialised and stigmatised minorities finding themselves denied access to those celebrated pathways to integration held up as the very fabric of republican opportunity. As Simon underlines,

> Far from being a recent phenomenon linked to the crumbling of the republican model, discrimination is inscribed at the very heart of this political model. Voluntary blindness with regard to the republican legacy of slavery, colonialism and institutional xenophobia is one of the explanations for the power of a discriminatory system that we have labelled the 'French model of discrimination'.[32]

The emphasis on cultural difference as the defining feature of racialised individuals has enabled politicians, the media, reactionary intellectuals and sections of academia to cite their relegation as proof of their own inability to 'become French'. In 2003, the Interior Ministry commissioned a report on racism and antisemitism by the doctor and human rights activist Jean-Christophe Rufin. Confessing that he didn't know much about the subject,[33] Rufin nevertheless published his report the following year, in which he summed up what he considered to be the choices facing *banlieue* youth: 'Either immigrant-origin youth choose republican values and "fully participate in civic life via educational and cultural instruments that encourage social mobility and support the emergence of new elites", or they join various radical movements that preach war against the West and the rejection of its values.'[34]

As Bouamama highlights, persistent questioning of the compatibility between Islam and the Republic implicitly points the finger at the descendants of immigrants from France's former colonies, obscuring awkward social and political issues and presenting the precarity and poverty of the *banlieues* as symptoms of a 'ghetto' culture produced by the rule of criminal gangs and Islamic fundamentalists. Social questions are viewed through the prism of an 'enemy within'.[35] This enemy has been constructed by reconstituting the historic figure of the '*indigène*', the indigenous colonial subject, or native. This construction sometimes takes place surreptitiously, via terms denoting an 'exterior' status without explicitly naming it: 'young Arab', 'young immigrant',

'immigrant-origin youth'. There has been a tendency to refer to black and Arab youth with both parents born in France as third, fourth or fifth generation immigrants, as if their origins, unlike people of European descent, are as indelible as their skin colour. 'Condemned for life,' as the former government minister Christiane Taubira put it, 'to come from elsewhere'.[36] In the wake of the 2005 riots, a more subtle term was used: 'youth of French nationality'. Sagot-Duvauroux notes that behind this term the same essential element remained constant:

> the mark of exteriority, even when euphemised in the extreme like this. The youth who does not need to have any particular qualification appended is still at the centre of the circle. 'A' youth. But for what deep and unseen reason, in response to what obscure doubt, do we feel the need to signal that the others, the youths 'of French nationality,' have their French papers? Already in the Republic and still on the margins of the Empire?[37]

The systematic characterisation of Islam as a threat to *laïcité* and republicanism has been central to this construction of externality. It allows black and Arab French youth to be implicitly cast as 'foreign' not because of their skin colour but because of their religion, made into an object of suspicion and 'otherness' due to the threat posed by Islam's supposed incompatibility with republican values. Xavier Darcos, then a junior education minister, offered a perfect example of this technique in 2003, remarking that what had changed over the previous fifteen years was 'the insolence of these Arabo-Muslim immigrants of the third generation, who have problems integrating into the world of work and who yelled "Long live Bin Laden!" after 9/11.'[38] The choice then imposed on these 'third generation immigrants' is the same as the choice articulated above by Rufin, the same as the choice offered to the indigenous subjects of the French Empire: 'break with what is supposed to link you to the "enemy within" (religion, culture, language, clothes, language, family, etc) and integrate, or refuse this "break" and be excluded, discriminated against and stigmatised with entirely respectable legitimacy.'[39]

President Hollande also presented inequality as a choice. 'Today's veiled woman,' he confided to journalists in 2016, 'will be the Marianne [the symbolic incarnation of the Republic] of tomorrow.' Naturally, this was conditional on her making the right choice, in order to become French: 'If we manage to provide her with the conditions to flourish, she will liberate herself from the veil and become a Frenchwoman... this woman will choose freedom over enslavement.'[40] In other words, success is available to those who break with their culture of origin; the outcome is simply a matter of will.[41]

The depiction of the *banlieues* as 'lost territories of the Republic' reinforces these culturalist prejudices, contributing to the generation of a collective fear of young immigrants in French society.[42] It is a depiction given credence, as Michel Kokoreff points out, by academics from various disciplines who have contributed to a vision of the *banlieues* and the young people who have grown up there that is 'miserablist, sensationalist and homogenous', relying on generalisations based on the most marginalised or excluded fringes.[43] The fears conjured up as a consequence have found a prime target to latch on to in the form of the Arab male, or '*garçon arabe*'. Embodying, as Nacira Guénif-Souilamas explains, issues of both ethnicity and gender, the *garçon arabe* is the negative alter ego of the veiled girl, crystallising repressed colonial memories and a sexualised angst and loathing:

> There are multiple uses and abuses of the figure of the *garçon arabe*. The 'integration deficit' of these postcolonial Frenchmen does not come from their social inadequacy or their unsuitability for the job market. It derives from their bodies, from their incapacity to submit to the rules of self-restraint prescribed by the process of French civilisation. They

> embody proof that in France sexism is peculiar to ethnicised minorities because of their Arab and/or Muslim origins... In short, for the time being, the *garçon arabe* epitomises the ideal culprit.[44]

The *garçon arabe* is the archetypal troublemaker: a potential rapist, violent, brutal, barbaric and uncivilised. He is the Socialist Jean-Pierre Chevènement's 'little savage', former SOS Racisme president Malek Boutih's 'little Nazi of the *banlieue*' and Nicolas Sarkozy's '*racaille*'.[45] In the autumn of 2005 he fought back.

The 2005 *banlieue* uprising

For three weeks in October and November 2005, thousands of young people took part in what is best described as an urban uprising against police violence, discrimination, inequality, Islamophobia and racism.[46] It was the biggest social upheaval since May 1968, engulfing huge swathes of urban France. The uprising was sparked by the deaths of two teenagers in Clichy-sous-Bois, north of Paris, who were electrocuted while hiding from the police in an electricity sub-station. The tragedy came in the wake of then interior minister Sarkozy's characterisation of *banlieue* youth as 'scum' or 'riffraff'. These are areas of profound social deprivation: in 2005, over 700 of them, with a combined population of 4.5 million, were officially classified as 'in difficulty'. Around 300 areas were affected nationally. 10,000 cars were burnt out, 5,000 arrests made and over £100 million worth of damage caused to property.

Interviewed by the author towards the end of the uprising, some of those involved saw the rioting as a way of throwing the Republic's values back in its face. For Malik from Aulnay-sous-Bois, north of Paris, France had 'two faces':

> The first is the one they show the world—we're a democratic country, lots of museums, the Champs Élysées, the Eiffel Tower, the Arc de Triomphe, the good life, fine wine, and all that. It's not true. Here, it's

> miserable poverty. We live here, we grew up here. And now we've started burning it, they're talking about doing this up, renovating that. But until we did something, they'd left us for dead... The gymnasium round here is always closed—so we burn it. We were always getting thrown out of the schools—we burn them. The shops and malls where we never get jobs—we burn them. A hundred people work at Renault here, but not a single young person from this estate—so we burn it. If there's no change, it's not going to stop.

In the Seine-Saint-Denis area, youth unemployment was running at close to 50 per cent. 'They don't talk about jobs,' argued Rachid. 'If we had more jobs, young people wouldn't hang around the area in the evening. They would've been thinking about work the next morning. If we had a job we wouldn't be against anything. But we've got nothing, that's why we're against everything.'

Islam was never a point of reference in these interviews, except in relation to the tear gas canister thrown by the police into a Clichy-sous-Bois mosque, an event understood, like Sarkozy's *racaille* outburst, as a provocation. Others were at pains to point out that the uprising was about more than racism and discrimination. 'You mustn't say it's just the immigrants taking part in all this,' was one view. 'It's not just the Muslims and the blacks and the Arabs involved. There's the Portuguese, the Vietnamese, the French. They always generalise and say, "It's the blacks and the Arabs." But it's all races together, all those who live in the *banlieues*.'

Mainstream political reaction to the revolt asserted the physical and metaphorical role of the state, which was to defend the nation against an enemy generally portrayed through crude racist and colonial stereotypes. The sense of an enemy within, of communities that had set their face against the rest of French society, was reinforced by the imposition of the temporary state of emergency and by the interpretation given to the crisis by prominent political figures.[47] Faced with the most widespread and sustained rioting ever seen in metropolitan France, politicians found ingenious means to obscure what lay behind the revolt. In 2005, the unemployment rate for university graduates from North African backgrounds stood at 26.5 per cent, against a national graduate unemployment rate of 5 per cent. The overall unemployment rate for people of French origin was 9.2 per cent. It stood at 14 per cent for those of foreign origin.[48] The employment minister presiding over this state of affairs was Gérard Larcher. When the riots broke out he chose to address the issue that he claimed was contributing to discrimination in the job market: polygamy. It was the absence of a father figure in polygamous families, he explained, that left children prone to anti-social behaviour. This, in turn, made ethnic minority young people less attractive to employers. 'Since part of society displays this anti-social behaviour,' he mused, 'it is not surprising that some of them have difficulties finding work ... Efforts must be made by both sides. If people are not employable, they will not be employed'.[49]

Other mainstream figures backed up these assertions. Although polygamy had been outlawed in 1993 and affected only a tiny minority of families nationwide,[50] Bernard Accoyer, president of the UMP parliamentary party, claimed that it was undoubtedly one of the causes of the riots since it prevented the provision of an education, 'as it is needed in an organised, normative society' like France. Stressing the difficulties of integrating certain immigrants and their children, he told RTL radio that the government would have to tighten up its policies on (post-immigration) family reunification.[51] Sarkozy concurred: 'Most of the rioters are French, legally speaking,' he noted, 'but let's say things as they are: polygamy and the acculturation of a certain number of families mean it's more difficult to integrate young French people of sub-Saharan African origin than young French people from other backgrounds'.[52] Such crassness was not confined to politicians. The historian Hélène Carrère d'Encausse, permanent secretary of the prestigious Académie française, shared her view of the rioters with the Russian media:

> These people come directly from their African villages. But Paris and other European cities are not African villages. For example, everyone's amazed that African children are in the street and not at school. Why can't their parents buy an apartment? It's obvious why: many of these Africans, I'm telling you, are polygamous. In their apartments there are three or four wives and twenty-five children... It's understandable that the children are running about in the street.[53]

The reactionary right-wing blogosphere duly translated the French elite's message into an easily digestible format: 'Too many wives causes unrest'.[54]

It was not poverty or discrimination, then, but cultural and ethnic differences that were offered as explanations for the uprising. This, as Joël Roman notes, marked a departure from attitudes that had greeted previous revolts, for example those in Les Minguettes in 1981 or Vaux-en-Velin and Mantes-la-Jolie in 1991. Now it was Islam—contrary to all available evidence—that was held to be a major factor in the revolt, threatening France's secular values.[55] As Hargreaves notes, Islamic organisations consistently called for an end to the disorder, while 'not a single statement is on record of rioters saying the disturbances were motivated by an Islamic agenda.'[56] Nevertheless, the media's favourite philosopher, Alain Finkielkraut, expanded on the theme: the revolt was 'an anti-republican pogrom.' Events in the *banlieues* had the same roots as the 9/11 attacks:

> In France, they would like very much to reduce these riots to their social dimension, to see them as a revolt of youths from the suburbs against their situation, against the discrimination they suffer from, against unemployment. The problem is that most of these youths are blacks or Arabs, with a Muslim identity. Look, in France there are also other immigrants whose situation is difficult—Chinese, Vietnamese,

> Portuguese—and they're not taking part in the riots. Therefore, it is clear that this is a revolt with an ethno-religious character. What is its origin? Is this the response of the Arabs and blacks to the racism of which they are victims? I don't believe so, because this violence had very troubling precursors, which cannot be reduced to an unalloyed reaction to French racism... All of this hatred and violence is now coming out in the riots. To see them as a response to French racism is to be blind to a broader hatred: the hatred for the West, which is deemed guilty of all crimes. France is being exposed to this now.[57]

Finkielkraut responded to the furore over his remarks by claiming that he did not recognise himself in the way they had been portrayed. Sarkozy was less inhibited: 'Monsieur Finkielkraut,' he told reporters, 'is an intellectual who brings honour and pride to French wisdom ... If there is so much criticism of him, it might be because he says things that are correct.'[58]

Finkielkraut was not alone in evoking the Israeli occupation of Palestine. The head of the police officers' union wrote to Sarkozy complaining that forces in the *banlieues* were faced with 'a permanent intifada', a civil war orchestrated by 'radical Islamists'. Fox News ran televised reports of the upheaval with the strapline 'Muslim riots'. According to Prince Alwaleed bin Talal bin Abdul aziz Al-Saud, a Saudi Arabian shareholder in News Corporation, his phone call to Rupert Murdoch complaining about the coverage resulted in the strapline being changed to 'civil riots' within half an hour.[59] If any calls were being made to government ministers in France, however, they weren't having any impact. Despite the heightening tensions nationwide, Sarkozy was unrepentant: 'I've said it once and I'll say it again, they are thugs, scum.'[60]

The disdain shown by Sarkozy, Finkielkraut and others for understanding what was going on explains their refusal to acknowledge what research had been showing for some time: the young people involved in the uprising were not primarily motivated by religion. The children of Algerian immigrants were far less likely to attend a place of worship than their parents and twice as likely to have no religion. Rather, their attitudes towards religion were much more in line with everyone else of their age living in France.[61] When it came to those rioting, according to a secret service report circulated in the aftermath of the uprising, the protagonists were motivated by a strong sense of identity, not primarily based on ethnic or geographic origins so much as their social condition, notably their exclusion from French society. The state's preoccupation with Islamic fundamentalism and terrorism meant that it had neglected the problem of the *banlieues*. The heads of both branches of the secret service units administered by Sarkozy went on to assert that the part played by Islamic fundamentalists in the violence was 'nil'.[62] Yet the report's findings did nothing to dispel the obsessive focus on isolating and berating elements in society that could be portrayed as irrevocably dysfunctional and divisive. Instead, this was to become a defining feature of the post-Gaullist right. The Socialist Party adopted a more measured tone, but came to the same conclusion. The president of its parliamentary group, Jean-Marc Ayrault, noted that 'Too many young Frenchmen... hold an identity card but feel like foreigners in their own country.' The solution? In their 2007 manifesto the Socialists proposed an annual event where naturalised French citizens would meet their mayor, an opportunity to 'remind them of the fundamental principles of the Republic'.[63]

As Beaud and Masclet argue, the 2005 revolt underlined how little public debate has taken seriously the question of recognition for migrants and their descendants, and in particular those from former French colonies, an issue raised explicitly by the 1983 March for Equality and Against Racism:

> The parties of the left have done very little to further the aspirations of the Beur generation [French-born of Arab background], and have [made] virtually no room in their ranks for the most active among them. A sec-

> tion of this generation, which has become radicalised, now displays an intransigent attitude towards the French Republic, which, to their eyes, treats them as '*Français sous condition* [conditionally French]'.[64]

Laurent Mucchielli attributes this 'blockage' in French society to the contradictions of the republican ideal and its reluctance to recognise people from Maghrebian and sub-Saharan African backgrounds. This, he argues, contributes to the construction of 'delinquent identities' via mechanisms of rejection, discrimination and non-recognition. A self-fulfilling prophecy is created, vindicating the adoption of the role of 'bad immigrant' by individuals confronted with a society that seems to want no part of them. Republican egalitarianism, moreover, increasingly functions like a myth, inducing belief and conformism on the one hand, but also the denunciation of another part of the population. Denied the equality of opportunity promised them by this myth, and discriminated against on the basis of their origins, these racialised individuals are instead assailed with the moral injunction to 'integrate', a state of affairs that will continue 'to produce incomprehension, frustration, resentment and despair'.[65]

Communitarianism

The narrative presented by various mainstream politicians in the wake of the uprising was that 'communitarian' impulses, rather than social inequalities, were to blame. Research indicating that people on the receiving end of racism and other discriminatory practices are more likely to retreat, particularly in situations where there appears to be no escape, was obscured by this rhetoric. Understanding social realities was not the point of the exercise. But, as Eric Maurin has shown, blaming the victims of social relegation for their plight simply masks the various processes that lead to segregation. In contemporary France, levels of immigrant 'ghettoisation' have remained unchanged for twenty years. Where 'communitarianism' does exist, it is likely to be a reaction to stigmatisation, rather than the result of voluntary secession.[66]

The areas most closed in on themselves, moreover, are not the *banlieues*, but 'the ghettos of the rich', the well-heeled gated enclaves of certain major cities and the luxury playgrounds of the south of France.[67] The communitarianism of the rich has been the subject of a series of studies by the sociologists Monique Pinçon-Charlot and Michel Pinçon, who have illustrated the closed, secretive and ruthless manner in which members of a small clique at the top of French society build ghettos for themselves and exercise all available means to defend their wealth and status. Describing a class in a permanent state of mobilisation, they document the various forms of violence, harassment, and coercion deployed to protect this status, and illustrate the means whereby ideological, social and cultural resources are mobilised to justify it, via symbols of prestige and networks of influence, creating the illusion that their domination is somehow natural and unassailable, rather than arbitrary and unjust.[68]

Unlike the poor, the rich choose their isolation from society. As Sylvie Tissot argues, the emphasis on the personal responsibility of the most impoverished for their situation not only distorts reality, it promotes the very ethnic divisions that such rhetoric claims to denounce. This discourse produces a vision of a Republic whose values are under threat and must be protected, thus shifting the focus of the state's role from a social to a penal function, a process reinforced by the paternalistic and colonial overtones of the debate.[69] Beyond the political arena, the prevalence of cultural prejudice, along with the mainstream left's lack of engagement with the political questions posed by poverty and discrimination, have given rise to a series of distorted interpretations of how patterns of inequality are playing out.

The notion that a 'white working class' is being left behind by a metropolitan elite in thrall to globalisation and multiculturalism has been the go-to analysis of uncritical sections of the media for some time. In France, the argument has found a comparatively nuanced exponent in Christophe Guilluy, who focuses on the insecurities of poor white voters, so-called '*petits blancs*', resentful of elites on the one hand, and immigrants on the other. Guilluy is a member of the Gauche Populaire grouping linked to the Socialist Party, a current that emerged in reaction to a cynical report by one of the party's think tanks, Terra Nova, which advocated abandoning efforts to retain a working-class electorate, since the latter had shifted so far to the right that it was effectively a lost cause. Instead, Socialists should pursue a younger, more female and more ethnically diverse electorate that represented 'the France of tomorrow'.[70]

Both sides of this argument rely on a pessimistic, racialised vision of the working class. It is implicitly white, and so disoriented and fragmented that its identity is characterised in abject terms: left behind, despised by elites, resentful of other, more 'recognised' minorities, consoling itself in ethno-centric retrenchment. One leading member of the Gauche Populaire, François Kalfon, has emphasised the need to 'fight against the systematic denigration by a left-wing elite of the ordinary Frenchman, the heterosexual "*petit blanc*" who lives with his classic family in a suburban house with a car and a television'.[71] These '*petits blancs*' are the people left abandoned by globalisation. Their response to this fate is to reject the metropolitan multiculturalism of the elites and seek solace in a communitarianism rooted in '*le terroir*'—local, rural or quasi-rural communities in villages, small towns or urban peripheries. The relocation of industry and the extortionate cost of metropolitan housing have clearly impacted on where people live, but attributing this to a conscious, rational choice on the part of '*petits blancs*' seeking to physically extricate themselves from multicultural France is as far-fetched as the notion that Muslim immigration is part of an international conspiracy to replace 'native' French stock.

Despite his use of catchy formulas contrasting the experience of 'popular classes' who live 'multiculturalism on €1,000 a month' with that of the ruling classes, who 'live multiculturalism on €5,000 a month', the fundamental divide in Guilluy's France is not class but identity. The principal cause of the anger gripping those who vote for the FN, for example, is not social inequality, but the failure of successive governments to limit immigration. The party's vote in 'peripheral France', small towns and villages and areas on the margins of big cities is reduced to a question of migration where different ethnic groups fight for symbolic resources. In many of these areas, an ageing 'native' population lives alongside a younger community of immigrant origin, engaging in an unspoken fight over emblematic spaces like the village square or the town centre. When social insecurity rises, argues Guilluy, so does sensitivity to demographic changes. But where does this sensitivity come from? Despite Guilluy's assertions, enthusiastically and uncritically taken up by politicians and journalists,[72] it does not come from contact with immigrants, as successive studies over the past three decades have shown. Not only have the highest votes for the FN frequently been recorded in areas of minimal immigration, but there is no meaningful correlation between the FN vote and the presence of immigrants.[73] This bears repeating: no convincing link has ever been identified between people voting FN and the presence or absence of immigrants in their neighbourhoods. On the contrary, research has consistently shown that the presence of immigrants in an area is not only a negligible influence on the FN vote, but that xenophobia tends to decrease as the presence of immigrants rises.[74] Guilluy and others, then, as Eric Charmes points out, are not so much describing a social reality as constructing one.[75]

The politics of immigration

In 1982, there were 4 million immigrants and 3.5 million foreigners living in France, where the total population was 55 million. In 2011, there were 5.4 million immigrants and 3.7 million foreigners amid a population of 65 million. Over a thirty-year period, then, the immigrant population had risen from 7.2 per cent to 8.4 per cent of the total population. The proportion of foreigners had fallen from 6.3 per cent to 5.8 per cent, considerably less than in fourteen of France's European neighbours, including Italy, Britain, Belgium, Germany and Spain.[76] Indeed, in terms of other OECD developed nations, France stands in seventeenth position.[77] While study after study has shown the impact of immigration on unemployment and on 'native' salaries to be negligible or non-existent, and the detrimental effects on public finances to be minimal or inconsequential,[78] myths persist about the drain of immigration on services and the threat it poses to jobs and wages. This is partly due to a political narrative that has been asserted with little to counter it since the 1980s, bolstered by the media, where privatisation and increased competition have fostered increasingly sensationalist reporting, notably of immigration. In France, since the 1990s, media reporting has tended to criminalise immigration, linking it to delinquency and urban violence, a pattern that echoed mainstream political preoccupations, as we saw in Chapter Two.[79]

One OECD report notes the impact on media reporting of a political shift, between 1983 and 1991, from policies promoting cultural diversity to a greater emphasis on integration:

> the number of stories stressing the positive aspects of cultural diversity fell to a quarter of what it had been eight years earlier, while more than a third of immigration stories addressed the problems caused by immigrants' cultural differences.[80]

By the turn of the century, polls indicated that 40 per cent of Europeans, and nearly half of French respondents, believed immigration to have a negative impact on salaries.[81] In 2016, only 11 per cent of French people surveyed in a Europe-wide Ipsos poll thought that there were positive aspects to immigration.[82] In the years since the financial crash, there has been a rapid acceleration in negative opinions on immigration. A report for France's CNCDH (National Consultative Commission on Human Rights) in December 2013 found 74 per cent of respondents believed there to be 'too many immigrants in France'. Five years earlier, in 2008, the percentage sharing this view had stood at 47 per cent.[83] As Ipsos director Brice Teinturier puts it, France 'is the country where we see the greatest gap between perception and reality on the question of immigration'. He notes in particular the role of leading politicians in fostering the notion that immigrants are coming to France to take advantage of social security payments.[84]

Polls assessing worldwide perceptions of immigrants in 2016 noted that 42 per cent of US and 45 per cent of British respondents believed the 'cultural impact' of immigration to be positive; in France the figure was only 17 per cent.[85] Such perceptions are based on a chronically distorted picture of what society looks like. One poll asked the question, 'Are there too many immigrants in your country?' In the US and in most European countries, between a third and a half of respondents answered Yes. Other respondents were asked the same question, but first told the actual number of immigrants in their country: the numbers responding in the affirmative fell by half.[86] One poll asked people to say what percentage of the French population was made up of immigrants. The response was 28 per cent. The real figure is around 10 per cent. When it came to Muslims, perceptions were even more distorted. Respondents believed that 31 per cent of the French population was Muslim, with the real figure closer to 8 per cent. Internationally, the average disparity between perception and reality was indicated by an imagined proportion of

Muslims in national populations at 16 per cent, with the reality at 3 per cent.[87] Just over half of French respondents, 51 per cent, believed there to be 'too many Muslims' in France, while around a third did not consider Muslims to be French 'like the others'. An identical proportion, 51 per cent, also found that there were too many Maghrebians in France. In 1966, this figure had stood at 62 per cent, a reminder that racist attitudes can be prevalent as latent views or sentiments without being taken up, legitimised and embedded in the political arena.[88]

The elevation of the notion of the '*petit blanc*' into a sociological category for contemporary France is a corollary of racialisation of other groups and the emergence of the spurious concept of 'anti-white racism'. Its use is significant as an indicator of widespread acceptance of the primacy of identity in shaping political cleavages, or at least perceptions of them. The use of such terms obscures not only the reasons why people vote for the Front National, attributing motives to imputed tribal instincts, but also the social changes that have underpinned the Front's rise. These are overwhelmingly related to the transformation of French society since the end of the long post-war boom—deepening inequalities, long-term structural unemployment, chronic job insecurity, the transformation of the world of work and blocked social mobility.

These processes have generated various forms of cultural pessimism, including racism, which—whether conscious or unconscious—played a part in breaking up workplace organisation and solidarity, part of a wider disintegration of associative and community networks linked to the traditional labour movement.[89] These social and economic factors, and the fragmentation and disorientation of working-class perspectives they have produced, have been the elements determining the life chances and expectations of working people in France—not the 1 per cent rise in the proportion of immigrants living amongst them. As Charmes notes, the left's role should not be to convince the white worker in 'peripheral France' that his enemy is the North African immigrant living in the *banlieues* of Paris or Marseille.[90]

Conclusion

Although this book focuses on the impact of Islamophobia, highlighting the pivotal role played by political and intellectual elites in its construction, society is not simply programmed by political ideas like a machine. It develops and shifts according to tendencies that are generally beyond the reach of political actors. Multiculturalism, as Bouamama points out, does not happen because of political choices—it is a social and historical fact. Feelings of similarity and difference 'are not decreed' but are produced by a process of socialisation:

> Cultural diversity is not a problem in itself, it all depends on whether the context is one of egalitarianism or domination. It's not cultural diversity that's problematic but the fact that cultural origins lead to inequality of opportunity. It's not difference that's shocking but the allocation of dominated roles based on origins. 'Communitarianism' is produced first of all by inequality, not by the existence of cultural differences.[91]

The capacity to assert an agenda, however—to develop a narrative that appears to make sense of society as part of an attempt to offer leadership to it—is an essential part of any contested political field. We saw in Chapter Two how the French right sought to capitalise on Chirac's 2002 victory by presenting it as some kind of republican resurgence, laying claim to the secular tradition that had until then been the preserve of the left. The absence of any coherent countervailing narrative to an increasingly strident new secularism has made it easier for myths about the nefarious influence of immigrants and Muslims to gain ground. Such views have a social impact. But, at the same time,

France continues to develop as a multicultural society. The response of political elites on both left and right has essentially been to deny this. In François Fillon's words: 'We have not chosen communitarianism, multiculturalism. It's not the choice I want for our country.'[92]

France today is a society where living standards are falling, poverty is endemic and inequality rising. The predominant explanatory framework adopted by mainstream parties has been a neoliberal outlook that essentially views inequality as inevitable and necessary, seeking to blame its effects on the consequences of immigration, notably the existence of several million people categorised as Muslim. This 'punitive' form of neoliberalism, more prominent since the 2008 crash,[93] has been bolstered rather than challenged by the authoritarian racism of the Front National. The failure of the left to confront this drift has been a significant feature of political competition since the 1980s. In the absence of a consistent, assertive, confident anti-racist movement, it becomes much easier for false polarisations to gain ground and for narratives to emerge that widen the gap between perception and reality.

As Guilluy notes, the racialisation of social relations is a form of social control.[94] Areas of social deprivation like the *banlieues*, defined in ethnic terms, are contrasted with 'middle-class' areas where 'middle-class' acts as a synonym for 'white', fostering the illusion that groups experiencing social relegation somehow have a stake in the system that is beyond the reach of second, third and fourth generation outsiders as well as their white working-class counterparts. The latter are no longer considered an active social force, regarded instead as mere victims of globalisation, left behind to stew in ignorance and lumpen prejudice: chavs, white trash, *petits blancs*.[95] These excluded losers only really come to life in public debate when the necessity of taking on board their 'concerns' about immigration is invoked. And yet one of the most important developments in contemporary France has been the emergence of a so-called 'social movement', capable not just of defending the conditions of working-class people in the face of neoliberal economic orthodoxy but also of asserting the possibility of alternatives to it. The inability of this movement to make common cause with stigmatised minorities and to confront prejudice with the same verve and *élan* it has deployed against neoliberalism has been the single greatest failure of France's nascent radical left. Underpinning this failure has been the lack of a concerted, organised challenge to Islamophobia, which we examine in the next chapter.

5

'TOUS ENSEMBLE'?

ISLAMOPHOBIA AND ANTI-RACISM

Friday 10 March 2006. Interior Minister Nicolas Sarkozy has just boarded a plane in Martinique. He has brought forward his departure after news reached him of an occupation of the Sorbonne university by around 200 students, part of a nationwide movement against the government's *Contrat Première Embauche* (First Job Contract, CPE), a plan to ease regulations on the employment of young people. The CPE protests have come barely half a year after the uprising that swept France's *banlieues*. Sarkozy is therefore on hand to oversee the government's riposte. From the plane he speaks to the head of the CRS riot police to finalise details of how they will break up the occupation. Why so much attention on a student protest? 'Tomorrow,' Sarkozy confides to journalists, 'there are all the demonstrations. There's no point in having crossovers.'[1]

Since the huge public sector strikes and demonstrations of late 1995, France's 'social movement' had exhibited a power unmatched anywhere else in Europe. Its capacity for organisation and coordination had seen an embryonic electoral alternative emerge on the radical left well before the development of similar initiatives in Spain, Greece, Portugal, Italy and Germany. Successive governments had seen attempts at dismantling the welfare state halted or defeated by the movement, which appeared able to regroup after defeats and grow stronger. In 2005 a major blow was dealt to the European Union's attempts to accelerate neoliberal reform when a proposed EU constitution was defeated in a French referendum dominated not by nationalism and xenophobia but by radical opposition to free market orthodoxies. The huge majority that rejected the treaty was overwhelmingly motivated by concerns that the project was too neoliberal and neglected social issues.[2]

For all the verve and dynamism of the movement, though—for all its organisational initiatives, for all the sophistication of the arguments it deployed against the neoliberal offensive—there was a problem. In the country that had seen the post-war far right reinvent itself and put racism at the centre of political life, anti-racism was not merely in disarray but in retreat. On the one hand, mainstream anti-racist organisations like SOS Racisme or the International League Against Racism and Anti-Semitism (LICRA) limited themselves to abstract denunciations of racism as morally wrong but offered little or no practical support to France's Muslim population, the most relentlessly stigmatised group in contemporary France. On the other, an enduring dislocation had developed between the radical left and those experiencing racism, dramatically highlighted by the 2005 *banlieue* uprising. By 2017, despite the alarming acceleration of Islamophobia over the previous decade, there had not been a single national mobilisation to counter it. Indeed, initiatives organised under an 'anti-Islamophobia' banner, from the Une école pour tous (One School for All) collective set up to counter the 2004 hijab law to the 'Against Islamophobia' conferences organised in 2015–17, had come under fierce attack. In other words, throughout the Sarkozy (2007–12) and Hollande (2012–17) presidencies, there was no major national anti-racist demonstration of any kind. This is in stark contrast to the mobilisation against austerity in the same period.

Why has there been so little 'crossover' between France's powerful anti-austerity movement and anti-racism? This chapter examines some of the fault-lines running through France's social movement and radical left, and traces the emergence of a combative, independent, black- and Arab-led current seeking to forge an alternative to institutional anti-racism, under the banner of 'political anti-racism'.

Confronting neoliberalism: the social movement

The emergence in the mid-1990s of a movement to counter attempts to break up the welfare state and deregulate the labour market was characterised from the outset by the coming together of various different strands of grassroots activism. Trade unions made common cause with organisations defending the homeless and the unemployed—the so-called '*sans*' movements of 'those without' that included the *sans papiers*, undocumented migrants. An early feature of the movement was the confidence it gave to activists in a range of struggles, breathing new life into anti-racist initiatives, with high-profile battles developing over undocumented migrants and legislation monitoring the movement of foreign visitors to France, alongside significant mobilisations against the Front National. These contributed to the damaging split in the organisation in the late 1990s and reached a crescendo between the two rounds of the 2002 election, which culminated in Jean-Marie Le Pen's defeat.[3] After this point, however, there were to be no more national demonstrations against the FN.

On the other hand, in the aftermath of Chirac's 2002 victory, the social movement continued to grow.[4] Mobilisations included widespread industrial action by trade unions against pension reform in 2003 and 2010, huge nationwide protests against moves to casualise youth labour in 2006, the first general strike against a major industrialised nation's response to the financial crisis in 2009, and angry demonstrations against the El Khomri law, the so-called *loi Travail* in 2016.[5] France also saw the development of a dynamic movement for 'another globalisation' that mobilised against the World Trade Organisation in 2003, briefly elevating the peasant trade union leader José Bové into an international symbol of revolt against transnational corporations. In the 2005 EU constitution referendum, these three elements came together in a campaign that saw the treaty rejected with a resounding No vote. A similar configuration came together—rather less successfully—in the form of the so-called '*Nuit Debout*' (Up All Night) protests of 2016, when the Place de la République in central Paris was occupied by activists in the wake of waves of mobilisation against the *loi Travail*'s deregulation of the workplace.

These mobilisations all involved the development of grassroots organisational networks that drew together associative, trade union, student and *altermondialiste* ('for another globalisation', or global justice) activists. With the exception of the Greek population's defiance of EU austerity, they represented the most sustained movement against the neoliberal policy agenda anywhere in Europe. The protests were sparked by reforms affecting the workplace and the social security and education systems, in a wider context of significant structural change in French society. This included, as we saw in Chapter Four, transformations in the world of work, with comparatively high unemployment and the development of non-standard forms of labour, generating greater precarity.

These changes have had an impact on what it means to be part of the working class. In the twentieth century, as Gerassimos Moschonas argues, the working class achieved a level of visibility and politicisation that was unprecedented for a dominated class.[6] The labour movement today, disoriented by defeat, structural unemployment and the rise of precarious work, no longer enjoys the same 'sociological and symbolic centrality' experienced by a once relatively compact and self-confident social force. However, periods of transition and transformation are nothing new in the history of the labour movement, and are not unique to France. The situation has been compounded by the decline of the Communist Party and by the Socialist Party's abandonment of any serious attempt to politicise working-class culture.[7] More generally, the sense that collective solutions are no longer possible, in a context of rising levels of insecurity, makes it easier for individuals to be pitted against each other. Patrick Savidan, founder of the French Observatory on Inequality, argues that the increasingly individualised nature of society, combined with a sense that governments are socially and politically impotent and that there is no collective political alternative, breeds the conviction 'that to avoid being dominated you have to find the means to dominate others'.[8]

By the mid-1990s, poor families in France were more likely to remain poor than in the 1980s, and rich families less likely to become so.[9] By 2016, 12 per cent of French jobs were categorised as 'precarious', against 5.3 per cent in 1982.[10] One in four under-25s were unemployed and nearly half of all young workers were on short-term contracts. Over time, such precarity takes a toll on confidence and organisation: working lives that are subject to insecurity and flux are prone to disorientation. Symptomatic of this is the FN's success in winning a significant number of votes from young workers, those most likely to endure precarious working conditions and to be least integrated into the political or trade union culture of their parents' generation.[11] Various sociologists have identified a decline in fraternity and solidarity,[12] but the rise of the FN and the disintegration of collective solidarities are not ineluctable processes.

The extent to which lives are shaped by individual rather than collective concerns often depends on the political responses to given situations. In the wake of the 2003 strikes over pension reform, one commentator wrote: 'In this splintered, reactive conflictuality, frequently conveying reactions of anger and revolt, there still exists a risk of spontaneous aggregation and open social crisis'.[13] The rage and frustration that led youths to burn schools and job centres, which for them had become symbols of the poverty and discrimination excluding them from 'republican' society, was not confined to France's impoverished urban fringes. In 2000, for example, textile workers threatened with redundancy at the Cellatex plant in the northern municipality of Givet occupied the factory and took charge of its 56,000 litres of sulphuric acid and 46 tonnes of carbon sulphide, threatening to blow it up, and eventually discharging thousands of litres of acid into the streets.[14] Several firms have experienced 'boss-napping' as employees exasperated by management intransigence have resorted to taking their CEOs hostage.[15] In October 2015, around 2,000 Air France employees, furious at management's restructuring plans, took part in a protest during which striking workers invaded the company headquarters and ripped the shirts from the backs of two senior managers, including the director of human resources.[16]

The social movement has not developed in a linear fashion. The period since 1995 has seen record low levels of strike action interspersed with some of the most explosive and significant protests of the post-war era. The movement has developed organisational tools, but not fashioned them into a durable form able to mount consistent action or deliver emphatic victories. The veteran commentator on French trade unions, René Mouriaux, has identified some of the movement's political weaknesses: the lack of a set of straightforward aims around which the trade movement could unite; the failure of the union leadership to develop radical alternative propositions to the state; and an inability to win over rank-and-file members to the positions it did develop. More generally, a global vision was lacking, a unifying political goal. To these fault-lines can be added a more basic failure: an inability to defend racialised minorities, to recognise and absorb the fact that the working class is changing, not just because of workplace pressure and regulations or the impact of unemployment and precarity, but because it is becoming more diverse. By the early twenty-first century, working-class identity had become much more heterogeneous, in terms of occupation, gender and ethnicity. As previous generations of workers have found, the emergence of a cohesive labour movement no longer just depends on the economic imperatives that brought women, Jews, Poles and Italians into the workplace. Political responses to prejudice and xenophobia have also become necessary.

Islamophobia and the radical left

In *Les filles voilées parlent*, a book of interviews with women who wear the hijab, the editors underline the extent to which watchwords like a 'ban on conspicuous symbols' or the 'neutrality of public space' are, for those interviewed, synonymous not with the 'reaffirmation of *laïcité*' or with 'emancipation' or 'encouraging living together', but rather 'with humiliations, exclusions, insults or even aggressions.' The testimonies in the book bear witness to the fighting spirit of Muslim women forced to justify their affiliation to a religion that, according to a majority of state actors, has made them submissive. One of them, Hanane, put it like this:

> I wear the veil out of submission to a God—a submission that I take full responsibility for—but that also means that I submit to nobody else. Even my parents. I respect them but I am not subordinate to them. That's the source of my strength: I give myself to a God and this God promises to protect and defend me.

Her message to those who wanted to dictate how she should behave? 'Go to hell!' Her message to other women who wear the veil? 'Let's stick together, don't give up on this!' As for those who point the finger at them, her message was straightforward: 'Fuck!'[17]

The book details dozens of ways in which the law gives rise to absurd situations, petty humiliations and indignities, but also to dashed hopes, the consequence of failed examinations and exclusions from school. Some students attempted to negotiate a path through the stipulations of the law, wearing bandanas instead of hijabs, since they could not be perceived as 'conspicuous' or 'manifest' religious symbols. Some teachers nevertheless interpreted them as such, while others gave detailed instructions on how to comply, generally by insisting that students made sure to display some hair, out of reverence for France's supposedly neutral public space.

The situation was sometimes made worse by the sheer vindictiveness of Islamophobic teachers, for whom the legislation had given discrimination the green light, and sometimes simply through a lack of solidarity or even basic human compassion on the part of others. One history teacher confided that her defence of a veiled student had led to staff room accusations of '*Islamo-gauchisme*' (Islamo-leftism) and 'green fascism'.[18]

Hanane, who had begun working in a school, was confronted one day by a senior member of staff who suggested she might wear shorter dresses, or trousers. She told the story to a colleague, a member of the Trotskyist Ligue communiste révolutionnaire (LCR), who then revealed that it was she who had informed management that Hanane wore a hijab outside school.[19] This was not an isolated incident. We saw in the last chapter how leading members of the far-left Lutte ouvrière party and the LCR played a key role in ensuring that two hijab-wearers were excluded from the Aubervilliers school where they taught in 2003. Such petty zealotry was countered by the active engagement of a relatively small minority of radical left activists in associations like the Collectif une école pour tous (One School for All), founded to defend Muslim students against stigmatisation, and in subsequent anti-Islamophobia initiatives and meetings. In general, however, the story of the radical left's attitude towards Muslims experiencing discrimination was one of abject abandonment, if not outright hostility. It was Lutte ouvrière members, for example, who initiated a vote to ensure that a group of Muslim feminists were not allowed to append their names to the call for an International Women's Day march in 2005.[20]

Organisations like Lutte ouvrière and the LCR identify themselves as Marxist, claiming an affiliation to the Bolshevik tradition. Although plenty of examples of crude anti-religious sentiment can be found within this tradition, it was nonetheless resolutely scornful of the petty anti-clericalism of the French left under the Third Republic. For Lenin, the practical unity of oppressed people in a revolutionary struggle to build a heaven on earth was more important than unity of opinion among workers about whether there was a heaven above. He urged Bolsheviks not to proclaim their atheism.[21] Along with Leon Trotsky and Rosa Luxemburg, he saw 'bourgeois anti-clericalism' as a distraction from working-class struggle. Indeed, as the essayist Pierre Tevanian points out, the struggle against religion should not simply be viewed as a distraction. It represents a form of idealism that actively prioritises the concerns of petty bourgeois rationalism over the social question.[22] In his classic account of the relationship between Marxism and Islam, Maxime Rodinson argues that this idealism served as a justification for French Communists to keep their distance from the struggle for Algerian independence. So steeped were they in 'Enlightenment ideology' that their polemics against religion 'brought them closer to the ambient implicit ideology of the non-communist French, who had nothing but contempt for Islam'.[23]

Such priorities have been a feature of the development of the anti-capitalist movement in France in a period of rising Islamophobia. Tim Peace's study of Muslim engagement in the anti-capitalist and anti-war movements in Britain and France highlights a paradox between the two countries. In Britain, Muslims have generally been welcomed and encouraged by activists, while in France 'they largely faced incomprehension'.[24] The subtitle of his book, 'Another World but with Whom?', was taken from an article by Dominique Sopo, leader of France's best known anti-racist organisation, SOS Racisme, that openly questioned the participation of Muslims in the movement. By contrast, when it came to the anti-capitalist movement, the involvement of French Muslims both has a longer history and, according to some accounts of the social forum events held in European cities in the early 2000s, has been more 'concrete and meaningful' than in Britain.[25]

A number of associations, like the MIB (Immigration and *Banlieues* Movement) that emerged in the 1990s, have built on the legacy of the associations that organised the 1983 March for Equality. In the Lyon area, DiverCité was an initiative set up in 1997 that encouraged participation between secular and religious activists. A key figure in the relationship between Muslim and secular activists has been the Swiss-based Muslim academic Tariq Ramadan. In the wake of the 1995 terrorist attacks on French soil by the Algeria-based Groupe islamique armé (GIA), he was banned from entering France by the centre-right interior minister, Jean-Louis Debré. Various anti-racist groups and senior Catholic clergy in Lyon, where Ramadan had developed links with young Muslim activists, formed a Committee for the Free Expression of Muslims in France. Other initiatives were to follow. An Islam and *Laïcité* Commission was established in 1996. Activists from the *banlieues* worked on campaigns over homelessness, in defence of undocumented migrants and on other questions ranging from Palestine to the US interventions in Afghanistan and Iraq. Following the success in 2002 of the first European Social Forum, where Ramadan and members of his Présence musulmane (Muslim Presence) group had played an active role, Muslim activists turned up at northern Paris' Saint-Denis Bourse du Travail to take part in preparing the next Forum, due to take place in Paris in 2003. They were met with bemusement and suspicion: 'What are you doing here?' 'What do you want?'[26]

Ramadan summed up the frustration of Muslims at anti-capitalists' reticence to work with them. Global justice activists, he argued, tended to consider religious and cultural diversity as matters requiring gestures of goodwill rather than as a practical reality that needed to be dealt with. Women and men with progressive views on social, political and economic issues would often hold views on cultural questions that were 'tainted by a colonial outlook'. Ramadan's conclusion was that 'there can be no future for the alter-globalisation movement without an open and sincere dialogue with the world of Islam.'[27]

Tariq Ramadan was to become the sustained focus of attempts to delegitimise the participation of Muslims in the European Social Forum process. It began with an article in which he argued that various intellectuals held political views that followed a communitarian or nationalist logic, based on their Jewish origins or support for Israel. Since Arab and Muslim figures were required—in the name of shared universal values—to condemn terrorism, violence, anti-semitism and Islamic dictatorships like Saudi Arabia or Pakistan, Ramadan pointed out that, by the same logic, it would make sense to expect Jewish intellectuals to condemn the repressive policies of the state of Israel.[28] SOS Racisme, the LICRA and a number of Socialist politicians called for him to withdraw from the Forum. Three feminists, including Maya Surduts of the LCR, produced a petition to the same effect that was published in *Libération*, questioning the motives of the 'ideologue' Ramadan and criticising alter-globalists for giving legitimacy to political Islam by working with someone who was advancing his own agenda by 'cloaking himself as a defender of the dignity of discriminated individuals'.[29] The polemicist Caroline Fourest waded in with a fierce book-length invective against Ramadan, deploying techniques that were to become her signature, relying on guilt by association, half-truths and wild generalisations about Islam (for example the claim that Muslim men are encouraged to marry women from other monotheistic religions in order to convert them).[30]

The furore coincided with the controversy over Lila and Alma Lévy in Aubervilliers, who explained that their conversion to Islam had partly come about through listening to Ramadan speak. Taken together, as Peace notes, this was enough to make him 'public enemy number one'.[31] The question of Muslim participation in the tax reform activist organisation ATTAC became a major debate within the association, contributing to its split in 2006. In their internal struggle for control of ATTAC, Bernard Cassen and Jacques Nikonoff frequently criticised their opponents for their inclusive attitude to Islam, Nikonoff going so far as to assert that 'gender equality and equality between all women on earth must take precedence over any ethnic or religious considerations. This idea is by no means shared by all members of the Administrative Council'.[32]

Tensions had grown in the wake of the 2004 law banning 'conspicuous' religious symbols in schools. Some members of ATTAC had helped set up the One School for All collective. In the words of one longstanding LCR and ATTAC member, Catherine Samary, those involved in the collective found themselves confronted with 'atheist activists who refused to share a platform with Muslim associations or, worse, veiled women'.[33] Some global justice activists went as far as to adopt an interpretation of *laïcité* that was so repressive that they even opposed Article II–70 of the EU's doomed constitutional treaty. This simply stated that 'Everyone has the ... freedom, either alone or in community with others and in public or private, to manifest religion or belief in worship, teaching, practice, and observance'.[34] Their radical anti-clericalism, supposedly part of a militant defence of universalism in the face of obscurantism, had taken them so far from an identification of basic rights, let alone solidarity with an oppressed minority, that they had become critical of a clause that those drafting the EU constitution had taken directly from the Universal Declaration of Human Rights.[35]

The emergence of an anti-war movement at the start of the twenty-first century offered possibilities for radical left activists in France to work with Muslims in building a united movement against intervention in Afghanistan and Iraq and to establish genuine cooperation between the political left and young people of immigrant heritage. Instead, the movement limited the prospects for such cooperation by putting terrorism on an equal footing with military intervention by the United States, and choosing not to march through areas with large black and Arab populations. The notion of a 'missed *rendez-vous*' between the left and the *banlieues* had long been noted, so this was nothing new.[36] Of course, there is no guarantee that the left, even if it had offered genuine, practical solidarity during the hijab affair or actively included them in the anti-war movement, would have found it possible to provide an alternative arena for the *banlieue* youths' expression of revolt in 2005. At the very least, however, it would have been better placed to engage in the political debate about what to do next that took place in the years following the uprising. It would also have opened up the possibility of a political challenge to the strategy adopted by the mainstream right: co-opting the left's preserve of *laïcité* and radicalising it.

For much of the 1980s and 1990s, the position of the radical left on such issues would have been largely irrelevant. It operated on the fringes of political debate, influential in an activist milieu but with little impact on national politics. One of the consequences of the resurgence of the social movement, however, was the emergence of radical left electoral alternatives, first in the unlikely form of Lutte ouvrière's Arlette Laguiller in 1995, and then with the more dynamic figure of Olivier Besancenot from 2002 to 2007. From 2012, Jean-Luc Mélenchon was to become the dominant electoral force for the so-called 'left of the left'. In the decade that spanned Chirac's 2002 success to the Hollande victory of 2012, the radical left managed a combined vote of close to 12 per cent in three successive presidential elections. Yet at no point did any of its candidates manage to offer a consistent or coherent defence against Islamophobia. Why was this so?

Part of the explanation lies with the historic difficulty encountered by the French left in establishing traditions and organisations genuinely independent from the Republic. Identification with republicanism was easy to understand. In simple terms, the Republic was better than a monarchy or a dictatorship. The left was prepared to tolerate the betrayals and atrocities of republican regimes if the alternative was something worse. In 1871, 30,000 Communards were massacred by an alliance of republican government troops, monarchists and the army of imperial Germany, united by a desire to crush the possibility of socialism represented by the Paris Commune. Those who were not killed were deported or imprisoned. Yet in 1914 former Communards were to rally to the 'sacred union' in defence of the 'Republic in danger'.

The historian Jacques Kergoat identifies the Dreyfus Affair (1894–1906) as a pivotal moment in the relationship between the left and the Republic. Leading figures on the socialist left, including Jean Jaurès and Jules Guesde, had initially adopted an abstentionist position towards Dreyfus, framed on spying charges because he was a Jew. When the danger posed by the anti-semitic leagues of the right became clear, the Socialists, led by Jaurès, then rallied to the defence of the Republic. It was there, argues Kergoat, that an opportunity to establish an independent Marxist alternative to the republican state was missed, hampering its development for the rest of the century.[37] The political impact of this failure can be seen in the tenacity of the republican myths fashioned in the aftermath of the Affair—primarily that the secular Republic was a bastion against reaction—and in the durability of the political tools the Republic deployed to mobilise against the right, notably anti-clericalism.

Vestiges of the crude Marxism that had characterised sections of the nineteenth-century French left have endured, and were accentuated by the anti-Muslim climate that gathered pace domestically from 1989, accelerating internationally from 2001. The first beneficiary of the revival of the social question in 1990s France was Lutte ouvrière, an insular grouping devoted to a fairly crude appropriation of Marxism. The organisation reacted to the November 2005 *banlieue* uprising by counterposing the insurgent youth and the working class, as if the two were somehow separate entities. Worse, Lutte ouvrière also echoed the racist stereotyping of the revolt as the work of 'yobs' and petty criminals, attacking those involved for having no social conscience, and deploring, with no sense of irony, their lack of solidarity. In 2017 the party confirmed its indifference to the various initiatives that had developed against Islamophobia, questioning the 'ambiguity' of the term as a 'trap' and arguing that the left's role should be to denounce the hold that Islam had over youth of immigrant backgrounds, seeking to win them instead to atheism.[38]

Such attitudes are explained in part by Lutte ouvrière's isolation from the wider world. The case of the Ligue communiste révolutionnaire (LCR) is more serious, has caused more damage and illustrates the extent of anti-Muslim sentiment on the radical left. As we saw in Chapter Four, in 2003–4 leading members of both organisations had led a campaign to get two students excluded from a school in Aubervilliers for wearing the hijab. The controversy had drawn the attention of politicians from across the spectrum. A junior education minister had gone so far as to declare that 'When you don't like the French Republic, you go elsewhere'.[39] As Laurent Lévy, the students' father, noted, divisions over the issue went beyond the *laïcité* debate. They had their roots in the social and political history of France via questions ranging from feminism, law and order, the nation state and colonialism to anti-racism, urban policy, wider geopolitical threats, and fears and fantasies arising from the rise of Islamic fundamentalism.[40] What successive headscarf affairs had done was to reduce these matters, almost to the point of absurdity, to a question of how a girl's hair should be covered. In Aubervilliers the head of the high school met with the other teachers. They came up with a compromise solution: the students could continue to receive an education there if they agreed to leave the base of their neck uncovered, along with their earlobes and the roots of their hair.[41] This occurred at a time when there was no law governing the wearing of the hijab, or any other 'visible' religious symbol, other than those stipulating that the buildings and personnel in public sector spaces should be neutral. In this instance the school, under the impetus of a campaign led by Trotskyist teachers, was effectively choosing its public.

A shift was taking place in the perception of *laïcité*. It was now being used to arbitrate a separation between the public sphere—the school—and the private sphere—religion. As Lévy points out, had such a distinction been in operation a century before there would have been no separation of church and state or indeed any need for non-denominational schools. What was to be made of the private sphere's invasion of every town, village and city across France, with churches, cathedrals and cemeteries everywhere to be seen?[42] *Laïcité* was no longer an instrument guaranteeing the independence of politics and the state from religion, but was instead becoming inscribed in the heart of all politics, as 'liberty, equality and fraternity combined'.[43] A concerted process of stigmatisation could be identified, underway since the 1980s, that fused together various trajectories of Islamophobic reaction: anti-immigrant racism; republican colonial tropes insinuating French superiority over 'backward' cultures; the post-9/11 myth of a 'clash of civilisations' putting all Muslims under suspicion; the targeting of 'dangerous classes' concentrated in the unruly metropolitan outskirts of the *banlieues*; various stereotypes of the violent, sexist 'Arab male' and the passive, submissive Muslim wife, sister, daughter with her yoke, the hijab, around her head. Each accumulated prejudice was crystallised into this one conspicuous symbol.

Into this racist climate marched the principal organisations of the radical left, castigating the use of the term 'Islamophobia' on the grounds that the right to criticise religion must be upheld and that, in any case, Muslims 'were not a race'. Yet, as Lévy notes, 'It's racism that constitutes races; it's the essentialisation of certain populations, to whom racism claims to attribute certain common, specific and socially significant characteristics, distinguishing them as objects of rejection or discrimination'.[44] How can this have escaped the radical left? Lévy puts it down to the influence, subconscious or otherwise, of the post-9/11 rise of the 'clash of civilisations' agenda. A powerful element of this narrative was the view that Muslim women were victims of a particular kind of sexism: more authoritarian, violent and pervasive than that experienced by Western women, a sexism that required the liberation of its victims, if necessary by repressive means.[45] There was also the historic role of French republican anti-clericalism, which by the late 1980s had morphed into an anti-Muslim stance that grew more intransigent with every headscarf affair. This was the radical left's version of the 'civilising mission': Muslims had to be convinced of the superiority of atheism before they could become part of the feminist struggle. The notion of an activism that could 'articulate, without putting them in hierarchical order, the oppressions of race, sex and class, and whose starting point was women's lived experience' was completely obscured by the debate.[46]

On a more rudimentary level, however, there was a simple failure to grasp the role of racism, and specifically Islamophobia, in reshaping contemporary French politics and society. Rather than put the changing social reality of contemporary France at the forefront of an analysis that took into account the reasons why Islam was now France's second most practised religion, Islam was instead identified as the problem. Rather than highlight the shortcomings of France's so-called model of integration in an increasingly multicultural (and racist) society, the far left chose instead to put the onus on the teenagers wearing the hijab, highlighting their need to integrate. In the Aubervilliers case, teachers from the secondary school in question (some of whom were affiliated to the radical left) even went so far as to publicly condemn a sixteen-year-old student for her 'militant affiliation' to the hijab and her desire to defend the right of all young women to wear it.[47] To put it in crude but nevertheless accurate terms, rather than stand with an oppressed minority, the two principal organisations of the radical left chose to side with racism and the state. This was effectively the position of the LCR nationally, summed up in shorthand terms as 'neither veil, nor law'. Its condemnation of the headscarf, put on the same plane as the law, meant that the Ligue was unable to mount any effective opposition to the discrimination institutionalised by the law, and indeed did not do so. Its condemnation of the law remained abstract, leaving Islamophobic elements in the party free to campaign for exclusions.

A leading LCR member at the time, Pierre-François Grond, was a history teacher at the Aubervilliers school. He led the agitation for the two students' exclusion. He and the other Ligue and Lutte ouvrière members teaching there defended the choice in the national press. One teacher pointed out that if the young women had been prepared to display a lock of hair and their earlobes then they would not have been excluded. All this in the name of combatting obscurantism. It is difficult, as Alain Badiou noted at the time, to ignore the implicit injunction that these women must reject 'modesty' and conform to French societal norms by declaring themselves sexually available.[48] In any case it is hard to see how the activists' decision to deprive these students, the daughters of a Jewish radical left activist, of a state education, would advance its two stated motivations—*laïcité* and women's rights—or how it tallied with their supposed opposition to the law itself. The Aubervilliers case, preceding the hijab ban, undoubtedly bolstered the prohibitionist camp. The ban itself, as Catherine Samary argued, would only strengthen the hand of the father, brother or husband in cases where the headscarf was being imposed. More widely, it came to foster a 'clientelist communitarianism' via the establishment of private faith schools—financed by the state as part of Interior Minister Sarkozy's project of promoting a 'French Islam'.[49]

The LCR's contrasting treatment of white male prohibitionists and female Muslims was striking. When the Saint-Denis branch of the LCR in northern Paris was approached by a Muslim activist who asked to join the organisation, she was given the same choice as that offered to Muslim school students by the Chirac administration: take off your hijab during political activity with us or be refused entry.[50] While women wearing the headscarf were prevented from joining, men who agitated for the exclusion of students faced no sanction. Grond was even to become a leading member of the organisation that succeeded the LCR in 2009, the New Anti-Capitalist Party (NPA). The LCR effectively aligned itself with the 'new secularist' turn in French society, an alignment that could be measured by the gulf between its positions in 1989, when it opposed school exclusions, and 2003/4, when its members agitated for them.

The NPA was an attempt to take advantage of the impressive scores achieved in presidential elections by the LCR's Olivier Besancenot and to build a durable organisation on the back of more than a decade of social movement struggles. Things began well. Where the LCR had around 3,000 members, the NPA recruited 9,000 on its formation. The radical left was also beginning to win support from racialised individuals, notably in the south of France. In the Vaucluse a Muslim woman, Ilham Moussaïd, was chosen as a candidate on the NPA list for the March 2010 elections. She wore a hijab. The decision caused uproar. National figures from all the major parties intervened to condemn the decision, trotting out clichés about the opium of the people. Hadn't the comrades read Marx? The then Socialist Party leader Martine Aubry claimed that she would not permit a veiled woman to stand as a candidate since it was a declaration of religious affiliation that should remain 'in the private sphere'.[51]

Leading radical left figure Jean-Luc Mélenchon argued that Moussaïd would not be able to 'represent the majority' because of her headscarf. She also faced considerable opposition from within her own party. Three candidates on the same NPA list in the Vaucluse stood down in protest at her candidacy, arguing that the hijab was a 'conspicuous' symbol of women's oppression, and therefore incompatible with the values of a secular and feminist organisation.[52] The Ni Putes Ni Soumises group (Neither Sluts Nor Slaves) took legal action against an 'anti-secular, anti-feminist and anti-republican' list (it was unsuccessful). Interviewed by this author at the time, Moussaïd countered that

> here's a woman with a headscarf, a Muslim, who's politically active—that also surprises them enormously because they think we're not capable of getting involved in politics ... If this had been about a woman wearing a

cross, or about someone with a kippah, there wouldn't have been such a fuss. There are politicians who wear crosses and who say openly that they're Christians and nobody is shocked. But this apparently shocks a lot of people even though there are 4 million Muslims in France.

Some accounts of the controversy had portrayed the NPA as an 'Islamo-leftist' party, courting the so-called *quartiers populaires* (working-class areas). 'I find it shocking,' remarked Moussaïd, 'that politicians haven't been able to realise that it's perhaps the other way round—that people from these areas are interested in the NPA. So I'm surprised they couldn't think for a moment that we might be concerned about our own lives, that we've got our own political consciousness and that we want to get involved.' As for those who argued that her hijab was a symbol of oppression and submission,

> For my part, I'm not submissive: it's a personal choice. I'm a feminist. I fight for women's rights with my women comrades. I fight for equality between men and women. I fight for the right to abortion, the right to contraception. It's true they see it as a symbol of oppression but unfortunately they forget that there are women who wear it out of choice. A certain number of women are made to wear it, of course, I don't deny that, and I'll fight for those women. But you can't say that all those who've chosen to wear a headscarf are submissive. It's not true ... For me, being a feminist means defending the right of women to have control over their own lives ... My response is that there's not just one way to be a feminist; there's not just one way to be a woman. We can't all be alike. We need to concentrate on what unites us, on the fight for equality between men and women, and not to say we should all dress the same way, that you can't wear a headscarf because otherwise you're not a feminist. I think that shows a lack of respect.[53]

Moussaïd's hope had been that her candidacy would encourage people from the *quartiers populaires* to get involved in politics, 'to stop them hesitating politically' once they saw that 'At last there's a party, the NPA, which is not Islamophobic and which is engaged in anti-capitalist struggle.' Such hopes were to be dashed. By the end of the year Moussaïd's name was among a dozen resignations from the party in Avignon in protest at the 'witch hunt' waged against them. At the following NPA congress the party adopted a motion welcoming members of all faiths and none, but stipulating that it could not be represented by anyone wearing the hijab.[54]

The debate underlined the profound impact that the rise of Islamophobia was having on the left, from the mainstream to the margins. Had the twenty-first-century left's intransigent secularism been adopted by previous generations when it came to 'conspicuous' religious garb, France would have been deprived of a number of key parliamentary figures, among them Abbé Sieyès (author of *What is the Third Estate?*), fellow revolutionary Abbé Grégoire, and Talleyrand, who wore a *soutane* (ecclesiastical robe) as first president of the revolutionary Constituent Assembly. There were no protests in the late nineteenth century when Philippe Grenier converted to Islam and became France's first Muslim deputy, wearing traditional Berber robes and a turban in the National Assembly. In modern, secular France, the celebrated homelessness campaigner Abbé Pierre wore his *soutane* in parliament from 1945 to 1951, as did Canon Kir, deputy for Dijon and doyen of the National Assembly from 1953 to 1967.[55] A deputy from the *harki* community (Algerians who fought on the French side during the independence war), Saïd Benaisse Boualam, wore a *burnous* (a Berber hooded cloak) and a white turban, and was unanimously elected vice-president of the National Assembly four times in the late 1950s and early 1960s.[56]

The Moussaïd affair emphasised the extent to which France's own secular tradition was being rewritten. The 1905 legislation that laid the basis for contemporary interpretations of *laïcité* had emphasised the need for neutrality of public space, as opposed to the individuals within it. This was about the protection, not the obliteration, of the rights of religious minorities, ensuring that the dominant group did not impose its will or render invisible other sensibilities. Public space had to be neutral so that individuals had the scope not to be.[57] The new secularism, however, was asserting the opposite and some of its most vociferous advocates were to be found on the radical left. This was particularly significant in a climate characterised by constant attempts to stigmatise Muslims as culturally inassimilable. Hargreaves' observation on this question bears repeating here. 'The principal obstacles to the incorporation of post-colonial minorities into French society,' he argues, 'lie not in cultural differences but in the radical restructuring of the labour market since the mid-1970s, greatly reducing the opportunities open to minority groups, and in the discriminatory treatment which they have suffered in the competition for jobs and scarce resources.'[58]

Since political issues, particularly the fight against discrimination, offered a potential means of establishing links between different groups of workers in a period of turbulence and transition for the labour movement, the radical left's position was entirely counter-productive. Its attitude highlighted a particular conception of what the working class represents in contemporary France. Both major revolutionary left currents, Lutte ouvrière and the LCR/NPA, formally recognise the diverse nature of the modern labour movement. Each has put forward presidential candidates who have emphasised their 'working-class' identity and been duly ridiculed for it in the media. Philippe Poutou, the candidate chosen to represent the NPA, often found himself in the role of fall guy on television shows where panels of presenters took it in turns, with barely disguised contempt, to mock him. On one occasion Poutou was asked about the NPA's decision to present a 'veiled' candidate, Ilham Moussaïd. His reaction was particularly abject. He immediately distanced himself from Moussaïd, reassuring his interviewers that he had always been opposed to her standing since the hijab was a reactionary symbol. In that moment, as Pierre Tevanian points out, Poutou made a very clear statement: his failure to display the slightest solidarity with his own comrade, a working-class Muslim woman attempting to assert anti-capitalist politics at a time of rampant Islamophobia, established Poutou as 'the candidate of white anti-capitalism'.[59]

Political anti-racism

The absence of an adequate response to Islamophobia from the radical left does not mean that there has been no response, however. Since the start of the Sarkozy presidency (2007), a series of initiatives have established networks of resistance to the prevailing climate. It is hard to underestimate the impact of the 2005 *banlieue* uprising in forging this resistance. For Yasser Louati, former president of the Collective Against Islamophobia in France (CCIF), it was a turning point, bringing into focus widespread disaffection with 'institutional anti-racism' and sparking the emergence of a new generation of activists: 'Every single person you see in the anti-racist camp today comes from the deaths of Zyed and Bouna [electrocuted while hiding from police in a power substation]. Every single one of them. To them it was, "That's it"'.[60] Fania Noël, an activist in decolonial and Afro-feminist networks, founder of the review *Assiégé*, reinforces the point, underlining the importance of the two boys' deaths in shaping the outlook of her generation:

> I was eighteen at the time. It was a catalyst. They say the revolution is impossible until it happens, well it was like that. The straw that broke the camel's back. There were other deaths at the hands of the police, there were other instances of police violence but it's because we can no longer breathe that we start screaming. It was a feeling of 'That's enough', of politics in the pure and literal sense of the term... Because it was Zyed and Bouna. It was Zyed who was Arab and Bouna who was black. It wasn't just Zyed, it wasn't just Bouna, it was a whole century

in perspective: slavery, colonialism, post-colonialism, post-colonial immigration, the *quartiers populaires*, the HLMs [rent-controlled housing] ... Zyed and Bouna: it was the blacks and the Arabs—in one phrase, the most problematic social category in this country.[61]

Groups and associations set up in the aftermath of the revolt include the CCIF, which records Islamophobic acts and provides a support network for victims, and the Indigènes de la République (Indigenous of the Republic), which identifies colonial racism as a defining element of the Republic and seeks to organise among those suffering from its consequences. Other initiatives have included the All Mothers Equal network, established by parents opposed to the exclusion of mothers wearing the hijab from school trips; the Social Forum of the *Quartiers Populaires*, set up in 2007 to affirm resistance to racism and stigmatisation, drawing on the experience and struggles of these working-class neighbourhoods; the Boycott, Divestment and Sanctions campaign; and various groups organising against police violence and stop and search legislation.

For Ndella Paye, a founder member of All Mothers Equal, the development of such organisations was a product of shortcomings in existing anti-racist institutions. The CCIF, for example, only exists 'because the traditional anti-racist organisations didn't take Islamophobia into account. If the MRAP [Movement Against Racism and for Friendship between Peoples] or the LDH [Ligue des Droits de l'Homme or Human Rights League] had taken it into account, alongside those directly affected by it, there wouldn't have been any need to form the CCIF.' Failure to combat Islamophobia, or to side with those involved in the 2005 uprising, widened a gulf that had already developed between racialised activists and the organisations of 'official' anti-racism:

They depoliticise struggles so much that we can't trust them ... Look at their campaigns—'everyone is beautiful, everyone is nice, we must love each other' ... It's horrible. They deny the violence of the system.

> They individualise racism ... 'It's your neighbour who doesn't like you.' I couldn't care less if my neighbour doesn't like me because I'm black. What am I supposed to do about that? Really! As long as it doesn't stop me having a job, from going to school, having a home, what do I care if he doesn't like me? I couldn't care less. They deny all the violence of the system, the racist system. Who experiences racism at work, in housing? Who is insulted, assaulted in the outside world? They don't want to see the system, it's individuals. There's a dividing line.[62]

This dividing line was emphatically asserted by the 'Appeal of the Indigenous of the Republic' in January 2005, giving rise to the Movement of the Indigenous of the Republic, which in turn became the Party of the Indigenous of the Republic in 2010. Houria Bouteldja, the party's founder and spokesperson, sees the division in similar terms:

> Moral anti-racism believes that racism is something individual, interpersonal. There are individuals who don't like other people, so they need to be reformed, taught a lesson. Political anti-racism offers an alternative. It can even provide the basis for a political movement. It knows that racism can't exist without imperialism and that racism is a structural question.[63]

The text of the 2005 Appeal detailed the discrimination suffered by people from France's colonies, old and new, and their descendants. This discrimination took place in the job market, housing, healthcare, in schools and in leisure activities. It made them the first victims of social exclusion and precarity. Whatever their origins, the population of the *banlieues*, or *quartiers populaires*, were 'indigenised', relegated to the margins of society, brutalised by the police and ignored by the justice system. The Republic was and remained a colonial Republic. Its anti-headscarf law was 'discriminatory, sexist, racist ... a law of exception with colonial overtones'. The document highlighted the way American neo-imperial interests, George W. Bush's neoconservatism and France's colonial legacy had combined to 'ravage' French society, imposing its rhetoric and spreading 'like gangrene' even among progressive forces. This reactionary offensive was reconfiguring French politics, 'fraudulently camouflaging itself under the flag of *laïcité*, citizenship and feminism'.

The 'Republic of Equality', the Appeal went on, 'is a myth'. French society and the French state must engage in a radical examination of its colonial past and present: 'It's time for France to interrogate its Enlightenment' and the Revolution's 'universal egalitarianism', the way it represses nationalism, 'propped up by a "chauvinism of the universal" supposed to "civilise" savages.' The Appeal ended with a call for urgent measures to end racist discrimination and a defiant declaration of solidarity with anti-colonial struggles: for the Indigenous of the Republic, Dien Bien Phu (the historic battle that effectively marked the end of French involvement in Indochina) was not a defeat but a victory for liberty, equality and fraternity. The signatories stood in solidarity with anti-imperialist struggles from Iraq to Palestine, calling for a common combat of all the oppressed and exploited for a truly egalitarian and universal society.[64]

The Appeal caused a certain amount of uproar. France's leading new reactionary intellectual, Alain Finkielkraut, called it a 'declaration of war'.[65] It was also vehemently criticised by the far left. Lutte ouvrière condemned it for 'reinforcing communitarianism',[66] while the LCR lamented its 'criminalisation' of differences of opinion among progressives, restating its condemnation of the hijab as a 'symbol of oppression' and offering the rather patronising observation that the Appeal showed how 'good sentiments can often lead to bad politics'.[67] Although the capacity of the Indigenous of the Republic to organise significant numbers of activists under their banner has been limited since 2005, its role has been an important one. It has played a major part in the organisation of various key events and demonstrations, notably the annual March for Dignity. It has also acted as a dissident, often provocative corrective to the complicity of the radical left with the Islamophobic drift in French society, and as a combative alternative to the stance offered by institutional anti-racism.

According to one leading anti-racist activist, Omar Slaouti, a former member of the LCR/NPA, 'The radical left is a prisoner of the radical left. It has continually ignored, put to one side, even undermined, any mobilisation or demand coming from those with an *indigène* background.' This is not a new phenomenon, he argues. In the 1970s a movement of Arab workers emerged in France 'because they felt their demands were not being taken into account by the white trade union movement or by white political parties'. In the same way, strikes in the early 1980s by mostly Arab workers in the car industry were condemned by sections of the left who warned of the dangers of communitarianism and the influence of Islam. For Slaouti, 'This says a lot about how the white workers' movement is a prisoner of itself, of its own representation, including racism, neo-colonialism and so on. We've still got the same problem today. When we assert the need to fight Islamophobic racial discrimination, we often hear, "But at the same time, feminism; but at the same time, *laïcité*; but at the same time, our values". The famous clash of civilisations.'

The assertion of an autonomous black and Arab led anti-racism has been necessary, then, and, according to Slaouti, has produced results:

> The white left has a major influence but things are changing, and they're changing solely because the *indigènes* have taken control of their fight, whether it's migrants, the *sans papiers*, or people in their neighbourhoods organising against police violence or Islamophobia. Today the term Islamophobia has been imposed on public debate in France because the *indigènes* have imposed it. In the same way that, if there have been feminist gains in France and elsewhere, it's because women have imposed their struggles, and the themes and the terms of debate.

Despite the crisis of anti-racism in France, and the very real divisions between the radical left and black- and Arab-led groups asserting the need for a more combative approach to problems like Islamophobia, Slaouti remains hopeful about the prospects for anti-racists and the left:

> When someone is oppressed they resist it, they're not just the victim of it. We *are* victims of it, but we also resist it. I feel very strongly that if things are going to move on a national level it will happen through the *indigènes* in the *quartiers populaires*. They're at the crossroads of social inequalities produced by the crisis of capitalism and at the same time they are very sharply subjected to the process of racialisation, from top to bottom. They're the ones with most interest in things moving. It's not a mechanical thing, but they're the ones with most interest in stopping the *loi Travail*, in stopping police violence, and racial discrimination, and in preserving public services. Because they're the ones who experience, before anyone else, the crisis of the capitalist system. So they're victims, they're resisters and they're also, as I see it, the hope for the labour movement in France ... they have the most to win from fighting.[68]

In 2011 a number of local committees were formed across France under the banner D'ailleurs nous sommes ici. This network, whose name plays on the two meanings of *d'ailleurs* (From elsewhere/Moreover, we are here), was established against racism and anti-immigrant legislation, and in defence of undocumented migrants, mounting demonstrations in Paris and other towns and cities on 28 May. Later that year, the Printemps des quartiers (Neighbourhood Spring) was launched, formed by associative networks from the *quartiers populaires* and by anti-racist activists from the radical and trade union left. Taking inspiration from the 2005 *banlieue* uprising, the Arab Spring of 2011, the Palestinian struggle and the Indignados movement worldwide, its networks organised a series of national and local initiatives. In March 2014 a group of teachers launched a petition calling for the repeal of the 2004 hijab law, collecting over 30,000 signatures.[69] Alongside such developments, a series of arguments and analyses of

Islamophobia have been developed by academics, activists and journalists in a range of books and articles.[70]

Such developments meant that, in the climate of moral panic created after the January 2015 attacks, there was a means of organising resistance to scapegoating. When dozens of organisations signed up to an appeal for a unity rally against Islamophobia in Paris on 6 March 2015, it provoked a debate on the left. Signatories were asked to justify their support for a meeting that was also backed by the Union of French Islamic Organisations. How, opponents asked, could left-wing activists make common cause with such conservative, sexist forces that had opposed gay marriage? Under pressure from new secularist commentators like Caroline Fourest, who argued that the meeting amounted to 'spitting on the dead of 7 January',[71] the Greens withdrew their support for the meeting, a decision publicly condemned by a number of leading party figures.[72] Members of the ATTAC gender commission opposed the association's participation,[73] as did Jean-Luc Mélenchon's Front de gauche coalition, arguing that the term 'Islamophobia' blurred the distinction between racism and legitimate criticism of religion.[74] The Front's Ensemble current, however, did offer clear backing for the initiative. The Communist Party and the NPA also held firm in their support. The meeting itself was a success, with over 500 people attending.

Such was the situation facing anti-racist activists a decade after the law on the hijab. Former CCIF president Yasser Louati underlines their exasperation with leading radical left figures who objected to the use of the term 'Islamophobia' while supporting laws that promoted it: 'If minorities tell you the racism they live is called Islamophobia, you accept it and then you help them fight it'.[75] The right, under Sarkozy's leadership, had clearly understood much better than the left the power that racism could have, both in preventing 'crossovers' and in distracting from other issues. As Louati puts it, 'The world is about to collapse and they created a debate on national identity. It meant they could avoid talking about the banks ripping us off, because they were talking about the enemy within.'[76] The balance of forces, then, is unfavourable to anti-racists. But such a balance can be reversed. As Ndella Paye notes, it took fifteen years for the tide to turn in favour of Islamophobia, between the first headscarf affair in 1989 and the 2004 law.[77] Fania Noël stresses the same theme: 'My activism is based around the question, "How do we create a balance of forces?" And then, "How do we create a balance of forces within the balance of forces?" Who, then, does this mean engaging with?

> The first are those who are closest, the far left. They have an economic and social capital that we don't have. We want to get them moving. To do that they have to recognise that they're always going to remain where they are if they don't move ... I think it's inevitable that the far left will move: the question is how.[78]

Various obstacles remain to be overcome. Meriem is one of the organisers of a group set up to combat Islamophobia in north-eastern Paris. She is also a member of the NPA. Before joining she asked herself the question 'a thousand times'. Interviewed in March 2017, she recalled bursting into tears before joining the organisation,

> Alone, without anybody seeing, because I had the impression that I was betraying myself, my family. When I took that step and went home there was a pain, a burden, a weight, something so painful. As if I was betraying my father, my mother, my sister, my brother ... it floored me.

Her personal reaction was part of a wider dilemma. 'As long as we don't grasp the relationship between questions of class and race,' she argues, 'we won't be able to reconcile them. The NPA has been very workerist on these issues. It puts race second.' Moreover, 'As long as the far left does not have a clear position on Islamophobia, it's missing something':

> They hope for a revolution but there won't be one as long as the most oppressed category of our class is not a driving force, is not at the heart of building something to create another kind of society ... The far left should be closer to such an over-marginalised population. They're part of the new working class, the blackest of the blacks. There were missed opportunities in 2005 but young people couldn't stand institutional racism any more: police violence, unemployment, discrimination, being stigmatised as the enemy within. Did you see the far left [then]? They're absent from these areas.[79]

For Omar Slaouti, Islamophobia is a governmental response to heightened tensions in French society, one in which questions of race and class are entwined:

> Neoliberalism creates very deep social inequalities and creates a very strong potential for revolt. It creates a fear of social relegation even among whites, the middle classes who, like in the United States, are afraid of losing their few advantages. And if they lose these little advantages they risk ending up on the same level as Afro-Americans or Mexicans in the US or, in France, in the *quartiers populaires*, in deep poverty. So attempts by governments to foster Islamophobia are a response to fears of social relegation among whites. It's working quite well ... Islamophobia and the 'clash of civilisations' allows an 'us' to form. Where the working class has lost many of its collective reflexes, there's a white 'us' that can be created. Instead of attacking the neoliberals who create injustice, they direct their fear towards Muslims, migrants, foreigners, and so on. This works even better when there's a retreat of the labour movement. So Islamophobia is linked to social questions; it's also the result of the retreat of the labour movement on these questions.[80]

Islamophobia is a political construction that has drawn strength from the convergence of a number of separate but related dynamics: the 'war on terror', colonialism, authoritarian neoliberalism and inequality. Its tenacity in France is due less to any inherent national characteristic revolving around a 'tradition of secularism' than to the way in which this tradition, in both its narrowly distorted and more progressive liberal forms, has rallied forces from across the political spectrum to a defence of state authority. If such prejudice is to be contested, let alone dismantled, it is hard to see how this will happen without the development of a political anti-racist response among the radical and wider left—one that identifies a clear set of priorities, beginning with the most basic question that can be asked of anyone confronted with injustice: which side are you on?

CONCLUSION

Global Islamophobia

France is by no means the only country where anti-Muslim prejudice has become a respectable form of racism. In the wake of the 9/11 attacks the Italian political scientist Angelo Panebianco remarked that 'If the war on terror lasts for years, we shall have to be ready to neutralise... Bin Laden's principal ally in the West, his most precious fifth column: cultural relativism'.[1] The trajectory of this backlash—against Muslims, 'communitarianism', multiculturalism and minorities more generally—has taken different forms in different contexts, intersecting with issues of race and class, advancing or retreating in relation to the opportunities and opposition encountered, but always finding vindication and momentum in the framework for discrimination provided by global Islamophobia and the 'war on terror'. State actors have made ample use of this framework, seeking wherever possible to extend and deepen its reach in order to marshal support from broader sections of society, reinforcing the authority of the state in the process. In this sense, as Nilüfer Göle underlines, 'France, with its republican model and attachment to secularism, is not an exception... despite differences in historical heritage and national particularities, we are observing... a convergence in ways of trying to frame Islam'.[2]

In *The Manchurian Candidate* (1962), John Frankenheimer's lampoon of Cold War paranoia, a Chinese hypnotist overseeing measures of Communist control and indoctrination observes that the brain of one of his victims 'has not only been washed, as they say, it has been dry cleaned'. Half a century later, governments around the world appeared to be drawing on the film to inform their understanding of the radicalisation process supposedly underpinning Islamist violence. Donald Trump's route to the White House was signposted by repeated Islamophobic outbursts that evoked 'red scare' rhetoric by imagining Islamists, rather than reds, under the bed. 'Just as we won the Cold War, in part by exposing the evils of communism and the virtues of free markets, so too must we take on the ideology of radical Islam', he declared.[3] 'If there is a Trump doctrine,' wrote one commentator in the wake of his election, '"war on Islam" has to be a strong contender.'[4]

Trump's victory in the 2016 US presidential election marked a new stage in the mainstreaming of Islamophobia, drawing on a combination of rehashed Cold War insecurities and anti-Arab racism. For years he had indulged in crude attacks on Muslims, likening their presence on American soil to a Trojan horse advancing the interests of ISIS,[5] threatening to close mosques and establish a database of all Muslims resident in the US, relaying far-right conspiracies about President Obama being a Muslim and repeating lies about crowds in New Jersey cheering the destruction of the World Trade Centre.[6] Islam hated the US and Muslims were 'sick people' who could not assimilate. In a bestselling book on how to defeat radical Islam, Trump's former national security advisor Michael Flynn asked, 'Do you want to be ruled by men who eagerly drink the blood of their dying enemies?'[7]

One of Trump's first acts in office was to ban citizens of seven predominantly Muslim countries (Syria, Iraq, Libya, Somalia, Iran, Sudan and Yemen) from entering the US for ninety days. The initiative had much more to do with religion-based prejudice than confronting terrorism. The Cato Institute observed that 'Foreigners from those seven nations have killed zero Americans in terrorist attacks on US soil between 1975 and 2015.'[8] Meanwhile, countries with documented and proven links to terrorism, but which happened to be US allies (Saudi Arabia, Egypt, Qatar and the UAE), were excluded from the ban. As the journalist Glenn Greenwald noted, Trump did not 'appear out of nowhere'; he was simply the 'logical and most grotesque expression' of trends that had been allowed to develop under both George W. Bush and Obama, from the erosion of civil liberties in the name of the security agenda to the executive's accumulation of powers on the back of 'sustained demonisation of Muslims as scary, primitive, uniquely violent Others'.[9]

For Greenwald, it was clear: the priority was not to confront terrorist organisations, but to dehumanise Muslims. How else, he asks, could successive governments have got away with 'bombing, invading and droning the same group of people for more than 15 years'?[10] This was not a view confined to critical journalists. Some FBI operatives were more than ready to acknowledge that they saw the main problem to be Islam rather than terrorism. In 2011 the Bureau's William Gawthrop told a gathering of law enforcement officials that going after al-Qaida was a 'waste' and that the real targets were Muslim clerics and scriptures. He drew a parallel between the targeting of Islam and the taking down of the Death Star in *Star Wars*. Using language that would not have been out of place in *The Manchurian Candidate*, Gawthrop compared the link between Islamic 'ideology' and the world's estimated 1.6 billion Muslims with the relationship between iron filings and a 'very powerful magnet':

> We are not discussing Muslims. What we are interested in is the magnetic force, the radiating force of the ideology ... we are not talking about the goodness or the badness of the iron filings. We are only interested in the force that this ideology exerts on its surroundings. That force is also exerted against you.[11]

'This', as one former intelligence analyst put it, 'is McCarthysim on steroids'.[12] But Gawthrop's views were simply an expression of FBI policy. By 2013 the Bureau's Terrorist Screening Center had compiled a watch list of 680,000 names, of which 280,000 had no known links to any network deemed to be terrorist by the US government. A further 320,000 people were being monitored on the government's wider Terrorist Identities Datamart Environment (TIDE) database, which comprised over a million names. Under President Obama, 47,000 people were put on a no-fly list without being informed they were on it, or offered an explanation when they found out.[13] All this in a country where the death toll from right-wing nationalist violence stands at double the number of those killed by Islamist terrorists since 9/11.[14] Yet in the years since the attack on the Twin Towers more than 700,000 Muslims have been interviewed by the FBI—which means that over half of Muslim households in the US have been affected by federal investigations.[15]

The factors mobilised by Trump, targeting an 'enemy within' threatening Western values, implying that all Muslims were potential accomplices to Islamist violence and using the law to reinforce and normalise their stigmatisation, have become the common currency of Islamophobia worldwide. In Britain, the Conservative party's candidate for London mayor in 2016, the urbane and unctuous Zac Goldsmith, ran what many considered to be a dubious election campaign, frequently accusing his Muslim opponent, Labour candidate Sadiq Khan, of 'giving cover' to extremists, notably for repeatedly sharing a platform with the imam of his local mosque, Suliman Gani, described by Goldsmith as 'one of the most repellent figures in this country'.[16] The campaign was enthusiastically supported by Prime Minister David Cameron, who spoke in parliament about Gani's description of women as 'subservient to men' and his objection to homosexuality as 'an unnatural act'.[17] The slurs against Khan, who won the election, backfired embarrassingly when it emerged that Gani was a Conservative supporter who had been invited by the Conservative Muslim Forum to recruit Muslims to the party.[18] Cameron was later obliged to apologise for falsely labelling him a supporter of ISIS.[19]

In 2011 Cameron had launched a vigorous attack on multiculturalism, arguing that 'passive tolerance' of extremists needed to end and be replaced by what he called 'muscular liberalism'. Muslims needed to identify with Britain and 'British values' or risk becoming rootless and drawn into extremism via internet chat rooms. Cameron was able to draw on flawed research into 'radicalisation', which posited a continuity between 'non-violent' extremism and terrorist acts. Shoddy analyses in this vein, often drawn up by government-funded researchers, allowed Cameron to pay lip service to the notion that Islamist extremism had nothing to do with Britain's Muslim population as a whole while insinuating that it was nevertheless somehow implicated in the problem. At issue, he felt, was 'a question of identity', since some young Muslims found it hard to embrace traditional Islam but didn't see enough white multiculturalists standing up to its excesses, such as forced marriage.[20] Cameron therefore managed to link both the Muslim community and multiculturalism itself to the problem of Islamist violence. He also gave credence to the notion that radical ideology was the starting point for extremism, ignoring both the role of state violence in creating a context for radicalisation and the obvious point that very few radicals become violent extremists, while not all terrorists are necessarily radicals. The result of such muddled thinking was the government's Prevent strategy, building on groundwork laid by previous Labour governments.

The Prevent scheme developed a special mechanism, Channel, for 'deprogramming' suspects. It attempted to amass lists of suspects via a national network of informants—teachers, lecturers and other public sector workers—instructed to report evidence of radicalisation to the police. Questioned about its plans to require nursery staff to refer toddlers to the authorities, a Home Office spokesperson insisted that 'We would expect staff to have the training they need to identify children at risk of radicalisation.'[21] In 2014, 44,000 nurses were given training to spot the signs of extremism and instructed to relay to the authorities concerns about patients whom they thought might have been radicalised. In March 2016, a Bedfordshire nursery attempted to report a four-year-old boy to Channel after he drew a picture of a man cutting a cucumber and mispronounced it 'cooker bomb'.[22] In East London, a nine-year-old boy suspected of extremism was sent to Channel to be 'deprogrammed'.[23] A fourteen-year-old Muslim boy at a North London school was called to an interview after he referred to 'eco-terrorism' in a classroom discussion on the environment. The child was asked if he was affiliated with ISIS. 'I didn't know what was going on,' he recalled. 'They said there had been safety concerns raised. If you are taken out of French class and asked about ISIS, it is quite scary. My heart skipped a beat.'[24] One boy was considered to hold 'terrorist-like' views by a policeman when found in possession of pro-Palestinian Boycott, Divestment and Sanctions leaflets.[25] In East London, when a two-year-old Muslim child with a learning disability sang an Islamic song and said 'Allahu Akbar', he was referred to social services for 'concerning behaviour'.[26]

British counter-terrorism measures, in line with the global pattern, disproportionately target Muslims. Between 2007 and 2010, there were 1,120 cases of individuals classed by Channel as being 'on a pathway to radicalisation'. Over 90 per cent of them were Muslim and nearly a third were under sixteen.[27] Between 2012 and 2015 nearly 2,000 children under fifteen were referred to counter-radicalisation programmes. Over 400 of them were under ten.[28] In 2010 it emerged that police in Birmingham had used counter-terrorism funds to install £3 million worth of CCTV cameras in predominantly Muslim areas, including 150 automatic number plate recognition devices—three times more than in the entire city centre. According to the National Police Chiefs' Council, 'The greatest threat the UK currently faces is from terrorists who claim to act in the name of Islam, and who specifically target Muslims. Therefore Prevent activity such as the support offered through Channel predominately takes place in and with Muslim communities.'[29] This logic has contributed to a dynamic that puts Muslim areas under greater scrutiny, subjects Muslims to vetting procedures when invited to speak in colleges and universities,[30] and forces Muslim children and parents to suffer the indignity and humiliation of being treated like potential terrorists.

Projects involving Muslim youth associations and mental health initiatives have been subjected to conditions that do not apply to other groups, with access to public funding made conditional on the sharing of data and information with law enforcement agencies.[31] Youth project managers and colleges have also faced pressure to hand over data about young Muslims to the authorities.[32] A report for the Institute of Race Relations in 2009 showed a clear correlation between Prevent funding and the size of the Muslim population in a given area.[33] In 2014 Britain's most senior Muslim police officer, Mak Chishty, asserted the need to 'move into the private space' of Muslims in order to spot signs of radicalisation as early as possible. Confiding that even he felt his own children to be at risk of recruitment to ISIS, he drew attention to examples of subtle changes of behaviour that could indicate radicalisation, including abruptly adopting a negative stance towards alcohol, social occasions and Western clothing and refusing to shop at Marks and Spencer.[34]

In 2015, the Counter Terrorism and Security Act created a duty on public sector institutions to comply with the provisions of the

Prevent agenda, vetting speakers and reporting signs of radicalisation among individuals who came into contact with public sector workers. As in France, legislation targeting Muslims had a significant impact in both normalising and fostering discrimination. It gave a green light to racists who wanted to make vindictive claims about Muslims, and demanded compliance from non-racists with procedures that made them complicit in discriminatory practices. The 'surveillance gaze', as Arun Kundnani notes, 'is a racial gaze', involving 'the social construction of racial others'.[35]

When it came to the question of stripping naturalised Britons of their citizenship, the UK government went much further than the ultimately abortive efforts of François Hollande or Manuel Valls. As far as Amnesty International was concerned, the July 2014 amendment to the Immigration Act put the UK at 'the extreme end of the spectrum in the EU'. It meant that a foreign-born naturalised British citizen could be deprived of their nationality even if it rendered them stateless, stripping them, to use Hannah Arendt's phrase, of the 'right to have rights'. This could be done at the home secretary's discretion, with no judicial authorisation.[36] Appeals against such decisions were to be referred to a Special Immigration Appeals Commission authorised to conduct hearings in closed session, with the government permitted to use secret evidence, on public interest and national security grounds, and deny the individual concerned access either to the hearing or to the secret evidence submitted. Such opaque and unaccountable methods have become a defining feature of British counter-terrorism efforts. Indeed, the police's own watchdog, the Independent Police Complaints Commission (IPCC), had to threaten the Metropolitan Police with legal action when forced to act upon complaints from British Muslims alleging discrimination in the police's use of Schedule 7 of the 2000 Terrorism Act, which allowed officers to stop individuals even where there was no suspicion of any wrongdoing. Those from ethnic minorities were up to forty-two times more likely to be stopped than white people. Instructed by the IPCC to conduct an investigation into the matter, the force then refused to hand over its findings.[37]

The credibility of programmes like Prevent has also been undermined by the chronic inability of state actors to define precisely what is meant both by 'British values', and by 'extremism'. As home secretary, Theresa May found it difficult to come up with anything of particular significance that set British values apart from those of most other nations. Her list generally stalled beyond 'democracy, the rule of law, tolerance ... acceptance of different faiths'.[38] As prime minister in 2017, she had still not managed to develop a more comprehensive or distinctive list, having produced a counter-terrorism bill that defined extremism as 'the vocal or active opposition to our fundamental values, including democracy, the rule of law, individual liberty and the mutual respect and tolerance of different faiths and beliefs'. The bill itself ran into the ground when the government was given legal advice that its proposed legislation could not adequately define what 'non-violent extremism' or 'British values' were, and therefore ran the risk of subjecting law-abiding people to unnecessary scrutiny.[39]

Part of the difficulty in defining extremism in relation to British values was that Cameron's 'muscular liberalism', when translated into the Prevent strategy, meant a draconian clampdown on freedom of speech, supposedly one of those very values. Cameron explicitly declared that speakers at odds with British values should be denied a platform, singling out four universities who, he alleged, had regularly hosted 'extremist preachers'.[40] Such heavy-handedness over this and other incidents prompted conservative commentator Peter Oborne to ask whether the Tories had 'a problem with Muslims'.[41] Sayeeda Warsi, a former co-chair of the party and the first Muslim woman to hold a cabinet post in Britain, who left office when the government failed to condemn Israel's assault on Gaza in 2014, dismissed Prevent as 'broken' and 'toxic'. 'The way we're starting to operate now with the Muslims is McCarthyistic', she argued. 'One of my colleagues would refer to the crocodiles in the swamp and we had to drain the swamp, but all the policy ever did was grow the swamp.' Since individuals were radicalised for all kinds of reasons—a criminal past, alienation from their family, confused sexuality—why, she asked, the focus on 'one single ideology'? 'If it's not all ideology, it's stupid to keep saying it's all ideology.' Claiming that she was the only high-profile politician to have made a speech on Islamophobia, she called on Prime Minister May publicly to condemn it, adding, 'I think Islamophobia is Britain's bigotry blind spot. It's a form of racism still rationalised by the respectable.'[42]

The dangers of the escalating security measures that have accompanied the rise of Islamophobia are clear, whether in terms of unlawful rendition, torture, enforced disappearance, erosion of civil liberties, freedom of expression and democratic accountability, or racism. The construction of 'suspect communities', turning Muslims into 'objects of surveillance' is, Kundnani points out, part of a wider pattern, overlapping 'with other systems of security surveillance that feed deportation of immigrants and mass incarceration'.[43] Indeed, for Amnesty International,

> the threat to the life of a nation ... does not come from the isolated acts of a violent criminal fringe, however much they may wish to destroy these institutions and undermine these principles—but from governments and societies that are prepared to abandon their own values in confronting them.[44]

The normalisation of racist scapegoating, constructing 'a suitable enemy' within[45] completely disproportionate to the actual threat posed by terrorism, and the multiplication of authoritarian measures to deal with it—fuelling a multi-trillion-dollar international industry with close links to political elites[46]—are both part of a radicalisation taking place in mainstream politics that is not confined to France. As Domenico Losurdo warns, the 'catastrophe of the twentieth century' was not 'a new barbarian invasion that unexpectedly attacked and overwhelmed a healthy, happy society'.[47] Rather, it developed out of the legacy of imperial and colonial rule already normalised by liberal democracy, with its baggage of elitism, anti-egalitarianism, racial supremacy, concentration camps and mass exterminations. These horrors may seem to belong to a distant past yet, as Amnesty warns, 'Brick by brick, the edifice of rights protection that was constructed after the Second World War is being dismantled.'[48] This is not primarily the work of politicians confined to a so-called 'populist' fringe. Liberalism, as Kundnani argues, 'plays more than just a secondary enabling role in Islamophobia' and the domestic and international security agenda; the latter's calls for 'mass violence against racialised populations' are ostensibly to uphold liberal values.[49] The concentration of power in executive hands, bypassing the judiciary and reinforcing instead the security and intelligence services, is normalising an undemocratic drift across Western states, giving governments access to measures 'whose use is unlikely to be restricted to those involved in the commission of terrorist acts'.[50]

Global Islamophobia has created a powerful means of isolating and demonising Muslims worldwide, legitimising stigmatisation and discrimination by reviving centuries-old caricatures of Islam as a violent and lascivious religion[51] and remodelling them for the post-Cold War era, placing Muslims across the world on a spectrum linking them to ISIS and al-Qaida. The precise way in which this international context intersects with domestic politics is dependent on various factors, determining the extent to which Islamophobia is able to penetrate national life. British state actors, for example, have amassed a powerful armoury of anti-terror laws that has successfully drawn sections of society, notably public sector workers, into practices of monitoring, scrutiny and denunciation that are Islamophobic. Trump's immigration hotline serves a similar purpose, seeking popular participation in state-directed stigmatisation of minorities. Nowhere, however, have efforts to generate Islamophobia and to unite cross-spectrum Islamophobes behind the state's authority been as successful as in France.

Muslims, class and the state

Universalism, the rights of man, *laïcité* and citizenship are heralded as the founding principles of republican society, forming the basis of a 'national civil religion'.[52] The particular slant given to *laïcité* since the late 1980s, along with the enduring emphasis on integration as a duty to be performed by people of immigrant background, have contributed to giving the hijab greater prominence in public debate in France than anywhere else, the issue feeding off the residual prejudices nurtured by an undigested colonial past and the persistence of latent anti-Arab racism.[53] But there is another element to this prominence. The hijab in France is worn by racialised and stigmatised women, many of them living in marginalised working-class neighbourhoods. It can therefore be seen, in Rivera's words, as a 'proletarian headscarf'. Marginalisation on economic, political and territorial grounds has been accelerated by various processes, notably the reactionary radicalisation of *laïcité*, that ethnicise and racialise working-class Muslims, creating a cultural barrier that marks them as incompatible, 'other'. Education offers a potential route out of this exclusion, which partly explains why school became the terrain on which state actors repeatedly chose to pursue their efforts to ban the hijab. One aspect of this marginalisation—the stigmatisation of particular areas, the so-called *banlieues*—is part of a wider process: the 'decomposition of the world of the industrial worker and its forms of organisation and representation'.[54] This is why debates on the left about the trajectory and meaning of the contemporary working class are significant.

As we saw in Chapter Four, according to the Terra Nova think tank, the Socialist Party's working-class electorate has been in decline, its numbers diminishing and values changing. While the left, the argument went, was becoming increasingly defined by its espousal of socially liberal values and an openness to Islam, gay rights and difference more generally, workers were going the other way. With their material security under threat, they were turning in on themselves, hostile to immigrants and welfare claimants, disoriented by the disorder of contemporary society and its loss of moral values.[55] Workers no longer recognised themselves in the values of the left, and no longer formed the bulk of its electorate. According to Terra Nova, the Socialist Party's coalition with workers would therefore be impossible to revive without embracing social populism.[56]

For the pro-immigration authors' collective Cette France-là (That Other France),[57] those contesting this argument simply turn it on its head: instead of an emphasis on visible minorities, the left should orient itself around the invisible majority, and respond to its imputed expectations and beliefs—secularism, morality, traditional values. Rather than offering naïve apologies for multiculturalism, the left should instead assert its opposition to communitarianism. The new working class, the argument goes, has few qualifications, works increasingly in services for low wages, and is defined by profound insecurity, fear of social relegation and a sense of being isolated before the threefold impact of the tyranny of financial markets, the rise of communitarianism and the impact of the debt crisis on individual households.

This combination of economic impotence and insecurity is therefore not simply economic but also physical and social. The complaint of those seeking a more trenchant line from the left on immigration was that the FN was offering people protectionism, both domestically and internationally, and parties that rejected populism were not.[58] The consensus, then, for authors linked to the Gauche Populaire network, was that identity-based *laïcité* must be defended against multiculturalism, and that economic protectionism must be tied to the protection of identity.[59] Immigration is persistently linked in these accounts to economic liberalism. 'By moving around,' Christophe Guilluy argues, 'the immigrant reinforces his integration into the world economy and the logic of liberal globalisation.'[60] Globalisation and the cosmopolitan immigrant are two sides of the same coin, mutually dependent on each other and subjecting the '*petit blanc*' to economic tyranny on the one hand, and the 'over-delinquency' of immigrant youth on the other—itself accentuated by governmental inability to curb migratory flows.[61]

What is common to the perspectives outlined by Terra Nova and those of its opponents is an assumption that ethnic divisions are a fundamental aspect of the choices made by a predominantly 'white' majority in response to the intrusion of a non-white minority.[62] Society, in other words, is riven along racial lines. This outlook is common to discussions of immigration and the rise of populist parties elsewhere, notably in Britain and the US, where the category of 'white working class' has emerged as a key element informing academic research and media commentary. The conclusion of such studies, from Guilluy and Bouvet in France to Ford and Goodwin in Britain,[63] is that impoverished white working-class men have been 'left behind' by globalisation, ignored by political elites who refuse to 'listen to the concerns of ordinary voters on immigration'. Ford and Goodwin's *Revolt on the Right* is an excellent example of researchers waging a political argument in defiance of the evidence they present themselves. What their data shows is that prior to 2017 a section of working-class votes went to UKIP from the Conservatives in Labour areas. They choose to argue that this represents an existential threat to the Labour Party, requiring an understanding of anti-immigrant concerns. Despite ubiquitous analyses to the same effect from pundits and commentators, in the 2017 election UKIP was crushed in a post-Brexit landscape where Labour's offer, although by no means progressive on the immigration question, was primarily based on policies of redistribution, nationalisation and an end to austerity, rather than an anti-immigrant agenda.

The lazy assumption that workers' political choices are largely determined by their ethnicity, and that anti-immigrant sentiment is something that emerges bottom-up from the depths of society, only feeds prevailing myths, rather than illuminating or explaining them. Following the Front National's electoral breakthrough in the 1980s, academics and journalists promoted the notion that immigration was the primary motivation behind the FN vote, producing studies analysing the FN vote in relation to either the presence or absence of immigrants, in defiance of any kind of real-world correlation between the two. In fact, there was a much greater correlation between the FN vote and unemployment or poor housing.[64]

This desire to pin the blame for anti-immigrant sentiment on the 'white working class', itself an arbitrary construction, feeds a sense of inevitability about perceived 'levels of tolerance' of migrants and their descendants. It also obscures the more complicated reality of perceptions of immigrants. As the Cette France-là collective has shown, since 1994 polls have consistently indicated that a majority of the population is in favour of granting the right to vote to foreign residents in local elections. By November 2011 this majority stood at 61 per cent. It included 60 per cent of workers and up to three quarters of voters aged eighteen to thirty-four.[65] In 2003 and 2005 polls also revealed that a large majority of the population supported positive discrimination in favour of people with an immigrant background.[66] Thus, as Cette France-là argues, the notion of a population naturally inclined to reject immigrants and visible minorities is false, and needs to be rejected as part of breaking with the politics of xenophobia. Opinion is neither automatically racist or anti-racist, but is shaped in part by the narrative frameworks on offer. In the absence of a clear alternative politics to the mainstreaming of racism, parties that promote or pander to bigotry are likely to make headway. Academics and journalists who counterpose minorities to the population at large, as if the population were white and ethnic minorities not of the people, are part of the problem.

Understanding the experience of immigrants and their descendants has been made more difficult in French society in particular by the pervasiveness of the integration myth. This is generally presented as harmonious, conflating the fact of integration (which can take myriad forms, often by sub-cultural means) with the abstract universal 'model' that allegedly underpins it. The illusion that integration is a process achieved or sustained by a 'republican model' is bolstered by counterposing it to an 'Anglo-Saxon model'. These constructions, as Bouamama outlines, 'homogenise and globalise' respective realities in France, Britain and the US, implying that some kind of 'essence' intrinsic to each nation is at play, rather than shifting social, political and economic contexts.[67] Bouamama outlines two key factors that influence integration today. Firstly, the destabilisation of working-class culture—formerly a much more prolific and effective pathway to integration than any French 'model'—has disrupted the process.[68] The participation, politicisation and representation of workers once played a significant role in giving symbolic meaning and value to the status of being working-class. The fragmentation of this sense of collective identity, and the absence of 'political and ideological cement', has had a profound impact both in devaluing the figure of the worker and in contributing to an ongoing sense of atomisation.[69] Secondly, the legacy of colonialism weighs heavily, for the simple fact is that the majority of immigrants to France are from former colonies. Their acceptance is therefore partly shaped by the meaning given by the French state to the colonial legacy.[70]

More broadly, the myth of a unified national identity obscures the reality of contemporary society. Diversity, as Bouamama insists, is irreducible to questions of folklore or culture and has always been a characteristic of France, in spite of the persistent ideological assertion to the contrary. This will continue to be the case, since 'human societies do not evolve by decree and are not restricted to ideological models'.[71] The myth of an 'integrated' national culture—in which 'new arrivals take their place by making the elements that specify them disappear'—shifts economic and social questions onto a cultural plane.[72] In particular, social inequality and racist discrimination are masked. The institutional framework that blocks social mobility for racialised individuals is ignored when the focus is placed on the extent to which such individuals' culture, religion or traditions can be considered 'compatible' with the norms of French national identity.[73] This necessarily involves a denial of the true cultural and social diversity of France, both in terms of ignoring the multi-ethnic reality of French society and obscuring the genuine, concerted efforts of the richest sections of society to create communitarian enclaves for themselves.[74] By contrast, various studies have underlined the fact that 'recognition of differences' is much less important a demand for French Muslims than the demand for equality.[75]

The radical left, as we saw in Chapter Five, has not yet adapted to the 'new sociology' of the working class. It has been slow to comprehend the implications of a growing element of racialised individuals of immigrant background within a social category rendered more fragmented by precarity and unemployment, and less unified by shared conditions of employment, in a world of work in transition.[76] The relative indifference of both the mainstream and radical left towards questions of discrimination has accelerated the development of an autonomous anti-racist current highly conscious of the need to confront Islamophobia. This, as Talpin et al note, could be seen as a sign of weakness, evidence of a lack of support or means to relay campaigns more widely.[77] The cynicism felt by racialised activists towards the so-called 'white left', however, is not the cause of division. Here the damage had already been done by the failed organisations of 'moral anti-racism', such as SOS Racisme; by the discriminatory and racist policies and rhetoric of leading Socialists; and by radical left groups that have chosen not to confront Islamophobia.

The emergence of black- and Arab-led organisations has been a significant development in contemporary France. As one CCIF activist interviewed by Houda Asal notes, this partly explains the hostility towards such groups and the demonisation of the leading figures of political anti-racism, from Tariq Ramadan to Houria Bouteldja: 'What troubles people is that Muslims are leading the struggle.'[78] The vehemence of reactions to independent initiatives like the Decolonial Summer Camp, organised by and for black and minority ethnic anti-racist activists in the summer of 2016, reinforces the point. 'Rosa Parks must be turning in her grave,' complained Alain Jakubowicz, president of the LICRA (International League Against Racism and Anti-Semitism), arguing that the notion that one must have been a victim of discrimination to fight it marked the organisers out as 'imposters' whose desire to segregate blacks from whites put them on a par with the Ku Klux Klan.[79] SOS Racisme denounced the camp as 'openly racist', organised by people who had turned their 'neuroses about identity into political hate'.[80] Three government ministers, including then Prime Minister Valls, intervened to denounce the gathering, amid calls for it to be banned altogether on grounds of 'anti-white racism'. The constant vilification of Houria Bouteldja, routinely denounced as homophobic, anti-semitic and racist, is part of the same reaction against the emergence of 'political anti-racism', a vilification often bound up with condemnations of the concepts of 'race' and 'Islamophobia'.[81]

As Asal observes, 'the struggle against Islamophobia is part of an older battle, a long battle by those living in the *quartiers populaires* and by victims of racism, to exist politically'.[82] Her formulation draws on the question asked by Abdelmalek Sayad in the 1990s: 'How to exist in a socio-political order called the nation—even this minor, accidental, inessential, fragile, narrow, mutilated existence granted to immigrants—without existing politically?'[83]

The construction of national identity as a central theme in public debate since the 1980s is part of a wider crisis of identity in contemporary France. This crisis, as Bouteldja argues, is not about a Muslim problem: 'There's a white problem. There's a French problem. There's a crisis of French identity. There's a problem of French decline.'[84] As the rest of this book has outlined, there are multiple issues, in addition to the question of imperial power, that have fed the rise of Islamophobia. These include the refusal to come to terms with the social reality of a modern, multicultural society and to face up to the legacy of French colonialism in the context of deepening social and political polarisation. Symptoms of this polarisation include the ongoing disintegration of the party system that dominated post-war politics and the resurgence of an extreme-right tradition with fascist roots, all against a backdrop of structural unemployment, institutional racism and widening inequalities.

In trying to develop an explanatory framework to address—or, more often, distract from—this situation, politicians, and in particular state actors, have consciously created a 'Muslim problem', drawing on resources provided by the 'war on terror's' global

Islamophobia, by France's colonial legacy and by the lexicon of 'cultural racism' fashioned by a radicalising right since the 1970s. It is a racism, says Rancière, driven not by 'retrograde social groups' but by a section of the intellectual elites, a 'rationalisation of the state' rather than a popular passion.[85] The reactionary trajectory of republican secularism today, moulded into a weapon of discrimination and exclusion by parties of left and right, has bolstered the state's authority as the primary and intransigent arbiter of social relations—an arbitration perceived increasingly through the lens of culture and ethnicity. The dynamics of Islamophobic scapegoating and creeping authoritarianism, involving withdrawal from democratic accountability and hostility to cultural pluralism, are mutually reinforcing. They require compliance and assent from wider sections of the population to operate. They will, therefore, require non-compliance and dissent—as well as meaningful, practical solidarity and a concerted political will—if they are to be interrupted, challenged and halted.

NOTES

INTRODUCTION

1. Kundnani, Arun, *The Muslims are Coming! Islamophobia, Extremism and the Domestic War on Terror*, London: Verso, 2015; Kumar, Deepa, *Islamophobia and the Politics of Empire*, New York: Haymarket, 2012; Lean, Nathan, *The Islamophobia Industry. How the Right Manufactures Fear of Muslims*, London: Pluto, 2012; Tyrer, David, *The Politics of Islamophobia. Race, Power and Fantasy*, London: Pluto, 2013; and Fekete, Liz, *A Suitable Enemy: Racism, Migration and Islamophobia in Europe*, London: Pluto, 2009.
2. Ahearne, Jeremy, *Government Through Culture and the Contemporary French Right*, Basingstoke: Palgrave Macmillan, 2014.
3. See, for example, Baubérot, Jean, *Les 7 laïcités françaises*, Paris: Maison des sciences de l'homme, 2015 and *La laïcité falsifiée*, Paris: La Découverte, 2012; and, from a different perspective, Pena-Ruiz, Henri, *Qu'est-ce que la laïcité?*, Paris: Gallimard, 2003.
4. Hargreaves, Alec, *Multi-Ethnic France: Immigration, Politics, Culture and Society*, Abingdon: Routledge, 2007. See also Beauchemin, Cris, Christelle Hamel and Patrick Simon (eds), *Trajectoires et origines. Enquête sur la diversité des populations en France*, Paris: Ined, 2015, http://teo.site.ined.fr/fichier/rte/General/Publications/Grandes%20enqu%C3%AAtes/TeO-fascicule.pdf, last accessed 8 May 2017.
5. Muscati, Sina Ali, 'Arab/Muslim "Otherness": The Role of Racial Constructions in the Gulf War and the Continuing Crisis with Iraq',

Journal of Muslim Minority Affairs, vol. 22, no. 1 (2002). See also, Peters, Cynthia, *Collateral Damage: The 'New World Order' At Home and Abroad*, New York: South End Press, 1999.

6. Silverstein, Paul A., 'The context of antisemitism and Islamophobia in France', *Patterns of Prejudice*, vol. 42, no. 1 (2008).
7. On the 2004 law and its implications see Scott, Joan Wallach, *The Politics of the Veil*, New Jersey: Princeton University Press, 2007; Bouamama, Saïd, *L'affaire du foulard islamique—La production d'un racisme respectable*, Lille: Geai Bleu, 2004.
8. Escalona, Fabien, 'Comment le thème de l'identité nationale a été capturé par la droite et le FN', *Mediapart*, 3 March 2017, https://www.mediapart.fr/journal/france/030317/comment-le-theme-de-l-identite-nationale-ete-capture-par-la-droite-et-le-fn?page_article=3, last accessed 10 June 2017. See also, Martigny, Vincent, *Dire la France. Culture(s) et identités nationales (1981–1995)*, Paris: Presses de Sciences Po, 2016.
9. Samary, Catherine, 'La Laïcité n'est pas anti-religieuse', *Que Faire?*, 28 May 2010, http://quefaire.lautre.net/La-laicite-n-est-pas-anti#nb10, last accessed 28 July 2017.
10. Sciolino, Elaine, 'Seeing Green; The Red Menace Is Gone. But Here's Islam', *The New York Times*, 21 January 1996, http://www.nytimes.com/1996/01/21/weekinreview/seeing-green-the-red-menace-is-gone-but-here-s-islam.html, last accessed 10 June 2017.
11. Ibid.
12. 'Macron: "nous ne cèderons rien à l'antisionisme", "forme réinventée de l'antisémitisme"', *Libération*, 16 July 2017, http://www.liberation.fr/societe/2017/07/16/macron-nous-ne-cederons-rien-a-l-antisionisme-forme-reinventee-de-l-antisemitisme_1584155, last accessed 25 July 2017.
13. See Deltombe, Thomas, *L'Islam Imaginaire. La construction médiatique de l'Islamophobie en France, 1975–2005*, Paris: La Découverte, 2007.
14. Redeker, Robert, 'Face aux intimidations islamistes, que doit faire le monde libre?', *Le Figaro*, 19 September 2006, http://www.lefigaro.fr/debats/2006/09/19/01005-20060919ARTFIG90134-face_aux_intimidations_islamistes_que_doit_faire_le_monde_libre_.php, last accessed 22 June 2017.

15. Brenner, Emmanuel, *Les territoires perdus de la République*, Paris: Fayard, 2015. For a critique of this book see Segré, Ivan, 'On Ethno-Cultural Sociology', in Badiou, Alain, Eric Hazan and Ivan Segré, *Reflections on Anti-Semitism*, London: Verso, 2013, pp. 99–149.
16. Peters, 'Collateral Damage', p. 124.
17. See Wolfreys, Jim, 'The Disposable Heroes of Hypocrisy', *International Socialism* (Autumn 2002), http://pubs.socialistreviewindex.org.uk/isj96/wolfreys.htm, last accessed 22 June 2017.
18. Chabal, Emile, *A Divided Republic: Nation, State and Citizenship in Contemporary France*, Cambridge: Cambridge University Press, 2015, p. 26.
19. Lindenberg, Daniel, *Le Rappel à l'ordre. Enquête sur les nouveaux réactionnaires*, Paris: Seuil, 2016.
20. 'The construction of *laïcité* as a republican value in contemporary France cannot simply be seen as an exercise in "domination" or as a thin justification for "racism" or "exclusion"', Chabal argues. 'Rather, it is a story of republican triumph that rests on partial readings of the Revolution, the Third Republic and the impact of the 1905 law.' Chabal, A *Divided Republic*, p.31.
21. Fysh, Peter and Jim Wolfreys, *The Politics of Racism in France*, Basingstoke: Palgrave Macmillan, 2003.
22. Cohen, Patrick, 'Elisabeth Badinter: "Il ne faut pas avoir peur de se faire traiter d'islamophobe,"' *France Inter*, 6 January 2016, https://www.franceinter.fr/emissions/l-invite/l-invite-06-janvier-2016, last accessed 22 June 2017.
23. Redeker, 'Face aux intimidations islamistes, que doit faire le monde libre?'.
24. Fallaci, Oriana, *The Rage and the Pride*, New York: Rizzoli, 2002.
25. Mishani, Dror and Aurelia Smotriez 'What Sort of Frenchmen Are They?', *Haaretz*, 17 November 2005, http://www.haaretz.com/what-sort-of-frenchmen-are-they-1.174419, last accessed 22 June 2017.
26. De Cabarrus, Thierry, 'Invité par l'UMP, Finkielkraut stigmatise "l'accent des Beurs": des propos dangereux', *L'Obs*, 6 February 2014, http://leplus.nouvelobs.com/contribution/1142505-finkielkraut-stigmatise-l-accent-des-beurs-et-des-banlieues-des-propos-dangereux.html, last accessed 22 June 2017.

27. Mishani and Smotriez, 'What Sort of Frenchmen Are They?'.
28. Zemmour, Eric, *Le Suicide français. Ces quarante années qui ont défait la France*, Paris: Albin Michel, 2014. See also Baverez, Nicolas, *La France qui tombe*, Paris: Tempus Perrin, 2004 and De Villiers, Philippe, *Les Cloches sonneront-elles encore demain? La vérité sur l'islamisation de la France*, Paris: Albin Michel, 2016.
29. 'Le dérapage de Brice Hortefeux à l'université d'été de l'UMP', *Le Monde*, 10 September 2009, http://www.lemonde.fr/politique/article/2009/09/10/le-derapage-de-brice-hortefeux-a-l-universite-d-ete-de-l-ump_1238744_823448.html, last accessed 22 June 2017.
30. AFP, 'Pour Valls, "les Roms ont vocation à rentrer en Roumanie ou en Bulgarie,"' *Libération*, 24 September 2013, http://www.liberation.fr/societe/2013/09/24/pour-valls-seule-une-minorite-de-roms-veulent-s-integrer-en-france_934265, last accessed 22 June 2017.
31. 'Taubira traitée de "guenon" par une enfant de la "Manif pour tous" à Angers', *Le Parisien*, 27 October 2013, http://www.leparisien.fr/societe/taubira-traitee-de-guenon-par-une-enfant-a-angers-27-10-2013-3263151.php, last accessed 22 June 2017.
32. Anyangwe, Eliza, 'Brand new Macron, same old colonialism', *The Guardian*, 11 July 2017, https://www.theguardian.com/commentisfree/2017/jul/11/slur-africans-macron-radical-pretence-over, last accessed 11 August 2017.
33. For a discussion of the relationship between domestic and international trajectories of Islamophobia see Kumar, Deepa, 'Islamophobia and Empire: An Intermestic Approach to the study of Anti-Muslim Racism', in Massoumi, Narzanin, Tom Mills and David Miller (eds), *What is Islamophobia? Racism, Social Movements, and the State*, Chicago: University of Chicago Press, 2017.
34. Will Hutton offers a fairly standard version of this: 'Macron has led a brilliant coup—could the British do the same?', *The Observer*, 18 June 2017.
35. Amable, Bruno and Stefano Palombarini, *L'illusion du bloc bourgeois. Alliances sociales et avenir du modèle français*, Paris: Raisons d'agir, 2017, pp. 106, 115.
36. Ibid., p. 107.
37. Giudicelli, Vanina, 'Interview: The meaning of Macron', *International*

Socialism, (Summer 2017), http://isj.org.uk/interview-the-meaning-of-macron/, last accessed 25 July 2017.
38. Amable and Palombarini, *L'illusion du bloc bourgeois*, p. 122.
39. Stasi, Bernard, 'Commission de réflexion sur l'application du principe de laïcité dans la République: rapport au Président de la République', La Documentation Française, December 2003, http://www.ladocumentationfrancaise.fr/rapports-publics/034000725/index.shtml, last accessed 22 June 2017.
40. Brustier, Gaël, *La guerre culturelle aura bien lieu: l'occidentalisme ou l'idéologie de la crise*, Paris: Mille et une nuits, 2013, pp. 146–7.
41. Amable and Palombarini, *L'illusion du bloc bourgeois*, pp. 122–3.
42. 'Sarkozy: double ration de frites, sinon rien!', *Le Point*, 8 November 2016, http://www.lepoint.fr/presidentielle/les-primaires/sarkozy-double-ration-de-frites-sinon-rien-08–11–2016–2081581_3122.php, last accessed 28 July 2017.
43. Fillon, François, *Vaincre le totalitarisme islamique*, Paris: Albin Michel, 2016.
44. Bastié, Eugénie, '"Ali Juppé" et Tareq Oubrou: un surnom ravageur et un allié encombrant', *Le Figaro*, 24 November 2016, http://www.lefigaro.fr/elections/presidentielles/primaires-droite 2016/11/24/35004-20161124ARTFIG00175-ali-juppe-et-tareq-oubrou-un-surnom-ravageur-et-un-allie-encombrant.php, last accessed 18 September 2017.
45. Wolfreys, Jim, 'Can François Fillon stay the course?', *Prospect*, 8 February 2017, https://www.prospectmagazine.co.uk/world/francois-fillon-scandal-allegations-french-presidential-race-politics, last accessed 11 August 2017.
46. Jean-Luc Mélenchon, interview with the author, Hénin-Beaumont, 5 June 2012.
47. Bouvet, Laurent, *L'Insecurité culturelle. Sortir du malaise identitaire français*, Paris: Fayard, 2015.
48. Bastié, Eugénie, 'Laurent Bouvet: "Mélenchon a fait le choix de s'adresser aux Français plutôt qu'à la gauche," *Le Figaro*, 12 April 2017, http://www.lefigaro.fr/vox/politique/2017/04/12/31001–20170412 ARTFIG00302-laurent-bouvet-melenchon-a-fait-le-choix-de-s-adresser-aux-francais-plutot-qu-a-la-gauche.php, last accessed 28 June 2017.

49. Gendron, Guillaume, 'Au lancement du "Printemps républicain": "N'ayez pas peur du mot "islamophobe""', *Libération*, 21 March 2016, http://www.liberation.fr/france/2016/03/21/au-lancement-du-printemps-republicain-n-ayez-pas-peur-du-mot-islamophobe_1440912, last accessed 22 June 2017.
50. Manifeste pour un printemps républicain, 'Face aux attaques contre la République, le Printemps républicain commence aujourd'hui', *Marianne*, 20 March 2016, https://www.marianne.net/debattons/tribunes/face-aux-attaques-contre-la-republique-le-printemps-republicain-commence-aujourd, last accessed 22 June 2017.
51. Guillaume, 'Au lancement du "Printemps républicain"'.
52. Citron, Suzanne, *Le Mythe national. L'histoire de France revisitée*, Paris: Editions de l'Atelier, 2008.
53. Fernando, Mayanthi L., *The Republic Unsettled: Muslim French and the Contradictions of Secularism*, Durham, NC: Duke University Press, 2014, p. 7.
54. Ibid., pp. 7, 10, 11. See also Shepard, Todd, *The Invention of Decolonization: The Algerian War and the Remaking of France*, Ithaca, NY: Cornell University Press, 2006.
55. Fernando, *The Republic Unsettled*, p. 12.
56. Ibid., p. 20.
57. Savidan, Patrick, *Voulons-nous vraiment l'égalité?*, Paris: Albin Michel, 2015, pp. 329 and 332 (Kindle edition).
58. Ibid., pp. 496 and 501 (Kindle edition).
59. Maurin, Eric, *La peur du déclassement. Une sociologie des recessions*, Paris: Seuil, 2009, pp. 6–12.
60. Ibid., p. 6.
61. Savidan, *Voulons-nous vraiment l'égalité?*, p. 2801 (Kindle edition).
62. Savidan, *Voulons-nous vraiment l'égalité?*, p. 2819 (Kindle edition).
63. Cette France-là, *Xénophobie d'en haut. Le choix d'une droite éhontée*, Paris: La Découverte, 2012, pp. 172–3.

1. STATE OF EMERGENCY

1. 'Un cortège présidentiel aux allures de sommet international', *Le Journal du Dimanche*, 11 January 2015, http://www.lejdd.fr/Politique/Une-

cinquantaine-de-chefs-d-Etat-et-de-gouvernement-Merkel-Renzi-Netanyahou-Abbas-Cameron-ont-defile-aux-cotes-de-Francois-Hollande-711974, last accessed 19 March 2016.

2. Withnall, Adam, 'Paris march: TV wide shots reveal a different perspective on world leaders at largest demonstration in France's history', *The Independent*, 12 January 2015, http://www.independent.co.uk/news/world/europe/paris-march-tv-wide-shots-reveal-a-different-perspective-on-world-leaders-at-largest-demonstration-9972895.html, last accessed 25 March 2016.
3. Breton, Laure, 'Hollande: "Ceux qui sont tombées le 13 novembre étaient la France, toute la France"', *Libération*, 27 November 2015, http://www.liberation.fr/france/2015/11/27/hollande-ceux-qui-sont-tombes-le-13-novembre-etaient-la-france-toute-la-france_1416609, last accessed 19 March 2016.
4. Amnesty International, 'France: Emergency Measures Must Protect Public Without Trampling Human Rights', Press Release, 19 November 2015, http://www.commondreams.org/newswire/2015/11/19/france-emergency-measures-must-protect-public-without-trampling-human-rights, last accessed 19 March 2016.
5. 'Etat d'urgence (suite): interdiction de la marche pour le climat à Lyon', *Rue89Lyon*, 25 November 2015, http://www.rue89lyon.fr/2015/11/25/etat-durgence-suite-interdiction-de-la-marche-pour-le-climat-lyon/, last accessed 19 March 2016.
6. 'Pour Mélenchon, l'état d'urgence sert à "criminaliser les mouvements sociaux"', *20 Minutes*, 30 November 2015, http://www.20minutes.fr/politique/1741139–20151130-melenchon-etat-urgence-sert-criminaliser-mouvements-sociaux, last accessed 19 March 2015.
7. Todd, Emmanuel, *Qui est Charlie? Sociologie d'une crise religieuse*, Paris: Seuil, 2015.
8. Théobald, Marie, 'Le Medef demande aux patrons de signaler la radicalisation des salaries', *Le Figaro*, 20 November 2015, http://www.lefigaro.fr/societes/2015/11/20/20005–20151120ARTFIG00188-le-medef-demande-aux-patrons-de-signaler-la-radicalisation-des-salaries.php, last accessed 19 March 2016.
9. Guichard, Mourad, 'Dans le Loiret, l'éducation nationale rêve d'un

fichage des parents', *Libération*, 1 December 2015, http://www.liberation.fr/france/2015/12/01/dans-le-loiret-l-education-nationale-reve-d-un-fichage-policier_1417561, last accessed 4 June 2017.

10. 'Lionnel Luca: "La "libanisation" c'est quand on admet le communautarisme"', *Nice-Matin*, 14 November 2015, http://archives.nicematin.com/cagnes-sur-mer/lionnel-luca-la-%E2%80%9Clibanisation%E2%80%9D-cest-quand-on-admet-le-communautarisme.2396720.html, last accessed 19 March 2016.
11. 'Attaques à Paris: les politiques, entre émotion et récupération', *Le Monde*, 14 November 2015, http://www.lemonde.fr/attaques-a-paris/article/2015/11/14/attaques-a-paris-les-politiques-entre-emotion-et-recuperation_4809584_4809495.html, last accessed 19 March 2016.
12. 'Juppé: "Il faut que les français musulmans disent clairement nous ne voulons pas de cette religion"', BFMTV, 17 November 2015, http://www.bfmtv.com/mediaplayer/video/juppe-il-faut-que-les-francais-musulmans-disent-clairement-nous-ne-voulons-pas-de-cette-religion-696866.html, last accessed 19 March 2016.
13. Amnesty International, 'France: Emergency Measures'.
14. '"Repérer et traiter ceux qui ne sont pas Charlie", une brillante analyse de Nathalie Saint-Cricq', *La Rotative*, 14 January 2015, http://larotative.info/reperer-et-traiter-ceux-qui-ne-785.html, last accessed 25 March 2016.
15. Maillard, Matteo, 'Les mesures de l'après-"Charlie" au collège et au lycée', *Le Monde*, 22 January 2015, http://www.lemonde.fr/campus/article/2015/01/22/les-mesures-de-l-apres-charlie-au-college-et-au-lycee_4561097_4401467.html, last accessed 25 March 2016.
16. 'François Hollande veut célébrer la laïcité dans les écoles', *Le Monde*, 22 January 2015, http://www.lemonde.fr/politique/article/2015/01/22/francois-hollande-prone-l-autorite-a-l-ecole_4560936_823448.html, last accessed 25 March 2016.
17. Government of the French Fifth Republic, 'Radicalisation djihadiste. Les premiers signes qui peuvent alterter', http://www.stop-djihadisme.gouv.fr/decrypter.html, last accessed 25 March 2016.
18. CCIF, 'La guerre est déclarée?', 21 January 2015, www.islamophobie.net/articles/2015/01/20/marion-le-pen-chauprade, last accessed

25 March 2016; de Boni, Marc and Emmanuel Galiero, 'Marine Le Pen désavoue Aymeric Chauprade après ses propos sur les musulmans', *Le Figaro*, 19 January 2015, http://www.lefigaro.fr/politique/le-scan/couacs/2015/01/19/25005–20150119ARTFIG00131-marine-le-pen-desavoue-aymeric-chauprade-apres-ses-propos-sur-les-musulmans.php, last accessed 4 June 2017.

19. 'Eric Ciotti propose la suppression des allocations familiales aux parents des enfants qui ne respectent pas les valeurs de la République', 15 January 2015, http://www.eric-ciotti.com/2015/01/15/eric-ciotti-propose-la-suppression-des-allocations-familiales-aux-parents-des-enfants-qui-ne-respectent-pas-les-valeurs-de-la-republique/, last accessed 25 March 2016.
20. Hoberman, J., 'French mayor bans anti-Jihadist Muslim film', *Tablet Magazine*, 17 January 2015, http://tabletmag.com/scroll/188412/french-mayor-bans-oscar-nominated-muslim-film, last accessed 25 March 2016.
21. Stone, Jon, 'Firebombs and pigs' heads thrown into mosques as anti-Muslim attacks increase after Paris shootings', *The Independent*, 14 January 2015, http://www.independent.co.uk/news/world/europe/firebombs-and-pigs-heads-thrown-into-mosques-as-anti-muslim-attacks-increase-after-paris-shootings-9977423.html, last accessed 25 March 2016.
22. 'Un homme tué de 17 coups de couteau en Provence: geste islamophobe?', *L'Express*, 16 January 2015, www.lexpress.fr/actualite/societe/fait-divers/un-homme-tue-de-17-coups-de-couteau-en-provence-geste-islamophobe_1641676.html#, last accessed 25 March 2016.
23. Debnath, Neela, 'Paris kosher supermarket hero Lassana Bathily given French citizenship for bravery and calls for 'liberty, friendship and solidarity', *Independent*, 21 January 2015, http://www.independent.co.uk/news/world/europe/paris-kosher-supermarket-hero-lassana-bathily-given-french-citizenship-for-bravery-and-calls-for-9991738.html, last accessed 25 March 2016
24. 'Ahmed 8 ans, poursuivi pour apologie d'actes de terrorisme', CCIF, 29 January 2015, www.islamophobie.net/articles/2015/01/28/ahmed-huit-ans-apologie-acte-terrorisme, last accessed 25 March 2016.

Mouillard, Sylvie, 'Un enfant de 8 ans au commissariat pour apologie du terrorisme', *Libération*, 28 January 2015, http://www.liberation.fr/societe/2015/01/28/un-enfant-de-8-ans-au-commissariat-pour-apologie-du-terrorisme_1190778, last accessed 25 March 2016.

25. The Kouachi brothers, Saïd and Chérif, were the perpetrators of the *Charlie Hebdo* attack. 'Charlie Hebdo: Mise en examen à 14 ans pour apologie du terrorisme', *Ouest France*, 14 January 2015, http://www.ouest-france.fr/pays-de-la-loire/nantes-44000/apologie-du-terrorisme-14-ans-elle-se-dit-la-soeur-coulibaly-et-menace-3113610, 25 March 2016.
26. 'Apologie du terrorisme. Un lycéen nantais poursuivi pour un dessin', *Ouest France*, 16 January 2015, http://www.ouest-france.fr/pays-de-la-loire/nantes-44000/apologie-du-terrorisme-un-lyceen-nantais-poursuivi-pour-un-dessin-3119401, last accessed 1 June 2016.
27. 'Poitiers: l'enseignant soupçonné d'apologie du terrorisme ne sera pas poursuivi', *Le Monde*, 27 February 2015, http://www.lemonde.fr/societe/article/2015/02/27/poitiers-l-enseignant-soupconne-d-apologie-du-terrorisme-ne-sera-pas-poursuivi_4584972_3224.html, last accessed 25 March 2016; Boissel, Pascal, 'Jean François Chazerans est un non terroriste', *Ensemble!*, 28 February 2015, https://www.ensemble-fdg.org/content/jean-francois-chazerans-est-un-non-terroriste, last accessed 25 March 2016.
28. AFP, 'Béziers: M. Ménard demande aux dirigeants de mosquées de signer une "charte"', *La Croix*, 26 November 2015, http://www.la-croix.com/Actualite/France/Beziers-M.-Menard-demande-aux-dirigeants-de-mosquees-de-signer-une-charte-2015–11–26–1385249, last accessed 19 March 2016.
29. 'Béziers: Ménard veut une garde de bénévoles pour patrouiller dans les rues', *Le Parisien*, 1 December 2015, http://www.leparisien.fr/languedoc-roussillon/beziers-menard-veut-une-garde-de-benevoles-pour-patrouiller-dans-les-rues-01–12–2015–5329891.php, last accessed 19 March 2016.
30. Bonnefoy, Geoffrey, 'Expulsion, internement, bagne de Cayenne: les idées post-attentats de la droite', *L'Express*, 20 November 2015, http://www.lexpress.fr/actualite/politique/lr/expulsion-internement-bagne-

de-cayenne-les-idees-post-attentats-de-la-droite_1738074.html, last accessed 19 March 2016.

31. 'Wauquiez: "Ce ne sera pas Guantanamo car on ne torturera pas"', *Marianne*, http://www.marianne.net/wauquiez-ce-ne-sera-pas-guantanamo-on-ne-torturera-pas-100238105.html, last accessed 19 March 2016.
32. Vigogne, Ludovic, 'Après les attentats, le faux pas de la droite', *L'Opinion*, 18 November 2015, http://www.lopinion.fr/edition/politique/apres-attentats-faux-pas-droite-90837, last accessed 19 March 2016.
33. 'Manuel Valls veut interner les personnes fichées S avec l'aval du Conseil d'Etat', *20 Minutes*, 9 December 2015, http://www.20minutes.fr/societe/1747599–20151209-manuel-valls-veut-interner-personnes-fichees-aval-conseil-etat, last accessed 19 March 2016.
34. Le Cour Grandmaison, Olivier, 'Après les attentats: la Réaction qui vient', *Mediapart*, 26 November 2015, https://blogs.mediapart.fr/olivier-le-cour-grandmaison/blog/261115/apres-les-attentats-la-reaction-qui-vient, last accessed 19 March 2016.
35. 'Un état d'esprit pas un esprit d'État', *La Voix du Nord*, 11 January 2016, http://www.lavoixdunord.fr/france-monde/un-etat-d-esprit-pas-un-esprit-d-etat-ia70450b0n3263112, last accessed 19 March 2016.
36. Kundnani, Arun, *The Muslims are Coming: Islamophobia, Extremism and the Domestic War on Terror*, Verso: London, 2014, p. 56.
37. Marchand, Leila, 'Déchéance de nationalité: les sept questions clefs pour comprendre le débat', *Les Echos*, 28 December 2015, http://www.lesechos.fr/politique-societe/politique/021583631755-decheance-de-nationalite-les-sept-questions-clefs-pour-comprendre-le-debat-1187941.php, last accessed 19 March 2016.
38. 'Pascal Cherki: "La déchéanche de nationalité n'a aucune efficacité"', *Europe 1*, 3 December 2015, http://www.europe1.fr/politique/pascal-cherki-la-decheance-de-nationalite-na-aucune-efficacite-2630255, last accessed 19 March 2016.
39. Stephan, Bernard, 'Vaincre sans se renier', *La Montagne/Centre France*, 4 December 2015, http://www.lamontagne.fr/france-monde/actualites/

a-la-une/editorial/2015/12/04/vaincre-sans-se-renier_11691021.html, last accessed 19 March 2016.

40. Chapuis, Nicolas and Raphaëlle Besse Desmoulières, 'La décheánche de nationalité provoque un malaise à gauche', *Le Monde*, 24 December 2015, http://www.lemonde.fr/politique/article/2015/12/24/la-decheance-de-nationalite-provoque-un-malaise-a-gauche_4837458_823448.html#H3MSt4tJmIkWWY7L.99, last accessed 19 March 2016.
41. Faye, Olivier, 'L'inquiétude liée aux attentats renforce le FN', *Le Monde*, 24 November 2015, http://www.lemonde.fr/elections-regionales-2015/article/2015/11/24/le-fn-vise-desormais-les-indecis-et-les-abstentionnistes_4815995_4640869.html#oFr4hh5vBCT4hR3G.99, last accessed 25 March 2016.
42. Ahearne, Jeremy, *Government through Culture and the Contemporary French Right*, Basingstoke: Palgrave Macmillan, 2014, pp. 31–2.
43. Deltombe, *L'Islam Imaginaire. La construction médiatique de l'Islamophobie en France 1975–2005*, Paris: La Découverte, 2007, p. 81.
44. Tevanian, Pierre, 'Pour 100 pour cent des musulmans les sondages sont plutôt une menace', *Les mots sont importants*, 24 October 2012, http://lmsi.net/Pour-100-des-musulmans-les, last accessed 19 March 2016.
45. Mandraud, Isabelle, 'La police estime marginal le port de la burqa', *Le Monde*, 29 July 2009, http://www.lemonde.fr/societe/article/2009/07/29/la-police-estime-marginal-le-port-de-la-burqa_1223776_3224.html, last accessed 23 July 2017.
46. Ahearne, *Government through Culture*, p. 31. For a critical assessment of the role of opinion polling see Garrigou, Alain and Richard Brousse, *Manuel anti-sondages: la démocratie n'est pas à vendre*, Paris: Editions la Ville Brulle, 2011; Garrigou, Alain, *L'Ivresse des Sondages*, Paris: La Découverte, 2006; Lehingue, Patrick and Rémy Caveng, *Sondages: Souriez, vous êtes manipulés*, Paris: Graffic-Bruno Leprince, 2011.
47. Mélenchon, Jean-Luc, 'Je parle du voile intégral', *Le Blog de Jean-Luc Mélenchon*, 7 January 2010, http://www.jean-luc-melenchon.fr/2010/01/07/je-parle-du-voile-integral/, last accessed 19 March 2016.
48. Wolfreys, Jim, 'Making Racism Respectable: Islamophobia in Sarkozy's France', *Global Social Justice Journal*, vol. 1, no. 1 (2013).
49. Ahearne, *Government through Culture*, p. 35.

50. Government of the French Fifth Republic, 'Déclaration de M. Nicolas Sarkozy, candidat à l'élection présidentielle, sur la lutte contre le terrorisme, l'énergie nucléaire, l'immigration, l'Union européenne, l'emploi et sur les relations franco-allemandes, à Ormes (Loiret) le 26 mars 2012', Direction de l'information légale et administrative, http://discours.vie-publique.fr/notices/123000682.html, last accessed 7 August 2017.
51. 'Copé dénonce l'existence d'un "racisme anti-blancs"', *Le Figaro*, 26 September 2012, http://www.lefigaro.fr/politique/2012/09/26/01002–20120926ARTFIG00428-cope-denonce-l-existence-d-un-racisme-anti-blanc.php, last accessed 4 June 2017.
52. Chrisafis, Angelique, 'Pork or nothing: how school dinners are dividing France', *The Guardian*, 13 October 2015, https://www.theguardian.com/world/2015/oct/13/pork-school-dinners-france-secularism-children-religious-intolerance, last accessed 4 June 2017.
53. Elkabbach, Jean-Pierre, 'Interview de M. François Fillon, premier minister, à Europe 1 le 5 mars 2012...', *Vie Publique*, 5 March 2012, http://discours.vie-publique.fr/notices/123000514.html, last accessed 25 March 2016.
54. 'Claude Guéant associe vote des étrangers et halal à la cantine', *Le Monde* and AFP, 2 March 2012, http://www.lemonde.fr/politique/article/2012/03/02/gueant-si-on-recoit-moins-d-immigres-les-choses-se-passeront-mieux_1651344_823448.html, last accessed 4 June 2017.
55. 'Viande halal en prison: le gouvernement va faire appel', *Le Parisien*, http://www.leparisien.fr/societe/viande-halal-en-prison-le-gouvernement-va-faire-appel-29–11–2013–3362007.php, 29 November 2013, last accessed 25 March 2016.
56. 'La collégienne au bandeau à nouveau privée de cours', *Le Parisien*, 20 March 2013, http://www.leparisien.fr/villiers-sur-marne-94350/le-bandeau-de-la-collegienne-se-denoue-au-conseil-d-etat-19-03-2013-2651957.php, last accessed 4 June 2017.
57. Wolfreys, 'Republic of Islamophobia'.
58. Lafargue, Paul, 'Franc-maçonnerie', *Le Socialiste*, 15–18 September 1901.
59. Solis, René, 'Niqab à l'Opéra: un cas très rare', *Libération*, 20 October

2014, www.liberation.fr/culture/2014/10/20/niqab-a-l-opera-un-cas-tres-rare_1125897, last accessed 25 March 2016.

60. Tevanian, Pierre, 'L'Exception au pluriel—et au quotidian', *Les mots sont importants*, 4 March 2013, http://lmsi.net/L-exception-au-pluriel-et-au, last accessed 19 March 2016.
61. 'Argenteuil: la femme enceinte voilé qui a été agressée a perdu le bébé qu'elle portait', *L'Express*, 18 June 2013, http://www.lexpress.fr/actualite/societe/la-jeune-femme-agressee-a-argenteuil-a-perdu-le-bebe-qu-elle-portait_1258488.html, last accessed 4 June 2017.
62. CNCDH, 'La lutte contre le racisme, l'anti-semitisme et la xénophobie, Année 2012', report, http://www.cncdh.fr/sites/default/files/cncdh_racisme_2012_basse_def.pdf; CNCDH, 'La lutte contre le racisme, l'anti-semitisme et la xénophobie, Année 2013', report, http://www.cncdh.fr/sites/default/files/cncdh_racisme_2013_basse_definition.pdf, p. 22, both last accessed 25 March 2016.
63. See Fysh, Peter and Jim Wolfreys, *The Politics of Racism in France*, Basingstoke: Palgrave Macmillan, 2003.
64. Grosjean, Blandine, '"Toutes les civilisations ne se valent pas", c'est Guéant qui le dit', *L'Obs avec Rue 89*, 4 February 2012, http://rue89.nouvelobs.com/2012/02/04/gueant-t-il-vraiment-dit-toutes-les-civilisatiosn-ne-se-valent-pas-229090, last accessed 19 March 2016.
65. Deltombe, *L'Islam Imaginaire*, p. 96.
66. Kundnani, *The Muslims are Coming*, p. 58.
67. Gilroy, Paul, *Postcolonial Melancholia*, New York: Columbia University Press, 2005.
68. Rosso, Romain, 'L'Indochine: lendemains de défaite', *L'Express*, 21 February 2007, http://www.lexpress.fr/actualite/politique/l-indochine-lendemains-de-d-eacute-faite_478164.html, last accessed 19 March 2016.
69. On the role of the headscarf affair in producing a 'respectable racism' see Bouamama, *L'Affaire du foulard islamique*. On the efforts of the right and far-right to focus on culture rather than race see Fysh and Wolfreys, *The Politics of Racism in France*.
70. Kundnani, *The Muslims are Coming*, p. 58.
71. 'Manuel Valls: "L'islamophobie est le cheval de Troie des salafistes"',

L'Obs, 31 July 2013, http://tempsreel.nouvelobs.com/politique/20130731.OBS1612/manuel-valls-l-islamophobie-est-le-cheval-de-troie-des-salafistes.html, last accessed 1 June 2016.

72. Fourest, Caroline and Fiammetta Venner, 'Ne pas confondre islamophobes et laïcs', *Libération*, 17 November 2003, last accessed 7 August 2017; Caroline Fourest and Fiammetta Venner, 'Islamophobie', *ProChoix*, 26–27, (Autumn/Winter 2003), http://www.prochoix.org/pdf/Prochoix.2627.interieur.pdf, last accessed 7 August 2017.
73. Hajjat, Abdellali and Marwan Mohammed, *Islamophobie. Comment les élites françaises fabriquent le problème musulman*, Paris: La Découverte, 2013.
74. Kersimon, Isabelle and Jean-Christophe Moreau, *Islamophobie, la contre-enquête*, Paris: Plein Jour, 2014, pp. 271–5.

2. MAKING RACISM RESPECTABLE

1. 'Discours de M. Jacques CHIRAC place de la République à Paris (campagne électorale pour l'élection présidentielle)', http://www.jacqueschirac-asso.fr/archives-elysee.fr/elysee/elysee.fr/francais/interventions/discours_et_declarations/2002/mai/fi002048.html, last accessed on 4 June 2017.
2. Colombani, Jean-Marie, *Le Résident de la République*, Paris: Stock, 1998.
3. Tevanian, Pierre, *La République du mépris. Les métamorphoses du racisme dans la France des années Sarkozy*, Paris: La Découverte, 2007.
4. Mair, Peter, *Ruling the Void: The Hollowing of Western Democracy*, London: Verso, 2013.
5. Macron's En Marche movement was renamed after his presidential victory.
6. Interior Ministry of the Fifth French Republic, 'Résultats des élections législatives de 2017', https://www.interieur.gouv.fr/Elections/Les-resultats/Legislatives/elecresult__legislatives-2017/(path)/legislatives-2017/FE.html, last accessed 7 August 2017.
7. Sayad, Abdelmalek, 'Qu'est-ce que l'intégration?', *Hommes et migrations*, vol. 182, no. 1 (1994), pp. 8–14.
8. Conan, Eric, 'Jospin cherche sa ligne', *L'Express*, 28 October 1999, http://

www.lexpress.fr/informations/jospin-cherche-sa-ligne_635462.html, last accessed 4 June 2017.

9. Wacquant, Loïc, 'Pénalisation de la misère et projet politique néo-libéral', in Collectif contre la répression, *Répressions, la Cagnotte et le Bâton*, Paris: L'Esprit Frappeur, 2000. See also Loïc Wacquant, *Les Prisons de la misère*, Paris: Raisons d'agir, 1999.
10. Pujadas, David, 'Interview de M. Jean-Pierre Raffarin, Premier Ministre, à France 2 le 7 mai 2003...', *Vie publique*, 7 May 2003, http://discours.vie-publique.fr/notices/033002493.html, last accessed 30 April 2016.
11. Barbier, Christophe and Eric Mandonnet, 'Raffarin contre la rue', *L'Express*, 29 May 2003, http://www.lexpress.fr/informations/raffarin-contre-la-rue_651781.html, last accessed 30 April 2016.
12. Yasser Louati, interview with the author, Paris, 23 April 2016.
13. Collectif Les Mots Sont Importants, 'Chronique du Racisme Républicain (Quatrième Partie). Les Années Sarkozy: 2005', 26 April 2007, http://lmsi.net/Chronique-du-racisme-republicain#nb3, last accessed 20 June 2016.
14. TF1, 'Une Présence Durable des CRS dans les Banlieues', 12 November 2005, http://lci.tf1.fr/france/2005–11/presence-durable-crs-dans-banlieues-4860968.html, last accessed 20 June 2016.
15. 'Emmanuel Todd: "rien ne sépare les enfants d'immigrés du reste de la société"', *Le Monde*, 13 November 2005, http://www.lemonde.fr/societe/article/2005/11/29/emmanuel-todd-rien-ne-separe-les-enfants-d-immigres-du-reste-de-la-societe_709613_3224.html, last accessed 4 June 2017.
16. 'What France Needs', *The Economist*, 26 October 2006, http://www.economist.com/node/8080753, last accessed 30 April 2016.
17. Fukuyama, Francis, cited in Ariès, Paul, *Misère du sarkozysme: Cette droite qui n'aime pas la France*, Paris: Parangon, 2005, p. 251.
18. See, for example, Musso, Pierre, *Le Sarkoberlusconisme*, Paris: Editions de L'Aube, 2008; Hewlett, Nick, *The Sarkozy Phenomenon*, Exeter: Imprint Academic, 2011; Ariès, Paul, *Misère du Sarkozysme: Cette droite qui n'aime pas la France*, Lyon: Parangon, 2005.
19. 'Sarkozy: "J'irai chercher les électeurs du FN"', *L'Obs*, 29 March 2006, http://tempsreel.nouvelobs.com/politique/20060329.OBS2148/sar-

kozy-j-irai-chercherles-electeurs-du-fn.html, last accessed 11 April 2016.

20. 'A Strasbourg, Sarkozy déclare la guerre aux "voyous"', *Le Parisien*, 25 October 2002, http://www.leparisien.fr/faits-divers/a-strasbourg-sarkozy-declare-la-guerre-aux-voyous-25–10–2002–2003516169.php, last accessed 20 June 2016.
21. Chevalier, Louis, *Classes laborieuses et classes dangereuses*, Paris: Plon, 1958.
22. 'Sarkozy veut "débarasser la France des voyous,"' *Le Monde*, 3 June 2005, http://www.lemonde.fr/societe/article/2005/06/03/sarkozy-veut-debarrasser-la-france-des-voyous_658188_3224.html, last accessed 20 June 2016.
23. France 2, 'Journal de 20 heures', 26 October 2005.
24. TF1 News, 6 May 2007, http://lci.tf1.fr/politique/2007–05/sarkozy-concorde-vous-trahirai-4886749.html, last accessed 22 June 2016.
25. Chrisafis, Angelique, 'Cheering crowds hail Sarkozy's triumph', *The Guardian*, 7 May 2007, www.guardian.co.uk/world/2007/may/07/france.angeliquechrisafis2, last accessed 2 May 2017.
26. Coulomb, Renaud and Marc Sangnier, 'Media coverage of Impacts of Political Majorities on French Firms: Electoral Promises or Friendship Connections?', PSE Working Paper 2012–08, http://marcsangnier.free.fr/divers/coulomb_sangnier_media.pdf, last accessed 22 June 2016.
27. Pinçon, Michel and Monique Pinçon-Charlot, *Le President des riches. Enquête sur l'oligarchie dans la France de Nicolas Sarkozy*, Paris: La Découverte, 2011.
28. In fact, as *Le Monde* reported, the pay rise turned out to be even bigger, at 172 per cent: Gurrey, Béatrice and Patrick Roger, 'Nicolas Sarkozy est augmenté de 172% et non de 140%', *Le Monde*, 6 November 2017, http://www.lemonde.fr/sarkozy-un-an-a-l-elysee/article/2007/11/06/le-president-de-la-republique-est-augmente-de-172-et-non-de-140_974995_1036775.html, last accessed 7 August 2017.
29. Ahearne, Jeremy, *Government through Culture and the Contemporary French Right*, Basingstoke: Palgrave Macmillan, 2014, p. 154.
30. Ahearne, *Government through Culture*, p. 153.
31. 'Sarkozy reçu par le pape', *L'Express*, 20 December 2007, www.lex-

press.fr/actualite/monde/sarkozy-recu-par-le-pape_468799.html, last accessed 21 June 2016.

32. 'Sarkozy à un visiteur: "casse toi, pauvre con"', *Le Nouvel Observateur*, 2 March 2008, http://tempsreel.nouvelobs.com/societe/20080223.OBS1979/sarkozy-a-un-visiteur-casse-toi-pauvre-con.html, last accessed 21 June 2016.
33. Brustier, Gaël and Jean-Philippe Huelin, *Voyage au bout de la droite. Des paniques morales à la contestation droitière*, Paris: La Découverte, 2011, pp. 192–3.
34. Sgard, Jérôme, 'Nicolas Sarkozy, lecteur de Gramsci. La tentation hégémonique du nouveau pouvoir', *Esprit*, July 2007, http://www.esprit.presse.fr/archive/review/article.php?code=14113, last accessed 22 June 2016.
35. Brustier and Huelin, *Voyage au bout de la droite*.
36. Haegel, Florence, *Les Droites en fusion. Transformations de l'UMP*, Paris: Presses de Sciences Po, 2012.
37. Godin, Emmanuel, 'The Porosity between the Mainstream Right and Extreme Right in France: *Les Droites Décomplexées* under Nicolas Sarkozy and Marine Le Pen's Leadership', *Journal of Contemporary European Studies*, vol. 21, no. 1 (2013), pp. 53–67, http://dx.doi.org/10.1080/14782804.2013.766476, last accessed 22 June 2016.
38. Haegel, *Les Droites en fusion*, p. 19.
39. Tissot, Sylvie, 'Le Repli communautaire: un concept policier. Analyse d'un rapport des Renseignements Généraux sur les "quartiers sensibles"', *Les mots sont importants*, 29 October 2004, http://lmsi.net/Le-repli-communautaire-un-concept, last accessed 22 June 2016.
40. Fourcade-Gourinchas, Marion and Sarah L. Babb, 'The Rebirth of the Liberal Creed: Paths to Neoliberalism in Four Countries', *The American Journal of Sociology*, vol. 108, no. 3 (2002).
41. See Hutton, Will, 'Macron has led a brilliant coup—could the British do the same?', *The Observer*, 18 June 2017.
42. Clift, Ben, 'French Responses to the Global Economic Crisis', in Wyn Grant and Graham K. Wilson, *The Consequences of the Global Financial Crisis: The Rhetoric of Reform and Regulation*, Oxford: OUP, 2012, p. 213.

43. Hall, Peter A., 'Introduction: the Politics of Social Change in France', in Culpepper, Pepper D., Peter A. Hall and Bruno Palier, *Changing France: The Politics that Markets Make*, Basingstoke: Palgrave Macmillan, 2006, p. 13.
44. Peck, Jamie, *Constructions of Neoliberal Reason*, p.30, cited in Mirowski, Philip, *Never Let a Serious Crisis Go to Waste: How Neoliberalism Survived the Financial Meltdown*, London: Verso, 2013, p. 54.
45. Harvey, David, *A Brief History of Neoliberalism*, Oxford: OUP, 2005, p. 3.
46. Pickett, Kate and Richard Wilkinson, *The Spirit Level: Why Equality is Better for Everyone*, London: Allen Lane, 2009, p. 4.
47. Mair, *Ruling the Void*.
48. Cerny, Philip G., 'Restructuring the Political Arena: Globalization and the Paradoxes of the Competition State', in Germain, Randall D., *Globalization and its Critics: Perspectives from Political Economy*, Basingstoke: Palgrave Macmillan, 2000, p. 118.
49. Brustier and Huelin, *Voyage au bout de la droite*, pp. 191–253.
50. Hall, 'Introduction: the Politics of Social Change in France', p. 17.
51. Giddens, Anthony, *The Third Way: The Renewal of Social Democracy*, Cambridge: Polity, 1996, pp. 15–16. See also Callinicos, Alex, *Against the Third Way: An Anticapitalist Critique*, Cambridge: Polity, 2001.
52. Goar, Matthieu and Cécile Chambraud, 'L'islam, variable électorale de Sarkozy', *Le Monde*, 3 June 2015, http://www.lemonde.fr/politique/article/2015/06/03/entre-sarkozy-et-l-islam-une-relation-opportuniste_4646083_823448.html#l0w91GfzFao9jwMZ.99, last accessed 22 June 2016.
53. '"Nous Protestons Contre la Dénomination et les Pouvoirs Dévolus à ce Ministère,"' *Libération*, 22 June 2007, http://www.liberation.fr/evenement/0101105693-nous-protestons-contre-la-denomination-et-les-pouvoirs-devolus-a-ce-ministere, last accessed 22 June 2016.
54. 'Polémique autour du ministère de l'immigration proposé par Sarkozy', *La Croix*, 11 March 2007, http://www.la-croix.com/Actualite/France/Polemique-autour-du-ministere-de-l-immigration-propose-par-Sarkozy-_NG_-2007–03–12–597289, last accessed 22 June 2016.

55. Chrisafis, Angelique, 'Nicolas Sarkozy says sorry for national identity ministry', *The Guardian*, 17 November 2010, https://www.theguardian.com/world/2010/nov/17/nicolas-sarkozy-immigration-apology, last accessed 8 August 2017.
56. 'Syndicat de Policiers: "Pas de Quotas Pour les Êtres Humains"', Contre-info, 12 September 2007, http://contreinfo.info/article.php3?id_article=1231, last accessed 2 May 2017.
57. Galaud, Flore, 'Sommet sur l'intégration à Vichy', 3 November 2008, http://www.lejdd.fr/International/Actualite/Sommet-sur-l-integration-a-Vichy-84814, last accessed 22 June 2016.
58. Ba, Diade, 'Africans still seething over Sarkozy speech', *Reuters*, 5 September 2007, http://uk.reuters.com/article/uk-africa-sarkozy-idUKL0513034620070905, last accessed 4 June 2017.
59. A full, unofficial translation of the speech can be found at *africaResource*, 'The Unofficial English Translation of Sarkozy's Speech', 13 October 2007, http://bit.ly/KqqR2y, last accessed 21 June 2016.
60. Guerrier, Sophie, 'Le discours de Grenoble de Nicolas Sarkozy', *Le Figaro*, 27 March 2014, http://www.lefigaro.fr/politique/le-scan/2014/03/27/25001–20140327ARTFIG00084-le-discours-de-grenoble-de-nicolas-sarkozy.php, last accessed 11 April 2016.
61. Haegel, *Les Droites en fusion*, pp. 252, 265–9.
62. Henley, Jon, 'French elections: 'Front National is different. The knee-jerk racists are out', *The Guardian*, www.guardian.co.uk/world/french-election-blog-2012/2012/may/02/french-elections-front-national-different, last accessed 11 April 2016.
63. Du Roy, Ivan, '"Rassemblement Bleu Marine": bienvenue au musée des horreurs de l'extrême droite', *Basta!*, 6 June 2012, www.bastamag.net/article2452.html, last accessed 11 April.
64. Clérin, Cédric, 'France. A propos des "Faux-semblants du Front national. Sociologie d'un parti politique,"' interview with Sylvain Crépon, *À l'encontre*, http://alencontre.org/europe/france/france-a-propos-des-faux-semblants-du-front-national-sociologie-dun-parti-politique.html, last accessed 22 June 2016.
65. Mestre, Abel, 'Marine Le Pen, la "candidate antisystème" contre le "fascisme doré"', *Le Monde*, 9 April 2012, www.lemonde.fr/election-presidentielle-2012/article/2012/04/07/marine-le-pen-la-candidate-anti-

systeme-contre-le-fascisme-dore_1682247_1471069.html, last accessed 8 August 2017.

66. 'Marine Le Pen: "La bataille ne fait que commencer"', *Le Monde*, 22 April 2012, http://www.lemonde.fr/election-presidentielle-2012/article/2012/04/22/marine-le-pen-la-bataille-ne-fait-que-commencer_1689472_1471069.html, last accessed 31 July 2017.
67. See Fysh, Peter and Jim Wolfreys, *The Politics of Racism in France*, Basingstoke: Palgrave Macmillan, 2003.
68. Mathiot, Cédric, 'Immigration: Montebourg et le "consensus" PS-UMP-FN', *Libération*, 24 April 2012, http://www.liberation.fr/france/2012/04/24/immigration-quand-montebourg-evoque-un-consensus-ps-ump-fn_814026, last accessed 22 June 2016.
69. AP, 'République/Le Pen: compatible (Sarkozy)', *Le Figaro*, 27 April 2012, http://elections.lefigaro.fr/flash-presidentielle/2012/04/27/97006-20120427FILWWW00317-republique-le-pen-compatible-sarkozy.php, last accessed 22 June 2016.
70. Igounet, Valérie, *Le Front national de 1972 à nos jours, Le parti, les hommes, les idées*, Paris: Seuil, 2014, p. 420.
71. Mayer, Nonna, 'Le mythe de la dédiabolisation du FN', *La Vie des idées*, 4 December 2015. http://www.laviedesidees.fr/Le-mythe-de-la-dediabolisation-du-FN.html, last accessed 22 June 2016.
72. Lemarié, Alexandre, 'Halal: l'affirmation erronée de M. Sarkozy', *Le Monde*, 6 March 2012, www.lemonde.fr/election-presidentielle-2012/article/2012/03/06/halal-l-affirmation-erronee-de-m-sarkozy_1652325_1471069.html, last accessed 22 June 2016.
73. Tassel, Fabrice, 'Sarkozy désintègre l'immigration', *Libération*, 8 March 2012, www.liberation.fr/societe/01012394606-sarkozy-desintegre-i-immigration, last accessed 22 June 2016.
74. Equy, Laure, 'Appels de Ramadan et des 700 mosquées à voter Hollande, l'intox', *Libération*, 26 April 2012, www.liberation.fr/politiques/2012/04/26/l-intox-des-appels-de-tariq-ramadan-et-des-700-mosquees-a-voter-pour-hollande_814519, last accessed 22 June 2016.
75. 'Polémique Zemmour: "Vichy, une collaboration active et lamentable"', *Le Monde*, 18 October 2014, http://www.lemonde.fr/politique/article/2014/10/18/polemique-zemmour-vichy-une-collaboration-active-et-lamentable_4508542_823448.html, last accessed 8 August 2017.

76. 'La "machine" Zemmour', *Le Monde*, 4 April 2011, http://www.lemonde.fr/actualite-medias/article/2011/04/04/la-machine-zemmour_1502695_3236.html#d7OczHjQ00AaTRr3.99, last accessed 22 June 2016.
77. Stille, Alexander, 'The French Obsession with National Suicide', *The New Yorker*, 11 December 2014, http://www.newyorker.com/news/daily-comment/french-obsession-national-suicide, last accessed 21 June 2016.
78. Montefiori, Stefano, 'Zemmour e la rabio anti-élite', *Corriere della Serra*, 31 October 2014, http://lacittanuova.milano.corriere.it/2014/10/31/zemmour-e-la-rabbia-anti-elite/?refresh_ce-cp, last accessed 4 June 2017. See also Mélenchon, Jean-Luc, 'Zemmour se lâche en Italie: déporter cinq millions de musulmans? Ça peut se voir!', *Le Blog de Jean-Luc Mélenchon*, 15 December 2014, http://www.jean-luc-melenchon.fr/2014/12/15/zemmour-se-lache-en-italie-deporter-cinq-millions-de-musulmans-ca-peut-se-voir/, last accessed 21 June 2016. Mamère, Noël and Patrick Farbiaz, *Contre Zemmour. Réponse au Suicide Français*, Paris: Les Petits Matins, 2014. For a broader overview see Cusset, François and Meyran Régis, *La Droitisation du Monde*, Paris: Textuel, 2016.
79. Schofield, Hugh, 'France shaken up by Zemmour and "new reactionaries"', BBC News, 14 December 2014, http://www.bbc.co.uk/news/world-europe-30436692, last accessed 22 June 2016.
80. Lévy, Elizabeth, 'L'antifascisme ne passera pas', *Le Figaro*, 24 April 2002.
81. 'Élisabeth Badinter déplore qu'"en dehors de Marine Le Pen", plus personne ne défende la laïcité', *Le Monde*, 29 September 2011, http://tinyurl.com/6e77z5e, last accessed 22 June 2016.
82. Raynal, Guillaume Weill, 'Raciste, Finkielkraut? Mais oui...' *Mediapart*, 18 April 2016, https://blogs.mediapart.fr/guillaume-weill-raynal/blog/180416/raciste-finkielkraut-mais-oui, last accessed 22 June 2016.
83. Redeker, Robert, 'Face aux intimidations islamistes, que doit faire le monde libre?', *Le Figaro*, 19 September 2006, http://www.lefigaro.fr/debats/2006/09/19/01005-20060919ARTFIG90134-face_aux_intimidations_islamistes_que_doit_faire_le_monde_libre_.php, last accessed 4 June 2017.

84. ReSPUBLICA. 'Pétition à signer. Contre la barbarie, le soutien à Robert Redeker doit être sans réserve', 1 October 2006, http://www.gaucherepublicaine.org/_archive_respublica/2,article,339,,,,,,_Contre-la-barbarie-le-soutien-a-Robert-Redeker-doit-etre-sans-reserve.htm, last accessed 4 June 2017.
85. Mondon, Aurélien, *The Mainstreaming of the Extreme Right in France and Australia*, Farnham: Ashgate, 2013, pp. 136–7.
86. Fourquet, Jérôme and Marie Gariazzo, 'FN et UMP: électorats en fusion?', Fondation Jean Jaurès, 2013, pp. 102, 110.
87. Ibid., p. 60.
88. Ibid., p. 62.
89. Ibid., pp. 110–13.
90. Ibid., pp. 72–3.
91. Ibid., p. 67.
92. Ibid., pp. 52–3.
93. Ibid., p. 92.
94. Ibid., pp. 84–5.
95. Mayer, 'Le mythe de la dédiabolisation du FN'.
96. Brustier, Gaël, *Le Mai 68 conservateur. Que restera-t-il de la Manif pour tous?*, Paris: Les Éditions du Cerf, 2014.

3. MORAL PANIC SECULARISM

1. According to Henri Pena-Ruiz the word's etymology invokes the indivisible unity of the people and represents the principles of liberty and equality. See Pena-Ruiz, *Qu'est-ce que la laïcité*? Paris: Gallimard, 2003, p.21.
2. Zola, Émile, *Lettre à la France*, 7 January 1898. Cited in Edwy Plenel, *For the Muslims. Islamophobia in France*, London: Verso, 2016.
3. Sand, Shlomo, 'Secularism, the Last Refuge of the Racist', Verso blog, 25 August 2016, http://www.versobooks.com/blogs/2814-shlomo-sand-secularism-the-last-refuge-of-the-racist, last accessed 3 September 2016.
4. 'Cannes bans burkinis over suspected link to radical Islamism', BBC News, 12 August 2016, http://www.bbc.co.uk/news/world-europe-37056742, last accessed 3 September 2016.
5. Zatat, Narjas, 'The more France tries to ban the Burkini, the more Non-

Muslims are buying it', *Indy 100*, 22 August 2016, http://indy100.independent.co.uk/article/the-more-france-tries-to-ban-the-burkini-the-more-nonmuslims-are-buying-it—WyzWQIfxpPb, last accessed 22 August 2016.

6. 'Le maire de Cannes interdit le port du burkini à la plage', *Le Figaro*, 12 August 2016, http://www.lefigaro.fr/flash-actu/2016/08/11/97001-20160811FILWWW00305-le-maire-de-cannes-interdit-le-port-du-burkini-a-la-plage.php, last accessed 12 August 2016.
7. AFP, 'Mayor of Cannes bans burkinis on resort's beaches', *The Guardian*, 11 August 2016, https://www.theguardian.com/world/2016/aug/11/cannes-mayor-bans-burqinis-beachwear-must-respect-secularism, last accessed 12 August 2016.
8. Poirier, Agnes, 'Burkini beach row puts French values to the test', BBC News, 17 August 2016, http://www.bbc.co.uk/news/world-europe-37093420?SThisFB, last accessed 18 August 2016.
9. Taub, Amanda, 'France's "Burkini" Bans Are About More Than Religion or Clothing', *The New York Times*, 18 August 2016, http://www.nytimes.com/2016/08/19/world/europe/frances-burkini-bans-are-about-more-than-religion-or-clothing.html?_r=0, last accessed 19 August 2016.
10. 'Le "burkini" de la discorde', *Le Monde*, 20 August 2016, http://www.lemonde.fr/idees/article/2016/08/20/le-burkini-de-la-discorde_4985415_3232.html#cHeEplkeXO6HPkJL.99, last accessed 22 August 2016.
11. 'Manuel Valls "soutient" les maires ayant interdit le "burkini"', *Le Monde*, 17 August 2016, http://www.lemonde.fr/religions/article/2016/08/17/manuel-valls-soutient-les-maires-ayant-interdit-le-burkini_4983667_1653130.html, last accessed 20 August 2016.
12. Manuel Valls, 'En France, les femmes sont libres', *Huffington Post*, 5 September 2009, http://www.huffingtonpost.fr/manuel-valls/manuel-valls-interdiction-burkini-islam-laicite_b_11865808.html, last accessed 4 May 2017.
13. 'Manuel Valls "soutient" les maires'.
14. Parti de Gauche, 'Le burkini: la polémique qui détourne des vrais problems', *Communiqué*, 18 August 2016, https://adhesion.lepartidegauche.

fr/communique/le-burkini-la-polemique-qui-detourne-des-vrais-problemes-35031, last accessed 5 May 2017.

15. Gérard, Aline, 'Interdiction du burkini: pour Rossignol, "procéder par amalgame n'est jamais utile,"' interview with Laurence Rossignol, *Le Parisien*, 16 August 2016, http://www.leparisien.fr/politique/proceder-par-amalgame-n-est-jamais-utile-16–08–2016–6043833.php, last accessed 20 August 2016.
16. Bowen, John R., *Why the French Don't Like Headscarves: Islam, the state and public space*, Princeton, NJ: Princeton University Press, 2007, p. 12.
17. Valls, 'En France, les femmes sont libres'.
18. Bowen, *Why the French Don't Like Headscarves*, p. 32.
19. Diallo, Rokhaya and Jean Baubérot, *Comment parler de laïcité aux enfants*, Paris: Le Baron Perché, 2015, p. 6.
20. Buresi, Pascal et al, *Histoire, Tle L-ES-S: livre de l'élève*, Paris: Hatier, 2014.
21. Bowen, *Why the French Don't Like Headscarves*, pp. 32–3.
22. Ahearne, Jeremy, *Government through Culture and the Contemporary French Right*, Basingstoke: Palgrave Macmillan, 2014, p. 25. See also Weil, Patrick, *La France et ses étrangers. L'aventure d'une politique de l'immigration de 1938 à nos jours*, Paris: Gallimard, 1995.
23. See Hennette-Vauchez, Stéphanie, and Vincent Valentin, *L'Affaire Baby Loup ou la Nouvelle Laïcité*, Paris: LGDJ, L'extenso éditions, 2014.
24. Government of the French Third Republic, 'Loi du 9 décembre 1905 concernant la séparation des Eglises et de l'Etat', http://www.legifrance.gouv.fr/affichTexte.do?cidTexte=LEGITEXT000006070169&dateTexte=20080 306, last accessed 5 May 2017.
25. Baubérot, Jean, 2011, 'Élisabeth Badinter et la laïcité lepénisée', *Mediapart* (30 September), http://blogs.mediapart.fr/blog/jean-bauberot/300911/elisabeth-badinter-et-la-laicite-lepenisee, last accessed 4 September 2016.
26. Ibid.
27. Baubérot, Jean, *L'intégrisme républicain contre la laïcité*, Paris: Aube, 2006.
28. National Assembly of the French Third Republic, 'Délibérations sur le projet et les propositions de loi concernant la separation des églises

et de l'État, 12e séance du 12 avril 1905', Chambre des députés, http://classiques.uqac.ca/collection_documents/assemblee_nationale/separation_Eglises_Etat/s eance_12/debat_12_1905.pdf, last accessed 3 September 2016.

29. Plenel, Edwy, *For the Muslims: Islamophobia in France*, London: Verso, 2016, p. 47.
30. Delphy, Christine, *Separate and Dominate: Feminism and Racism after the War on Terror*, London: Verso, 2015, p. xii.
31. Ibid., p. xiii.
32. Ibid., p. xi.
33. United Nations General Assembly, 'Universal Declaration of Human Rights, Article 18', http://www.un.org/en/universal-declaration-human-rights/, last accessed 5 May 2017. Emphasis added.
34. 'Chirac contre le port du voile à l'école', *L'Obs*, 6 December 2003, http://tempsreel.nouvelobs.com/politique/20031204.OBS0762/chirac-contre-le-port-du-voile-a-l-ecole.html, last accessed 5 June 2017.
35. Tevanian, Pierre, 'Une révolution conservatrice dans la laïcité: Retour sur la loi antifoulard du 15 mars 2004', *Les mots sont importants*, 28 January 2017, http://lmsi.net/Une-revolution-conservatrice-dans, last accessed 13 November 2017.
36. Mabilon-Bonfils, Béatrice and Geneviève Zaïa, *La laïcité au risque de l'Autre*, Paris: Editions de l'Aube, 2014, p. 104.
37. 'Peillon: "Je veux qu'on enseigne la morale laïque"', *Journal du Dimanche*, interview, 1 September 2012, http://www.lejdd.fr/Societe/Education/Actualite/Vincent-Peillon-veut-enseigner-la-morale-a-l-ecole-550018, last accessed 13 August 2016.
38. Weber, Eugen, *Peasants into Frenchmen: The modernization of modern France*, 1870–1914, Stanford, CA: Stanford University Press, 1976.
39. Citron, Suzanne, 'Identité nationale et histoire de France: déconstruire le mythe national', *Aggiornamento hist-geo*, 4 April 2011, http://aggiornamento.hypotheses.org/58, last accessed 3 September 2016.
40. Bourdieu, Pierre, *Acts of Resistance: Against the tyranny of the market*, New York: The New Press, 1998.
41. Mabilon-Bonfils and Zaïa, *La laïcité au risque de l'Autre*, pp. 9–11.
42. Fassin, Eric, 'Les femmes au service de l'identité nationale', L'Observatoire des questions sexuelles et raciales, 2 November 2009.

43. Valls, 'En France, les femmes sont libres'.
44. Milewski, Françoise, 'La précarité des femmes sur le marché du travail', *Observatoire des Inégalités*, 6 March 2006, https://www.inegalites.fr/La-precarite-des-femmes-sur-le-marche-du-travail, last accessed 15 November 2017.
45. 'Violences conjugales: 118 femmes tuées en 2014', *Libération*, 11 June 2015, http://www.liberation.fr/societe/2015/06/11/violences-conjugales-118-femmes-tuees-en-2014_1327822, last accessed 5 May 2017.
46. Thouny, Laura, 'Dérapages en série sur l'affaire DSK', *L'Obs*, 13 August 2012, http://tempsreel.nouvelobs.com/justice/l-affaire-dsk/20110519.OBS3517/derapages-en-serie-sur-l-affaire-dsk.html, last accessed 3 June 2017.
47. Davies, Lizzy, 'How Dominique Strauss-Kahn's Arrest Awoke a Dormant Anger in the Heart of France's Women', *The Observer*, 22 May 2011, https://www.theguardian.com/world/2011/may/22/dominique-strauss-kahn-arrest-dormant-anger-france-women, last accessed 5 May 2017.
48. 'Finkielkraut défend Polanski: à treize ans, "ce n'était pas une enfant"', *L'Obs*, 9 October 2009, http://tempsreel.nouvelobs.com/culture/2009 1009.OBS4087/finkielkraut-defend-polanski-a-treize-ans-ce-n-etait-pas-une-enfant.html, last accessed 24 July 2017.
49. Delphy, *Separate and Dominate*, pp. 47–8.
50. Plenel, *For the Muslims*, p. 72
51. Ibid., p. 71.
52. Ibid., p. 72.
53. Sylvie Tissot, 'Qui a peur du communautarisme?', *Le Blog de Christine Delphy*, March 2016, https://christinedelphy.wordpress.com/2016/03/28/qui-a-peur-du-communautarisme/, last accessed 5 May 2017.
54. Delphy, Christine, *Separate and Dominate*.
55. Sartre, Jean-Paul, 'Anti-Semite and Jew', cited in Plenel, *For the Muslims*, p. 71.
56. See Scott, Joan Wallach, *Only Paradoxes to Offer: French Feminists and the Rights of Man*, Cambridge, MA: Harvard University Press, 1996; Scott, Joan Wallach, *Parité! Sexual Equality and the Crisis of French Universalism*, Chicago, IL: Chicago University Press, 2005; McCaffrey,

Enda, *The Gay Republic: Sexuality, Citizenship, and Subversion in France*, Aldershot: Ashgate, 2005.

57. Plenel, *For the Muslims*, p. 72.
58. Fanon, Frantz, *A Dying Colonialism*, New York: Grove Press, 1967, pp. 37–8.
59. Ibid., p. 38.
60. Ibid., p. 41.
61. See Shepard, Todd, *The Invention of Decolonization: The Algerian War and the Remaking of France*, Ithaca, NY/London: Cornell University Press, 2006.
62. Ahearne, *Government through Culture*.
63. Halimi, Gisèle, 'Laïcité: Une loi pour la cohesion', *Le Monde*, 23 October 2003.
64. *France 2*, 19 January 2004. Cited in Pierre Tevanian, *Le voile médiatique. Un faux débat: 'l'affaire du foulard islamique'*, Paris: Raisons d'agir, 2005, p. 111.
65. National Assembly of the French Fifth Republic, 'Loi no 2004–228 du 15 mars 2004 encadrant, en application du principe de laïcité, le port de signes ou de tenues manifestant une appurtenance religieuse dans les écoles, collèges et lycées publics', Legifrance.gouv.fr, https://www.legifrance.gouv.fr/eli/loi/2004/3/15/MENX0400001L/jo/texte, last accessed 8 August 2017.
66. Vincent, Faustine, "La loi sur l'interdiction de signes religieux à l'école n'a pas réglé les problèmes", *20 Minutes*, interview with Jean Baubérot, 13 March 2014, http://tinyurl.com/p8k7rdz, last accessed 4 September 2016.
67. Collectif Une Ecole Pour Toutes, 'Eléments d'un futur "livre noir". La loi anti-foulard trois ans après: bilan d'une loi d'exclusion', 15 March 2014, http://lmsi.net/Elements-d-un-futur-Livre-noir, last accessed 4 September 2016. This is the Collectif's September 2005 report, republished online by *Les mots sont importants* to mark the tenth anniversary of the 2004 law.
68. Ibid. See also, Chouder, Ismahane, Malika Latrèche and Pierre Tevanian, *Les filles voilées parlent*, Paris: La Fabrique, 2008.
69. Ibid.
70. Gros, Marie-Joëlle, 'Deux soeurs voilées divisent un lycée', *Libération*,

22 September 2003, http://www.liberation.fr/societe/2003/09/22/deux-soeurs-voilees-divisent-un-lycee_445665, last accessed 4 September 2016.

71. Delphy, *Separate and Dominate*, p. 142.
72. Henley, Jon, 'Veil ban may extend to "religious" beards', *The Guardian*, 21 January 2004, www.theguardian.com/world/2004/jan/21/france.religion, last accessed 4 September 2016.
73. Collectif contre l'Islamophobie en France (CCIF), 'Délit de robe longue: le nouveau scandale islamophobe', *Saphir News*, 17 March 2011, www.saphirnews.com/Delit-de-robe-longue-le-nouveau-scandale-islamophobe_a12344.html, last accessed 4 September 2016; *Saphir News*, 2012, 'Islamophobie latente: un nouveau "délit de jupe longue" dans le Val-d'Oise', 29 March 2012, http://tinyurl.com/olm5w68, last accessed 4 September 2016.
74. Bernard Guetta, stepbrother of the jet-set DJ David Guetta, on *France-Inter*, 20 September 2013—see Teissier, Jacques, 'Sur France Inter, après le foulard, c'est la barbe!', *Mediapart*, 20 September 2013, http://tinyurl.com/mmfvfsh, last accessed 4 September 2016.
75. C.F. and *Reuters*, 'Laïcité: Le voile banni des sorties scolaires', *20 minutes*, 3 March 2011, http://www.20minutes.fr/societe/680352–20110303-societe-laicite-voile-banni-sorties-scolaires, last accessed 24 July 2017.
76. Malik, Maleiha, 'Full-face veils aren't barbaric—but our response can be', *The Guardian*, 17 September 2013, http://tinyurl.com/pgtbvpf, last accessed 4 September 2016.
77. National Assembly of the French Fifth Republic, 'Extrait du compte rendu du Conseil des ministres du 19/05/10', www.assemblee-nationale.fr/13/dossiers/dissimulation_visage_espace_public.asp, last accessed 4 September 2016.
78. Beyer, Caroline, 'Éric Raoult hospitalisé alors qu'il devait être jugé', *Le Figaro*, 30 November 2012, http://tinyurl.com/cbyc8tk, last accessed 5 May 2017.
79. Duportail, Judith, 'Eric Raoult accusé de harcèlement sexuel', *Le Figaro*, 17 March 2014, http://tinyurl.com/qy5y3a8, last accessed 4 September 2016.
80. Sulzer, Alexandre, 'Eric Raoult accusé de harcèlement sexuel: "Elle

n'hésitait pas à montrer son corps"', *L'Express*, 18 March 2014, http://www.lexpress.fr/actualite/politique/eric-raoult-accuse-de-harcelement-sexuel-elle-n-hesitait-pas-a-montrer-son-corps_1501175.html, last accessed 10 August 2017.

81. Mélenchon, Jean-Luc, 'Je parle du voile intégral', Le Blog de Jean-Luc Mélenchon, 7 January 2010, www.jean-luc-melenchon.fr/2010/01/07/je-parle-du-voile-integral, last accessed 4 September 2016.
82. Hennette-Vauchez, Stéphanie, and Vincent Valentin, *L'Affaire Baby Loup ou la Nouvelle Laïcité*, Paris: LGDJ, L'extenso éditions, 2014.
83. Mabilon-Bonfils and Zaïa, *La laïcité au risque de l'Autre*, pp. 8–9.
84. Ibid., p. 23.
85. Philippon, Baptistine, 'Bondy: une directrice d'école veut obliger les élèves à manger de la viande', *Le Figaro*, 23 April 2013, http://www.lefigaro.fr/actualite-france/2013/04/23/01016–20130423ARTFIG00535-bondy-une-directrice-d-ecole-veut-obliger-les-eleves-a-manger-de-la-viande.php, last accessed 5 May 2017.
86. Aphatie, Jean-Michel, 'Luc Chatel: "La réponse aux violences scolaires n'est pas que dans les moyens"', *RTL*, 17 February 2010, http://www.rtl.fr/actu/politique/luc-chatel-la-reponse-aux-violences-scolaires-n-est-pas-que-dans-les-moyens-video-5933073674, last accessed 4 June 2017.
87. 'Jugés trop communautaires, les hamburgers halal de Quick font polémique', *La Dépêche*, 17 February 2010, http://www.ladepeche.fr/article/2010/02/17/779369-juges-trop-communautaires-les-hamburgers-halal-de-quick-font-polemique.html, last accessed 4 September 2016.
88. Daboval, Adeline, 'Hauts-de-Seine: la supérette ne vend ni porc ni alcool, la mairie veut l'expulser', *Le Parisien*, 4 August 2016, http://www.leparisien.fr/colombes-92700/la-superette-ne-vend-ni-porc-ni-alcool-la-mairie-de-colombes-veut-l-expulser-03–08–2016–6013481.php, last accessed 4 September 2016.
89. Fruchard, Quentin, 'À Colombes, la mairie s'oppose à une supérette halal', *La Croix*, 11 August 2016, http://www.la-croix.com/France/A-Colombes-la-mairie-s-oppose-a-une-superette-halal-2016-08-11-1200781641, last accessed 5 September 2016.

90. Baubérot, Jean, 'Élisabeth Badinter et la laïcité lepénisée', *Mediapart*, 30 September 2011, http://blogs.mediapart.fr/blog/jean-bauberot/300911/elisabeth-badinter-et-la-laicite-lepenisee, last accessed 4 September 2016.
91. Mabilon-Bonfils and Zaïa, *La laïcité au risque de l'Autre*, p. 22.
92. Mabilon-Bonfils and Zaïa, *La laïcité au risque de l'Autre*, p. 104.
93. Ahearne, *Government through Culture*, pp. 19–20.
94. Ibid., p. 28.
95. Ibid., pp. 28–9.
96. Ibid.
97. Chrisafis, Angelique, 'Sarkozy declares war on elitism and offers return to liberty, equality and fraternity', *The Guardian*, 18 December 2008, https://www.theguardian.com/world/2008/dec/18/sarkozy-diversity-policy-france-obama, last accessed 16 August 2017.
98. Hargreaves, Alec G., 'Veiled truths: discourses of ethnicity in contemporary France', in Hsu, Roland (ed.), *Ethnic Europe: Mobility, Identity and Conflict in a Globalized World*, Stanford, CA: Stanford University Press, 2010, p. 98.
99. 'Lettre de Rachida Dati à François Fillon: 'Votre arrivée est une faute, une faute triste'', *Le Monde*, 12 December 2011, http://www.lemonde.fr/idees/article/2011/12/12/lettre-de-mme-dati-a-m-fillon-votre-arrivee-est-une-faute-une-faute-triste_1617473_3232.html, last accessed 24 July 2017.
100. 'Un ex-conseiller à l'Elysée accuse Copé d'islamophobie', *Le Point*, 22 March 2011, http://www.lepoint.fr/politique/un-ex-conseiller-a-l-elysee-accuse-cope-d-islamophobie-22–03–2011–1309850_20.php, last accessed 4 June 2017.
101. 'Un ex-conseiller de Sarkozy appelle les musulmans à porter une étoile verte', 28 March 2011, *Libération*, http://www.liberation.fr/france/2011/03/28/un-ex-conseiller-de-sarkozy-appelle-les-musulmans-a-porter-une-etoile-verte_725014, last accessed 4 June 2017.
102. Government of the French Fifth Republic, 'La laïcité aujourd'hui, note d'orientation de l'Observatoire de la laïcité', Observatoire de la laïcité, 27 May 2014, http://www.gouvernement.fr/la-laicite-aujourd-hui-note-d-orientation-de-l-observatoire-de-la-laicite, last accessed 7 September 2016.

103. Ba, Diadie, 'Africans still seething over Sarkozy speech', *Reuters*, 5 September 2007, http://uk.reuters.com/article/uk-africa-sarkozy-idUKL0513034620070905, last accessed 16 August 2017.
104. Ibid.
105. Ibid.
106. Pago, Gilbert, 'Fillon, à l'aise dans le cambouis identitariste!', *Mediapart*, 4 September 2016, https://blogs.mediapart.fr/gilbertpago/blog/040916/fillon-l-aise-dans-le-cambouis-identitariste, last accessed 8 September 2016.
107. 'Chevènement conseille la "discrétion" aux musulmans', *Le Figaro*, 15 August 2016, http://www.lefigaro.fr/actualite-france/2016/08/15/01016–20160815ARTFIG00078-chevenement-conseille-la-discretion-aux-musulmans.php, last accessed 8 September 2016.
108. 'Chevènement s'attire les foudres d'élus de Seine-Saint-Denis', *Libération*, 28 August 2016, http://www.liberation.fr/direct/element/chevenement-sattire-les-foudres-delus-de-seine-saint-denis_46264/, last accessed 8 September 2016.
109. 'Fondation de l'islam de France: M. Chevènement dénonce les 'procès d'intention fielleux', *Le Monde*, 31 August 2016, http://www.lemonde.fr/religions/article/2016/08/31/fondation-de-l-islam-de-france-m-chevenement-denonce-les-proces-d-intention-fielleux_4990144_1653130.html, last accessed 5 May 2017.
110. Bozzo, Anna, 'Islam et République: une longue histoire de méfiance', in Bancel, Nicolas, Pascal Blanchard and Sandrine Lemaire (eds), *La Fracture coloniale. La société française au prisme de l'héritage colonial*, Paris: La Découverte, 2006.
111. Lavisse, Ernest, *Histoire de France, cours élémentaire*, Paris: Armand Colin, 1913, available at http://ldh-toulon.net/Les-conquetes-de-la-France-par.html, last accessed 8 September 2016.
112. Valls, 'En France, les femmes sont libres'.
113. Lebrun, Céline, 'Une religion sous tutelle. Islam et État en France: de la république coloniale à la république post-coloniale (Deuxième partie)', *Les mots sont importants*, 26 July 2012, http://lmsi.net/Une-religion-sous-tutelle, last accessed 8 September 2016.
114. Valls, 'En France, les femmes sont libres'.

115. Tevanian, *Le voile médiatique*, pp. 118–9.
116. Chrisafis, Angelique, 'Nicolas Sarkozy says Islamic veils are not welcome in France', *The Guardian*, 22 June 2009, https://www.theguardian.com/world/2009/jun/22/islamic-veils-sarkozy-speech-france, last accessed 9 September 2016.
117. Piketty, Thomas, 'Le gouvernement souhaite-t-il vraiment la mixité sociale?', Le Blog de Thomas Piketty, *Le Monde*, 31 August 2016, http://piketty.blog.lemonde.fr/2016/08/31/le-gouvernement-souhaite-t-il-vraiment-la-mixite-sociale/, last accessed 9 September 2016.
118. Vallaud-Belkacem, Najat, 'On ne peut pas "imposer autoritairement la mixité sociale" au college', *Le Monde*, 7 September 2016, http://www.lemonde.fr/education/article/2016/09/07/mixite-au-college-il-faut-rompre-avec-le-mythe-francais-du-grand-soir-politico-technocratique_4993678_1473685.html, last accessed 9 September 2016.
119. Tevanian, *Le voile médiatique*, pp. 126–9.
120. Bouamama, Saïd, *Les classes et quartiers populaires. Paupérisation, ethnicisation et discrimination*, Paris: Editions du Cygne, 2009, pp. 70–71.
121. Delphy, *Separate and Dominate*, pp. 142–3.
122. Tevanian, *Le voile médiatique*, p. 127.
123. Martin, Guy, 'French Riviera 2015: On the Beach with Leo, Heidi, and King Salman of Saudi Arabia', *Forbes*, 31 July 2015, http://www.forbes.com/sites/guymartin/2015/07/31/french-riviera-2015-on-the-beach-with-leonardo-dicaprio-heidi-klum-simon-cowell-and-king-salman-of-saudi-arabia/2/#4b220244230b, last accessed 11 January 2017.

4. CONFRONTING INEQUALITY

1. Piketty, Thomas, *Capital in the Twenty-First Century*, Cambridge, MA/London: Harvard University Press, 2014.
2. 'Inherited Wealth', *The Economist*, 8 March 2014, http://www.economist.com/blogs/buttonwood/2014/03/inequality, last accessed 11 January 2017; Piketty, Capital, pp. 288–96.
3. 'Sondage IPSOS-SPF 2016', *Convergence*, September–October 2016, http://www.spf75.org/sites/default/files/les_francais_et_la_sante_sondage_ipsos-spf_2016.pdf, last accessed 11 January 2017.

4. 'Le inégalités continuent d'augmenter en France', *Observatoire des inégalités*, 24 September 2015, http://www.inegalites.fr/spip.php?page=article&id_article=2088, last accessed 11 January 2017.
5. OECD, 'Tous concernés: Pourquoi moins d'inégalité profite à tous', 21 May 2015, http://www.keepeek.com/Digital-Asset-Management/oecd/employment/tous-concernes-pourquoi-moins-d-inegalite-profite-a-tous_9789264235519-fr#page36, last accessed 8 May 2017.
6. OECD, 'In It Together: Why Less Inequality Benefits All', 21 May 2015, http://www.oecd.org/social/in-it-together-why-less-inequality-benefits-all-9789264235120-en.htm, last accessed 11 January 2017.
7. Boiron, Antoine, Michel Huwer and Julie Labarthe, 'Inégalités de niveaux de vie et pauvreté en 2013', in Boiron, Antoine and Julie Labarthe (eds), *Les revenues et le patrimoine des ménages, Edition 2016*, INSEE: Paris, 2016, p. 13.
8. *Observatoire des inégalités*, 'Un million de pauvres de plus en dix ans', 20 December 2016, http://www.inegalites.fr/spip.php?article270, last accessed 11 January 2017.
9. OECD, 'Tous concernés'.
10. Maurin, Louis, 'Non, on ne peut pas vraiment parler de baisse des inégalités en France', *Slate*, 29 September 2015, http://www.slate.fr/story/107495/non-inegalites-baisse-france, last accessed 11 January 2017.
11. Guilluy, Christophe, *Fractures françaises*, Paris: Flammarion, 2013, p. 81.
12. Chauvel, Louis, *Les classes moyennes à la derive*, Paris: Seuil, 2006, p. 23.
13. Ibid.
14. 'Une peur record de la pauvreté', *Convergence*, September–October 2015, https://www.secourspopulaire.fr/sites/default/files/atoms/files/convergence_344-dossier-barometre-une-peur-record-de-le-pauvrete.pdf, last accessed 11 January 2017.
15. 'La France inégale', *Alternatives économiques*, February 2006, http://www.alternatives-economiques.fr/la-france-inegale_fr_art_197_22786.html, last accessed 11 January 2017.
16. Chauvel, *Les classes moyennes*, pp. 11–12.
17. Furet, François, Jacques Julliard, Pierre Rosanvallon, *La République du centre. La fin de l'exception française*, Paris: Calmann-Lévy, 1988.

18. Chauvel, *Les classes moyennes*, pp. 88–9.
19. Simon, Patrick and Joan Stavo-Debauge, 'Les politiques anti-discrimination et les statistiques: paramètres d'une incohérence', *Sociétés contemporaines*, no. 54, 2004, pp. 57–84.
20. Simon, Patrick, 'L'arbre du racisme et la forêt des discriminations', in Guénif-Souilamas, Nacira, *La République mise à nu par son immigration*, Paris: La Fabrique, 2006, pp. 161–2.
21. Ibid., p. 172.
22. Simon and Stavo-Debauge, 'Les politiques anti-discrimination.'
23. Simon, Patrick, 'La question des statistiques ethniques en France', in Poinsot, Marie and Serge Weber, *Migrations et mutations de la société française, l'état des savoirs*, Paris: La Découverte, 2014, p. 304.
24. Beauchemin, Cris, Christelle Hamel and Patrick Simon (eds), *Trajectoires et origines. Enquête sur la diversité des populations en France*, Paris: Ined, 2015, http://teo.site.ined.fr/fichier/rte/General/Publications/Grandes%20enqu%C3%AAtes/TeO-fascicule.pdf, last accessed 8 May 2017.
25. Baumard, Maryline, 'Emploi, école: les réussites et le blocages de l'intégration en France', *Le Monde*, 8 January 2016, http://www.lemonde.fr/societe/article/2016/01/08/les-enfants-d-immigres-s-integrent-mais-restent-victimes-du-chomage-et-de-la-discrimination_4843872_3224.html#OTQiS70y6rq1Cp5I.99, last accessed 11 January 2017.
26. Baumard, 'Emploi, école'.
27. Baumard, Maryline, 'La population française a pris conscience qu'elle vit dans une société multiculturelle', interview with Patrick Simon, *Le Monde*, 8 January 2016, http://www.lemonde.fr/immigration-et-diversite/article/2016/01/08/la-population-francaise-a-pris-conscience-quelle-vit-dans-une-societe-multiculturelle_4843938_1654200.html, last accessed 8 May 2017.
28. Baumard, 'Emploi, école'.
29. Ibid.
30. Beauchemin et al, *Trajectoires et origines*, p. 14.
31. Beaud, Stéphane and Olivier Masclet, 'Des "marcheurs" de 1983 aux "émeutiers" de 2005. Deux générations sociales d'enfants d'immigrés', *Annales. Histoire, Sciences Sociales*, 2006, no. 4, pp. 809–43.

32. Simon, Patrick, 'L'arbre du racisme'.
33. Vidal, Dominique, 'Quand Jean-Christophe Rufin prône le délit d'opinion', *Le Monde Diplomatique*, 21 October 2004, https://www.monde-diplomatique.fr/carnet/2004–10–21-rufin, last accessed 11 January 2017.
34. Marelli, Joëlle, 'Usages et maléfices du thème de l'anti-sémitisme', in Guénif-Souilamas, *La République mise à nu*, p. 150.
35. Bouamama, Saïd, 'De la visibilisation à la suspicion: la fabrique républicaine d'une politique', in Guénif-Souilamas, *La République mise à nu*, p. 211.
36. Taubira, Christiane, 'Seule une mémoire vivante tient l'homme en état de parole', in Belaïd, Chakri (ed.), *Banlieue, lendemains de révolte*, Paris: La Dispute, 2006, p. 133.
37. Sagot-Duvauroux, Jean-Louis, 'Le "nous" manquant', in Belaïd (ed), *Banlieue, lendemains de révolte*, p. 111.
38. Cited in Esteves, Olivier, 'Quel sens y a-t-il à parler de "génération d'immigrés"?', *Délinquance, justice et autres questions de société*, https://www.laurent-mucchielli.org/index.php?post/2012/01/20/Quel-sens-y-a-t-il-a-parler-de-generation-d-immigres, last accessed 11 January 2017.
39. Bouamama, 'De la visibilisation à la suspicion', p. 212.
40. Les Décodeurs, 'François Hollande, Marianne et le voile: ce qu'il a vraiment dit', *Le Monde*, 12 October 2016, http://www.lemonde.fr/les-decodeurs/article/2016/10/12/francois-hollande-marianne-et-le-voile-ce-qu-il-a-vraiment-dit_5012374_4355770.html, last accessed 11 January 2017.
41. Bouamama, Saïd, *Les classes et quartiers populaires. Paupérisation, ethnicisation et discrimination*, Paris: Editions du Cygne, 2009, p. 165.
42. Mucchielli, Laurent, 'Immigration et délinquance: fantasmes et réalités', in Guénif-Souilamas, *La République mise à nu*, p. 58.
43. Kokoreff, Michel, *La Force des quartiers. De la délinquance à l'engagement politique*, Paris: Payot, 2003, p. 102.
44. Guénif-Souilamas, Nacira, 'La Française voilée, la beurette, le garçon arabe et le musulman laïc. Les figures assignées du racisme vertueux', in Guénif-Souilamas, *La République mise à nu*, pp. 118–21.

45. Ibid.
46. Mucchielli, Laurent and Véronique Le Goaziou, *Retour sur les émeutes de novembre 2005*, Paris: La Découverte, 2007; Collectif, *Une Révolte en toute logique. Des banlieues en colère, November 2005*, Sainte Colombe: L'Archipel des Pirates, 2006.
47. 'Une Présence durable des CRS dans les banlieues', *TF1*, 12 November 2005, http://lci.tf1.fr/france/2005–11/presence-durable-crs-dans-banlieues-4860968.html, last accessed 12 January 2017.
48. 'French Muslims Face Job Discrimination', *BBC News*, 2 November 2005, http://news.bbc.co.uk/1/hi/world/europe/4399748.stm, last accessed 12 January 2017.
49. Arnold, Martin, 'French Minister Says Polygamy to Blame for Riots', *Financial Times*, 15 November 2005, http://www.ft.com/cms/s/0/d6f1fe0a-5615–11da-b04f-00000e25118c.html#axzz2Tuzsn6c2, last accessed 12 January 2017.
50. Wakim, Nabil, 'Pourquoi les chiffres sur la polygamie sont inexactes', *Le Monde*, 10 June 2010, http://www.lemonde.fr/politique/article/2010/06/10/pourquoi-les-chiffres-sur-la-polygamie-sont-inexacts_1370633_823448.html, last accessed 12 January 2017.
51. *RTL*, 16 November 2005.
52. Jeambar, Denis, 'Nicolas Sarkozy contre-attaque', *L'Express*, 17 November 2005, http://www.lexpress.fr/actualite/politique/nicolas-sarkozy-contre-attaque_483925.html, last accessed 12 January 2017.
53. Millot, Lorraine, 'Beaucoup de ces Africains sont polygames', *Libération*, 15 November 2005, http://www.liberation.fr/evenement/2005/11/15/beaucoup-de-ces-africains-sont-polygames_539018, last accessed 11 January 2017.
54. Belien, Paul, 'Too Many Wives Causes Unrest', *The Brussels Journal*, 16 November 2005, http://www.brusselsjournal.com/node/479, last accessed 12 January 2017.
55. Joël Roman, 'Pourquoi la laïcité?', in Guénif-Souilamas, Nacira (ed.), *La République mise à nu par son immigration*, Paris: La Fabrique, 2006.
56. Hargreaves, Alec G., *Multi-Ethnic France: Immigration, Politics, Culture and Society*, Taylor and Francis, 2007, pp. 109, 5.
57. Mishani, Dror and Aurelia Smotriez, 'What Sort of Frenchmen are

They?', *Haaretz*, 17 November 17 2005, http://www.haaretz.com/what-sort-of-frenchmen-are-they-1.174419, last accessed 12 January 2017.

58. Ben Simon, Daniel, 'France's Sarkozy Backs Beleaguered Finkielkraut over Muslim Riot Comments', *Haaretz*, 6 December 2005, http://www.haaretz.com/print-edition/news/france-s-sarkozy-backs-beleaguered-finkielkraut-over-muslim-riot-comments-1.176010, last accessed 12 January 2017.
59. Cozens, Claire, 'Saudi prince changes Fox's Paris riots coverage', The Guardian, 12 December 2005, https://www.theguardian.com/media/2005/dec/12/newscorporation.rupertmurdoch, last accessed 11 August 2017.
60. 'Nicolas Sarkozy continue de vilipender "racailles et voyous"', *Le Monde*', 11 November 2005, http://www.lemonde.fr/societe/article/2005/11/11/nicolas-sarkozy-persiste-et-signe-contre-les-racailles_709112_3224.html, last accessed 11 August 2017.
61. Michèle Tribalat, *Faire France*, Paris: La Découverte, 1995, p. 97. Cited in Kokoreff, *La Force des quartiers*, p. 114.
62. Wolfreys, Jim, 'Regroupment and retrenchment on the Radical Left in France', *Journal of Contemporary European Studies*, vol. 16, no. 1 (2008), p. 76.
63. Szecinski, Romain, 'Les émeutes de novembre 2005, un an après. Une révolte salutaire délaissée par la gauche', *Socialisme international*, http://revuesocialisme.pagesperso-orange.fr/s17romain.html, last accessed 8 May 2017.
64. Beaud, Stéphane and Olivier Masclet, 'From the "Marchers" of 1983 to the "Rioters" of 2005: Two Generations of the Children of Immigration', *Annales Histoire, Sciences Sociales*, 2006/4, p. 809–43, http://www.cairn-int.info/article-E_ANNA_614_0809—fr/s17romain.html, last accessed 8 May 2017. See Chapter Five for a discussion of this supposed 'political vacuum' in the *banlieues*, and the relationship between the political left and those living in racialised communities.
65. Mucchielli, Laurent, 'Immigration et délinquance: fantasme et réalités', in Guénif-Souilamas, *La République mise à nu*, pp. 55–9.

66. Maurin, Eric, *Le Ghetto Français. Enquête sur le Séparatisme Social*, Paris: Seuil, 2004, p. 18.
67. Ibid., pp. 15–17.
68. See, for example, Pinçon-Charlot, Michel and Monique, *Sociologie de la bourgeoisie*, Paris: La Découverte, 2007; *Les ghettos du gotha. Comment la bourgeoisie défend ses espaces*, Paris: Seuil, 2007; Pinçon-Charlot, Michel and Monique, *La violence des riches. Chronique d'une immense casse sociale*, Paris: Zones, 2013.
69. Tissot, Sylvie, 'Le Repli communautaire: un concept policier. Analyse d'un rapport des Renseignements Généraux sur les "quartiers sensibles"', *Les mots sont importants*, October 2004, http://lmsi.net/Le-repli-communautaire-un-concept, last accessed 12 January 2017.
70. Ferrand, Olivier, Romain Prudent and Bruno Jeanbart, 'Gauche: quelle majorité électorale pour 2012?', 10 May 2011, http://tnova.fr/rapports/gauche-quelle-majorite-electorale-pour-2012, last accessed 8 May 2017.
71. Bekmezian, Hélène and Bastien Bonnefous, 'La bataille de la Gauche populaire pour éviter un "21 avril bis"', *Le Monde*, 14 November 2012, http://www.lemonde.fr/politique/article/2012/11/13/la-bataille-de-la-gauche-populaire-pour-eviter-un-21-avril-bis_1789688_823448.html, last accessed 12 January 2017.
72. Guilluy was invited to the Élysée palace by both Sarkozy and Hollande and was cited several times in Macron's book *Révolution*. The financial daily *Les Echos* referred to his *La France périphérique*, highly praised by Front National vice-president Florian Philippot, as the FN's 'beside reading': G.C., 'Opération séduction de Le Pen auprès de la France périphérique', *Les Echos*, 13 March 2017, https://www.lesechos.fr/13/03/2017/LesEchos/22402-011-ECH_operation-seduction-de-le-pen-aupres-de-la-france-peripherique.htm#3OFvIt5qYPHgt7qr.99, last accessed 11 August 2017. After the first round of the 2017 presidential election, Guilluy was presented by *Le Figaro* as the man who had foreseen the Macron/Le Pen stand-off: Devecchio, Alexandre, 'Guilluy, l'homme qui avait tout vu', *Le Figaro*, 27 April 2017, http://www.lefigaro.fr/vox/politique/2017/04/26/31001-20170426ARTFIG00356-guilluy-l-homme-qui-avait-tout-vu.php, last accessed 11 August 2017.

73. 'Immigration et vote FN', *Le Monde*, 28 May 2014, http://www.lemonde.fr/les-decodeurs/breve/2014/05/26/immigration-et-vote-fn_4426256_4355770.html, last accessed 8 May 2017.
74. For a discussion of this question see Fysh, Peter and Jim Wolfreys, *The Politics of Racism in France*, Basingstoke: Palgrave Macmillan, 2003, pp. 75–7; and Jolly, Seth K. and Gerald M. DiGiusto, 'Xenophobia and immigrant contact: French public attitudes toward immigration', *The Social Science Journal*, vol. 51, no. 3 (September 2014), pp. 464–73, http://www.sciencedirect.com/science/article/pii/S0362331913001468, last accessed 20 September 2017.
75. Charmes, Eric, 'Une France contre l'autre', *La vie des idées.fr*, 5 November 2014, http://www.laviedesidees.fr/Une-France-contre-l-autre.html, last accessed 12 January 2017.
76. Laurent, Samuel, '7 idées reçues sur l'immigration et les immigrés en France', *Le Monde*, 6 August 2014, http://www.lemonde.fr/les-decodeurs/article/2014/08/06/sept-idees-recues-sur-l-immigration-et-les-immigres_4467506_4355770.html, last accessed 20 September 2017.
77. 'L'immigration en France, quelles réactions des salaires et de l'emploi?', *La Lettre du CEPII*, no. 347 (September 2014).
78. See Mouhoud, El Mouhoub, 'Quelles sont les conséquences de l'immigration dans les pays riches?', *Regards croisés sur l'économie*, vol. 2, no 8 (2010), pp. 138–41; Chojnicki, Xavier, 'The Fiscal Impact of Immigration in France: A Generational Accounting Approach', *The World Economy*, no. 36, no. 8 (2013), pp. 1065–90; Borjas, George J., 'The labor demand curve is downward sloping: Reexamining the impact of immigration on the labor market', *Quarterly Journal of Economics*, no. 118 (2003), pp. 1335–74; Manacorda, Marco, Alan Manning and Jonathan Wadsworth, 'The impact of immigration on the structure of wages: theory and evidence from Britain', *Journal of the European Economic Association*, no. 10 (2012), pp. 120–51; Rowthorn, Robert, 'The fiscal impact of immigration on the advanced economies', *Oxford Review of Policy*, no. 24, vol. 3 (2008), pp. 560–80; Dustmann, Christian, Tommaso Frattini and Caroline Halls, 'Asssessing the fiscal costs and benefits of A8 migration to the UK', *Fiscal Studies*, no. 31, no. 1 (2010), pp. 1–41.
79. Héricourt, Jérôme and Gilles Spielvogel, 'Perception publique de

l'immigration et discours médiatique', *La vie des idées.fr*, 18 December 2012, http://www.laviedesidees.fr/Perception-publique-de-l.html, last accessed 12 January 2016.

80. OECD, *International Migration Outlook 2010*, OECD: Paris, 2010, p. 142, available at https://www.oecd.org/migration/48350703.pdf, last accessed 12 January 2016.
81. Héricourt and Spielvogel, 'Perception publique de l'immigration'; Mouhoud, 'Quelles sont les conséquences de l'immigration dans les pays riches?'
82. 'Immigration et réfugiés: France, pays d'accueil ou pays en repli?', *Ipsos*, 22 August 2016, http://www.ipsos.fr/decrypter-societe/2016–08-22-immigration-et-refugies-france-pays-d-accueil-ou-pays-en-repli, last accessed 12 January 2016.
83. Lacroix-Lanoë, Cécile, 'Les Français sont-ils racistes?', *Délits d'opinion*, 26 November 2014, http://delitsdopinion.com/1analyses/les-francais-sont-ils-racistes-17617/, last accessed 12 January 2017.
84. 'Immigration: Trop de migrants? Sondage Ipsos sur la perception mondiale vis-à-vis de l'immigration', *EU-Logos*, 30 August 2016, https://eulogos.blogactiv.eu/2016/08/30/immigration-trop-de-migrants-sondage-ipsos-sur-la-perception-mondiale-vis-a-vis-de-limmigration/, last accessed 12 January 2017.
85. 'Immigration: Trop de migrants?', *EU-Logos*.
86. Gemenne, François, 'Migration: réaligner les discours publics sur les réalités', *Alternatives Sud*, vol. 22, no. 1 (2015), pp. 7–23, http://www.cetri.be/Migrations-realigner-les-discours?lang=fr, last accessed 12 January 2017.
87. 'Vous avez dit préjugés?', *Ipsos*, http://www.ipsos.fr/decrypter-societe/2014–11–20-vous-avez-dit-prejuges, last accessed 12 January 2017. Full tables can be found here: http://perils.ipsos.com/archive/, last accessed 12 January 2017.
88. Lacroix-Lanoë, 'Les Français sont-ils racistes?'
89. See Pialoux, Michel and Stéphane Beaud, *Retour sur la condition ouvrière. Enquête aux usines Peugeot de Sochaux-Montbéliard*, Paris: La Découverte, 2012. See also Masclet, Olivier, *La gauche et les cités. Enquête sur un rendez-vous manqué*, Paris: La Dispute, 2003.

90. Charmes, Eric, 'Une France contre l'autre? À propos de: Christophe Guilluy, *La France périphérique. Comment on a sacrifié les classes populaires*, Flammarion', *La Vie des idées*, 5 November 2014, http://www.laviedesidees.fr/Une-France-contre-l-autre.html, last accessed 11 August 2017.
91. Bouamama, *Les classes et quartiers populaires*, pp. 77–8.
92. 'François Fillon: "La France n'est pas une nation multiculturelle"', *RTL*, 24 November 2016, http://www.rtl.fr/actu/politique/francois-fillon-la-france-n-est-pas-une-nation-multiculturelle-7785965830, last accessed 9 May 2017.
93. Davies, William, 'The New Neoliberalism', *New Left Review*, no. 101 (September–October 2016), https://newleftreview.org/II/101/william-davies-the-new-neoliberalism, last accessed 12 January 2017.
94. Guilluy, Christophe, *La France périphérique. Comment on a sacrifié les classes populaires*, Paris: Flammarion, 2014, pp. 84–8.
95. See, for example, Jones, Owen, *Chavs: The Demonization of the Working Class*, London: Verso, 2011; Isenberg, Nancy, *White Trash: The 400 Year-Old Untold Story of Class in America*, New York: Viking, 2016; and, from a less convincing perspective: Patricot, Aymeric, *Les Petits Blancs: Un voyage dans la France d'en bas*, Paris: Plein Jour, 2013.

5. '*TOUS ENSEMBLE*'? ISLAMOPHOBIA AND ANTI-RACISM

1. 'Sarkozy organise l'évacuation de la fac', *L'Obs*, 13 March 2006, http://tempsreel.nouvelobs.com/societe/social/20060311.OBS0159/sarkozy-organise-l-evacuation-de-la-fac.html, last accessed 10 June 2017.
2. Amable, Bruno and Stefano Palombarini, *L'illusion du bloc bourgeois. Alliances sociales et avenir du modèle français*, Paris: Raisons d'agir, 2017, pp. 85–6.
3. See Fysh, Peter and Jim Wolfreys, *The Politics of Racism in France*, Basingstoke: Palgrave Macmillan, 2003.
4. On the social movement to 2007 see Stathis Kouvelakis, *La France en Révolte. Luttes sociales et cycles politiques*, Paris: Textuel, 2007; and Jim Wolfreys, 'France in Revolt 1995–2005', *International Socialism*, no. 109 (Winter 2006).

5. The legislation's full title was 'Loi relative au travail, à la modernisation du dialogue social et à la sécurisation des parcours professionnels'.
6. With, Moschonas notes, the possible exception of the Enlightenment bourgeoisie.
7. See Moschonas, Gerassismos, *In the Name of Social Democracy: The Great Transformation, 1945 to the Present*, London: Verso, 2002.
8. Cassely, Jean-Laurent, 'Le temps des inégalités dont vous êtes le héros', *Slate*, 21 December 2015, http://www.slate.fr/story/109019/inegalites-dont-vous-etes-le-heros, last accessed 10 June 2017.
9. Maurin, Eric, *L'Egalité des possibles: La nouvelle société française*, Paris: Seuil, 2002, pp. 10–11.
10. *Observatoire des inégalités*, '3,4 millions de salariés précaires en France', 7 October 2016, http://www.inegalites.fr/spip.php?page=article&id_article=957&id_rubrique=131&id_groupe=11&id_mot=89, last accessed 10 June 2017.
11. See Mayer, Nonna, *Ces Français qui votent FN*, Paris: Flammarion, 1999, pp. 75–97.
12. Dubet, François (ed.), *Inégalités et justice sociale*, Paris: La Découverte, 2014; Savidan, Patrick, *Voulons-nous vraiment l'égalité?*, Paris: Albin Michel, 2015.
13. Pernot, Jean-Marie, 'Pleins et déliés de la contestation. Du repli de la grève au mouvement sur les retraites', in Sophie Béroud et René Mouriaux, *L'année sociale 2003–4*, Paris: Syllepse, 2004, p. 134.
14. Larose, Christain, Sophie Béroud, René Mouriaux and Maurad Rabhi, *Cellatex: Quand l'acide a coulé*, Paris: Syllepse, 2001.
15. Hayes, Graeme, 'Bossnapping: Situating Repertoires of Industrial Action in National and Global Contexts', *Modern and Contemporary France*, vol. 20, no. 2 (2012), pp. 185–201.
16. Borredon, Laurent, Soren Seelow and Guy Dutheil, 'Air France: récit d'une manifestation qui a dégénéré', *Le Monde*, 14 October 2015, http://www.lemonde.fr/entreprises/article/2015/10/14/air-france-recit-d-une-manifestation-qui-a-degenere_4789209_1656994.html, last accessed 10 June 2017.
17. Chouder, Ismahane, Malika Latrèche and Pierre Tevanian, *Les filles voilées parlent*, Paris: La Fabrique, 2008, p. 288.

18. Ibid., p. 74.
19. Ibid., pp. 226–7.
20. Ibid., p. 315.
21. Tevanian, Pierre, *La haine de la religion*, Paris: La Découverte, 2013, p. 92.
22. Ibid., pp. 95–100.
23. Rodinson, Maxime, *Marxism and the Modern World*, London: Zed Books, 1982, p. 47.
24. Peace, Timothy, *European Social Movements and Muslim Activism: Another World but with Whom?* Basingstoke: Palgrave Macmillan, 2015, p. 1.
25. Ibid., p. 71.
26. Ibid., p. 59.
27. Cited in ibid., p. 61
28. Ramadan, Tariq, 'Critique des (nouveaux) intellectuels communautaires', *Oumma*, 3 October 2003, http://tariqramadan.com/critique-des-nouveaux-intellectuels-communautaires/, last accessed 11 August 2017.
29. Chafiq-Beski, Chahla, Fatima Lalem and Maya Surduts, 'Ramadan antiféministe', *Libération*, 12 November 2003, http://www.liberation.fr/tribune/2003/11/12/ramadan-antifeministe_451498, last accessed 4 June 2017. See also Peace, *European Social Movements and Muslim Activism*, p. 63.
30. Fourest, Caroline, *Frère Tariq. Discours, stratégie et méthode de Tariq Ramadan*, Paris: Grasset et Fasquelle, 2004. See also Boniface, Pascal, *Les intellectuels faussaires. Le triomphe médiatique des experts en mensonge*, Paris: Jean-Claude Gawsewitch Éditeur, 2011.
31. Peace, *European Social Movements and Muslim Activism*, p. 63.
32. Ibid., p. 65.
33. Samary, Catherine, 'La laïcité n'est pas anti-religieuse', *Que faire*, 28 May 2010, http://quefaire.lautre.net/La-laicite-n-est-pas-anti#nb10, last accessed 4 June 2017.
34. 'A Treaty Establishing a Constitution for Europe', 2005, Article II-70, p.50, https://europa.eu/european-union/sites/europaeu/files/docs/body/treaty_establishing_a_constitution_for_europe_en.pdf, last accessed 18 September 2017.

35. United Nations, 'Universal Declaration of Human Rights', 1948, Article 18, http://www.un.org/en/universal-declaration-human-rights/index.html, last accessed 1 August 2017. See also Samary, 'La laïcité n'est pas anti-religieuse'.
36. Masclet, Olivier, *La Gauche et les cités. Enquête sur un rendez-vous manqué*, Paris: La Dispute, 2003; Fysh and Wolfreys, *The Politics of Racism in France*.
37. Kergoat, Jacques, *Histoire du Parti socialiste*, Paris: La Découverte, 1997.
38. 'Le piège de la "lutte contre l'islamophobie"', *Lutte de Classe*, no. 181, February 2017.
39. Boulangé, Antoine, 'The hijab, racism and the state', *International Socialism*, no. 102 (Winter 2004).
40. Lévy, Laurent, *'La Gauche', les Noirs et les Arabes*, Paris: La Fabrique, 2010, pp. 22–4 (Kindle edition).
41. Ibid., p. 122.
42. Ibid., pp. 312, 363.
43. Ibid., p. 371.
44. Ibid., pp. 713–14.
45. Papin, Marie and Thomas Voltzenlogel, 'Féminisme et anti-racisme: savoir d'où l'on part, pour savoir où aller', *Contretemps*, 9 December 2011, https://www.contretemps.eu/feminisme-et-anti-racisme-savoir-dou-lon-part-pour-savoir-ou-aller/#_ftn40, last accessed 10 June 2017.
46. Ibid.
47. Lafran, Anne, Marc Delval, Pierre-François Grond, Rémi Duloquin and Jean-Pierre Hennuyer, 'Une exclusion assumée', *Libération*, 22 October 2003, http://www.liberation.fr/tribune/2003/10/22/une-exclusion-assumee_448986, last accessed 10 June 2017.
48. FXavier, 'Derrière la loi foulardière: Alain Badiou', *Mediapart*, 22 November 2010, https://blogs.mediapart.fr/fxavier/blog/221110/derriere-la-loi-foulardiere-alain-badiou, last accessed 13 June 2017.
49. Samary, Catherine, 'Au-delà du voile et de la laïcité. Bilan de trois ans de controverses', *Les mots sont importants*, 1 June 2006, http://lmsi.net/Au-dela-du-voile-et-de-la-laicite#nb10, last accessed 10 June 2017.
50. Lévy, p. 1479.
51. Cited in Tevanian, *La haine de la religion*, p. 108.

52. Alemagna, Lilian, 'Le NPA mal fichu sur le foulard', *Libération*, 5 February 2010, http://www.liberation.fr/france/2010/02/05/le-npa-mal-fichu-sur-le-foulard_608241, last accessed 10 June 2017.
53. Wolfreys, Jim, 'Ilham Moussaid: A proud tribune of the oppressed', *Socialist Review* (March 2010).
54. Ducourau, Julie, 'Laïcité: le NPA ne lève pas tout à fait le voile', NPA, 5 February 2010, https://npa2009.org/content/la%C3%AFcit%C3%A9-le-npa-ne-l%C3%A8ve-pas-tout-%C3%A0-fait-le-voile, last accessed 10 June 2017.
55. Gresh, Alain, 'Le foulard, le moine et le député', *Le Monde Diplomatique*, 6 February 2010, http://blog.mondediplo.net/2010–02–06-Le-foulard-le-moine-et-le-depute, last accessed 10 June 2017.
56. Hammal, Samir, 'Quand la soutane et la gandoura siégeaient au Palais Bourbon', 27 January 2015, http://www.huffingtonpost.fr/samir-hammal/habits-deputes_b_6547672.html, last accessed 13 November 2017.
57. Tevanian, *La haine de la religion*, p. 112.
58. Hargreaves, Alec, *Multi-Ethnic France: Immigration, Politics, Culture and Society*, Abingdon: Routledge, 2007.
59. Ibid., p. 131.
60. Yasser Louati, interview with the author, Paris, 23 April 2016.
61. Fania Noël, interview with the author, Paris, 22 April 2016.
62. Ndella Paye, interview with the author, London, 10 June 2016.
63. Houria Bouteldja, interview with the author, Paris, 21 May 2016.
64. Parti des Indigènes de la République, 'L'Appel des Indigènes. NOUS SOMMES LES INDIGENES DE LA REPUBLIQUE!', January 2005, http://indigenes-republique.fr/le-p-i-r/appel-des-indigenes-de-la-republique/, last accessed 11 June 2017.
65. 'La France est-elle un état colonial?', *Le Point*, 12 May 2005, http://www.lepoint.fr/actualites-politique/2007–01–17/la-france-est-elle-un-etat-colonial/917/0/18263#, last accessed 4 June 2017.
66. 'L'appel des "Indigènes de la République": dénoncer le colonialisme... ou renforcer le communautarisme?', *Lutte Ouvrière*, no. 1910 (9 March 2005), http://journal.lutte-ouvriere.org/2005/03/09/lappel-des-indigenes-de-la-republique-denoncer-le-colonialisme-ou-renforcer-le-communautarisme_10376.html, last accessed 13 June 2017.

67. Ligue communiste révolutionnaire, 'Un débat dans la LCR sur l'appel aux "assises de l'anticolonialisme post-colonial"', *Rouge*, 7 April 2005, https://www.europe-solidaire.org/spip.php?article23080, last accessed 12 June 2017. See also Lévy, Laurent, 'Une voix de trop. Quand l'avant-garde révolutionnaire sermonne les indigènes', *Les mots sont importants*, 7 April 2005, http://lmsi.net/Une-voix-de-trop, last accessed 13 June 2017.
68. Omar Slaouti, interview with the author, Paris, 20 May 2017.
69. 'Nous demandons l'abrogation de la loi dite "sur le voile à l'école"', *Mediapart*, 12 March 2014, https://blogs.mediapart.fr/edition/les-invites-de-mediapart/article/120314/nous-demandons-l-abrogation-de-la-loi-dite-sur-le-voile-l-ecole, last accessed 4 June 2017.
70. See, for example, Pierre Tevanian and Sylvie Tissot's website, *Les mots sont importants* (http://lmsi.net). See also: Hajjat, Abdellali and Marwan Mohammed, *Islamophobie: Comment les élites françaises fabriquent le "problème musulman"*, Paris: La Découverte, 2013; Fassin, Didier, and Eric Fassin, *De la question sociale à la question raciale?*, Paris: La Découverte, 2006; Bouamama, Saïd, *L'affaire du foulard islamique: production d'un racisme respectable*, Lille: Le Geai bleu, 2004; Plenel, Edwy, *Pour les musulmans*, Paris: La Découverte, 2015.
71. Fourest, Caroline, 'Ces progressistes qui crachent sur les morts du 7 janvier', *Huffington Post*, 5 March 2015, www.huffingtonpost.fr/caroline-fourest/manifestation-islamophobie-pcf_b_6805882.html, last accessed 4 June 2017.
72. Khadre, Ayman, 'Clash chez les Verts à propos de l'islamophobie', *Politis*, 4 March 2015, www.politis.fr/Clash-chez-les-Verts-a-propos-de-l,30321.html, last accessed 4 June 2017.
73. Amitié entre les peuples, 'ATTAC GENRE: 9 protestations contre un meeting (6 mars)', *Mediapart*, 7 March 2015, http://amitie-entre-les-peuples.org/ATTAC-GENRE-9-protestations-contre, last accessed 4 June 2017.
74. Sulzer, Alexandre, 'Eric Raoult accusé de harcèlement sexuel: "Elle n'hésitait pas à montrer son corps"', *L'Express*, 18 March 2014, http://www.lexpress.fr/actualite/politique/eric-raoult-accuse-de-harcelement-sexuel-elle-n-hesitait-pas-a-montrer-son-corps_1501175.html, last accessed 4 June 2017.

75. Yasser Louati, interview with the author, Paris, 23 April 2016.
76. Ibid.
77. Ndella Paye, interview with the author, London, 10 June 2016.
78. Fania Noël, interview with the author, Paris, 22 April 2016.
79. Meriem, interview with the author, Paris, 20 March 2017.
80. Omar Slaouti, interview with the author, Paris, 20 May 2017.

CONCLUSION

1. Panebianco, Angelo, 'Smemorati tra noi', *Corriere della Sera*, 26 September 2001, cited in Rivera, Annamaria, *Les dérives de l'universalisme. Ethnocentrisme et islamophobie en France et en Italie*, Paris: La Découverte, 2005, p. 51.
2. Nilüfer, Göle, *The Daily Lives of Muslims: Islam and Public Confrontation in Contemporary Europe*, London: Zed Books, 2017, pp. 2411–12 (Kindle edition).
3. Sanger, David, E. and Maggie Habermanuag, 'Donald Trump's Terrorism Plan Mixes Cold War Concepts and Limits on Immigrants', *The New York Times*, 15 August 2016, https://www.nytimes.com/2016/08/16/us/politics/donald-trump-terrorism.html?_r=0, last accessed 19 July 2017.
4. Shariatmadari, David, 'How war on Islam became central to the Trump doctrine', *The Guardian*, 30 January 2016, https://www.theguardian.com/us-news/2017/jan/30/war-on-islam-central-trump-doctrine-terrorism-immigration, last accessed 19 July 2017.
5. Johnson, Jenna, 'Donald Trump: Syrian refugees might be a terrorist army in disguise', *The Washington Post*, 30 September 2016, https://www.washingtonpost.com/news/post-politics/wp/2015/09/30/donald-trump-syrian-refugees-might-be-a-terrorist-army-in-disguise/?utm_term=.39c1d301830e, last accessed 14 July 2017.
6. The Laura Ingraham Show, 30 March 2011. See MacNicol, Glynnis, 'TRUMP: Maybe Obama's Missing Birth Certificate Says He's A Muslim', *Business Insider*, 30 March 2011, http://www.businessinsider.com/trump-birther-obama-muslim-video-2011–3?IR=T, last accessed 19 July 2017.
7. Shariatmadari, 'How war on Islam became central to the Trump doctrine'.

8. Greenwald, Glenn, 'Trump's Muslim Ban Is Culmination of War on Terror Mentality but Still Uniquely Shameful', *The Intercept*, 28 January 2017, https://theintercept.com/2017/01/28/trumps-muslim-ban-is-culmination-of-war-on-terror-mentality-but-still-uniquely-shameful/, last accessed 19 July 2017.
9. Ibid.
10. Greenwald, Glenn, 'Donald Trump's Policies Are Not Anathema to U.S. Mainstream, but an Uncomfortable Reflection of It', *The Intercept*, 4 March 2016, https://theintercept.com/2016/03/04/trumps-policies-are-not-anathema-to-the-u-s-mainstream-but-an-uncomfortably-vivid-reflection-of-it/, last accessed 19 July 2017.
11. Ackerman, Spencer and Noah Shachtman, 'Video: FBI Trainer Says Forget "Irrelevant" Al-Qaida, Target Islam', *Wired*, 20 September 2011, https://www.wired.com/2011/09/fbi-islam-qaida-irrelevant/, last accessed 19 July 2017.
12. Ibid.
13. See Scahill, Jeremy and Ryan Devereaux, 'Watch Commander: Barack Obama's Secret Terrorist-Tracking System, by the Numbers', *The Intercept*, 5 August 2014, https://theintercept.com/2014/08/05/watch-commander/, last accessed 19 July 2017. See also Springer, Dan, 'Muslims, ACLU challenge the government's no-fly list', *Fox News*, 9 May 2012, http://www.foxnews.com/politics/2012/05/09/muslims-aclu-challenge-government-no-fly-list.html, last accessed 19 July 2017; and ACLU of Northern California, 'Court Rules No Fly List Process Is Unconstitutional and Must Be Reformed', 24 June 2014, https://www.aclunc.org/news/court-rules-no-fly-list-process-unconstitutional-and-must-be-reformed, last accessed 19 July 2017.
14. Shanejune, Scott, 'Homegrown Extremists Tied to Deadlier Toll Than Jihadists in U.S. Since 9/11', *The New York Times*, 24 June 2015, https://www.nytimes.com/2015/06/25/us/tally-of-attacks-in-us-challenges-perceptions-of-top-terror-threat.html?_r=0; see also Bergen, Peter, Albert Ford, Alyssa Sims and David Sterman, 'In Depth: Terrorism in America After 9/11', New America report, 2017, https://www.newamerica.org/in-depth/terrorism-in-america/, last accessed 19 July 2017.

15. Kumar, Deepa, *Islamophobia and The Politics of Empire*, New York: Haymarket, 2012, p. 197.
16. Syal, Rajeev, 'Imam called Isis supporter by Cameron was asked to recruit Muslims for Tories', *The Guardian*, 25 April 2016, https://www.theguardian.com/politics/2016/apr/25/imam-labelled-isis-supporter-cameron-invited-recruit-muslim-tories, last accessed 19 July 2017.
17. Williams, Richard A.L., 'Jeremy Corbyn reminds David Cameron the "extremist" imam he just described is a Tory', *The Independent*, 4 May 2016, http://www.independent.co.uk/news/uk/politics/jeremy-corbyn-reminds-david-cameron-suliman-gani-pmqs-video-extremist-imam-tory-conservative-voter-a7012941.html, last accessed 19 July 2017.
18. Hill, Dave, 'Cameron links Khan to Suliman Gani despite the cleric's Tory links', *The Guardian*, 20 April 2016, https://www.theguardian.com/uk-news/davehillblog/2016/apr/20/london-mayor-cleric-cameron-said-supports-is-confirms-he-backed-conservatives, last accessed 19 July 2017.
19. Cooper, Charlie and Caroline Mortimer, 'Suliman Gani: David Cameron apologises to imam for Isis link as he faces pressure over Khan claims', *The Independent*, 11 May 2016, http://www.independent.co.uk/news/uk/politics/suliman-gani-michael-fallon-forced-apologise-imam-isis-link-david-cameron-pressure-sadiq-khan-claims-a7024656.html, last accessed 19 July 2017.
20. 'Full transcript: David Cameron. Speech on radicalisation and Islamic extremism, Munich, 5 February 2011', *New Statesman*, 5 February 2011, http://www.newstatesman.com/blogs/the-staggers/2011/02/terrorism-islam-ideology, last accessed 11 August 2017.
21. Mendick, Robert and Robert Verkaik, 'Anti-terror plan to spy on toddlers "is heavy-handed"', *The Telegraph*, 4 January 2015, http://www.telegraph.co.uk/news/uknews/terrorism-in-the-uk/11323558/Anti-terror-plan-to-spy-on-toddlers-is-heavy-handed.html, last accessed 19 July 2017.
22. 'Radicalisation fear over cucumber drawing by boy, 4', BBC News, 11 March 2016, http://www.bbc.co.uk/news/uk-england-beds-bucks-herts-35783659, last accessed 2 August 2017.

23. Mohammed, Jahangir and Dr Adnan Siddiqui, 'The Prevent Strategy: A Cradle to Grave Police State', CAGE, 2013, https://cage.ngo/wp-content/uploads/report.pdf, last accessed 19 July 2017.
24. Dodd, Vikram, 'School questioned Muslim pupil about Isis after discussion on eco-activism', *The Guardian*, 22 September 2015, https://www.theguardian.com/education/2015/sep/22/school-questioned-muslim-pupil-about-isis-after-discussion-on-eco-activism, last accessed 19 July 2017.
25. Versi, Miqdaad, 'Meeting between David Anderson QC and the MCB. Concerns on Prevent', The Muslim Council of Britain, undated, http://www.mcb.org.uk/wp-content/uploads/2015/10/20150803-Case-studies-about-Prevent.pdf, last accessed 19 July 2017.
26. Ibid.
27. Kundnani, Arun, 'Still Spooked', Institute of Race Relations, 7 July 2011, http://www.irr.org.uk/news/still-spooked/, last accessed 19 July 2017.
28. Kotecha, Sima, 'More than 400 children under 10 referred for "deradicalisation"', BBC News, 21 January 2016, http://www.bbc.co.uk/news/uk-35360375, last accessed 19 July 2017.
29. 'National channel referral figures', NPCC, undated, http://www.npcc.police.uk/FreedomofInformation/NationalChannelReferralFigures.aspx, last accessed 19 July 2017.
30. This has been the case in my own university, King's College London, since 2015, and in other institutions. On the repercussions of the Prevent guidance for universities, see McGovern, Mark, 'The university, Prevent and cultures of compliance', *Prometheus*, vol. 34, no. 1 (2016). See also Mohammed and Siddiqui, 'The Prevent Strategy'.
31. Dodd, Vikram, 'Government anti-terrorism strategy "spies" on innocent', *The Guardian*, 16 October 2009, https://www.theguardian.com/uk/2009/oct/16/anti-terrorism-strategy-spies-innocents, last accessed 19 July 2017.
32. Mohammed and Siddiqui, 'The Prevent Strategy'. See also Kundnani, Arun, 'Spooked! How not to prevent violent extremism', Institute of Race Relations, 2009, http://s3-eu-west-2.amazonaws.com/wpmedia.outlandish.com/irr/2017/04/26154810/spooked.pdf, last accessed 19 July 2017.

33. Kundnani, 'Spooked!'
34. Dodd, Vikram, 'Jihadi threat requires move into "private space" of UK Muslims, says police chief', *The Guardian*, 24 May 2015, https://www.theguardian.com/world/2015/may/24/jihadi-threat-requires-move-into-private-space-of-uk-muslims-says-police-chief, last accessed 19 July 2017.
35. Arun Kundnani, 'Islamophobia as Ideology of US Empire', in Massoumi, Narzanin, Tom Mills and David Miller, *What Is Islamophobia? Racism, Social Movements and the State*, London: Pluto, 2017, p. 43.
36. See Amnesty International, 'Dangerously Disproportionate. The ever-expanding security state in Europe', 17 January 2017, https://www.amnesty.org/en/latest/campaigns/2017/01/dangerously-disproportionate/, last accessed 19 July 2017.
37. Dodd, Vikram, 'Police face court over refusal to hand over reports on anti-Muslim "bias"', *The Guardian*, 13 September 2013, https://www.theguardian.com/uk-news/2013/sep/13/police-court-reports-anti-muslim-bias, last accessed 19 July 2017.
38. Theresa May, 'Today' interview, BBC Radio 4, 13 May 2015, http://www.bbc.co.uk/programmes/p02r8z20, last accessed 14 July 2017.
39. Townsend, Mark, 'Theresa May's counter-terrorism bill close to "sinking without trace"', *The Observer*, 29 January 2017, https://www.theguardian.com/politics/2017/jan/29/theresa-may-counter-terrorism-bill-sinking-without-trace-extremism-british-values, last accessed 14 July 2017.
40. Cassidy, Sarah and Jonathan Owen, 'Soas hits back at David Cameron's accusations that it played host to "hate preachers"', *The Independent*, 17 September 2015, http://www.independent.co.uk/news/education/education-news/soas-hits-back-at-david-camerons-accusations-that-it-played-host-to-hate-preachers-10506676.html, last accessed 14 July 2017.
41. Oborne, Peter, 'Peter Oborne: What's the Conservative Party's problem with Muslims?', *Middle East Eye*, 7 October 2016, http://www.middleeasteye.net/columns/peter-oborne-whats-conservative-partys-problem-muslims-1757982215, last accessed 20 July 2017.
42. MEE staff, 'Baroness Warsi condemns UK's Prevent strategy as "bro-

ken, toxic'", *Middle East Eye*, 19 March 2017, http://www.middleeasteye.net/news/baroness-warsis-new-book-uks-prevent-strategy-broken-toxic-702187197, last accessed 14 July 2017.

43. Kundnani, 'Islamophobia as Ideology of US Empire', p. 43.
44. Amnesty International, 'Dangerously Disproportionate', p. 12.
45. Fekete, Liz, *A Suitable Enemy: Racism, Migration and Islamophobia in Europe*, London: Pluto, 2009.
46. See Rigouste, Mathieu, *Les Marchands de Peur. La bande à Bauer et l'idéologie sécuritaire*, Paris: Libertalia, 2011; and Stephen Graham, *Cities Under Siege. The New Military Urbanism*, London: Verso, 2010.
47. Losurdo, Domenico, *Liberalism: A Counter-History*, London: Verso, 2011.
48. Amnesty International, 'Dangerously Disproportionate', p. 6.
49. Kundnani, 'Islamophobia as Ideology of US Empire', p. 41.
50. Amnesty International, 'Dangerously Disproportionate', p. 8.
51. Kumar, *Islamophobia and The Politics of Empire*, p. 15.
52. Rivera, *Les dérives de l'universalisme*, pp. 52–3.
53. Ibid., p. 100.
54. Ibid., p. 101.
55. Cette France-là, *Xénophobie d'en haut. Le choix d'une droite éhontée*, Paris: La Découverte, 2012, p. 159.
56. Ibid., p. 160. See also Baumel, Laurent and François Kalfon, *L'équation gagnante. La gauche peut-elle enfin remporter la présidentielle?*, Paris: Le Bord de l'eau, 2011; and Baumel, Laurent and François Kalfon, *Plaidoyer pour une gauche populaire: La gauche face à ses électeurs*, Paris: Le Bord de l'eau, 2011.
57. Cette France-là, *Xénophobie d'en haut.*
58. Mergier, Alain and Jérôme Fourquet, *Le point de rupture. Enquête sur les ressorts du vote FN en milieux populaires*, Paris: Fondation Jean Jaurès, 2011.
59. Cette France-là, *Xénophobie d'en haut*, p. 165.
60. Guilluy, Christophe, *Fractures Françaises*, Paris: Flammarion, 2013, p.44.
61. Cited in ibid., pp. 165–8.
62. Cette France-là, *Xénophobie d'en haut*, p. 168.

63. Ford, Robert and Matthew J. Goodwin, *Revolt on the Right: Explaining Support for the Radical Right in Britain*, London: Routledge, 2011.
64. See Fysh, Peter and Jim Wolfreys, *The Politics of Racism in France*, Basingstoke: Palgrave Macmillan, 2003.
65. Cette France-là, *Xénophobie d'en haut*, p. 171.
66. IFOP poll in *le Journal du Dimanche*, 16 December 2003; BVA 2005, cited in Hargreaves, *Multi-Ethnic France: Immigration, Politics, Culture and Society*, Abingdon: Routledge, 2007, p. 162.
67. Bouamama, Saïd, *La France. Autopsie d'un mythe national*, Paris: Larousse, 2008, p. 112.
68. Ibid., p. 112.
69. Beaud, Stéphane and Michel Pialoux, *Violences urbaines, violences sociales: genèse des nouvelles classes dangereuses*, Paris: Fayard, 2003. Cited in Talpin, Julien, Julien O'Miel and Frank Frégosi (eds), *L'islam et la cité. Engagements musulmans dans les quartiers populaires*, Lille: Presses universitaires du Septentrion, 2017, p. 21.
70. Bouamama, *La France. Autopsie d'un mythe national*, p. 113.
71. Ibid., pp. 114.
72. Ibid., p. 115.
73. Ibid., p. 112.
74. Talpin et al., *L'Islam et la cité*, p. 25.
75. Ibid., p. 26.
76. Ibid., p. 21.
77. Ibid., p. 57.
78. Ibid., p. 161.
79. Eschapasse, Baudouin, 'Pourquoi le "camp décolonial" fait polémique', *Le Point*, 25 August 2016, http://www.lepoint.fr/societe/pourquoi-le-camp-decolonial-fait-polemique-25–08–2016–2063748_23.php, last accessed 16 August 2017.
80. SOS Racisme, '"Camp d'été décolonial": un rassemblement ouvertement raciste', 26 August 2016, http://sos-racisme.org/communique-de-presse/camp-dete-decolonial-un-rassemblement-ouvertement-raciste/, last accessed 16 August 2017.
81. See Birnbaum, Jean, 'La gauche déchirée par le "racisme antiraciste"', *Le Monde*, 9 June 2017, http://www.lemonde.fr/idees/article/2017/

06/09/la-gauche-dechiree-par-le-racisme-antiraciste_5141086_3232.html, last accessed 16 August 2016 and 'Vers l'émancipation, contre la calomnie. En soutien à Houria Bouteldja et à l'antiracisme politique', *Le Monde*, 19 June 2017, http://www.lemonde.fr/idees/article/2017/06/19/vers-l-emancipation-contre-la-calomnie-en-soutien-a-houria-bouteldja-et-a-l-antiracisme-politique_5147623_3232.html, last accessed 16 August 2016.

82. Ibid., p. 163–4.
83. Sayad, Abdelmalek, *L'immigration ou Les paradoxes de l'alterité: L'illusion du provisoire*, Paris: Raisons d'agir, 2006, p. 13.
84. Houria Bouteldja, interview with the author, Paris, 21 May 2016.
85. Rancière, Jacques, 'Racism, a Top-Down Passion', *Mediapart*, 22 October 2010, https://blogs.mediapart.fr/edition/english-club/article/221010/racism-top-down-passion, last accessed 16 August 2017. See also Noiriel, Gérard, *Racisme: la responsabilité des élites*, Paris: Textuel, 2007.

SELECT BIBLIOGRAPHY

News sources

BBC News
Le Figaro
Le Monde
Le Nouvel Observateur/L'Obs
Le Parisien
L'Express
Libération
Mediapart
The Guardian
The Independent
The New York Times

Articles, reports and book chapters

Ackerman, Spencer and Noah Shachtman, 'Video: FBI Trainer Says Forget 'Irrelevant Al-Qaida, Target Islam', *Wired*, 20 September 2011, https://www.wired.com/2011/09/fbi-islam-qaida-irrelevant, last accessed 27 July 2017.

Amnesty International, 'Dangerously Disproportionate. The ever-expanding security state in Europe', 17 January 2017, https://www.amnesty.org/en/latest/campaigns/2017/01/dangerously-disproportionate/, last accessed 19 July 2017.

Baubérot, Jean, 'Élisabeth Badinter et la laïcité lepénisée', *Mediapart*, 30 September 2011, https://blogs.mediapart.fr/jean-bauberot/blog/

300911/elisabeth-badinter-et-la-laicite-lepenisee, last accessed 27 July 2017.

Baumard, Maryline, 'Emploi, école', *Le Monde*, 8 January 2016, http://www.lemonde.fr/societe/article/2016/01/08/les-enfants-d-immigres-s-integrent-mais-restent-victimes-du-chomage-et-de-la-discrimination_4843872_3224.html, last accessed 27 July 2017.

Charmes, Eric, 'Une France contre l'autre', *La Vie des idées*, 5 November 2014, http://www.laviedesidees.fr/Une-France-contre-l-autre.html, last accessed 27 July 2017.

Clift, Ben, 'French Responses to the Global Economic Crisis', in Wyn Grant and Graham K. Wilson, *The Consequences of the Global Financial Crisis: The Rhetoric of Reform and Regulation*, Oxford: OUP, 2012.

Davies, William, 'The New Neoliberalism', *New Left Review*, no. 101, (September–October 2016), https://newleftreview.org/II/101/william-davies-the-new-neoliberalism, last accessed 12 January 2017.

Escalona, Fabien, 'Comment le thème de l'identité nationale a été capturé par la droite et le FN', *Mediapart*, 3 March 2017, https://www.mediapart.fr/journal/france/030317/comment-le-theme-de-l-identitenationale-ete-capture-par-la-droite-et-le-fn?page_article=3, last accessed 10 June 2017.

Fourcade-Gourinchas, Marion and Sarah L. Babb, 'The Rebirth of the Liberal Creed: Paths to Neoliberalism in Four Countries', *The American Journal of Sociology*, vol. 108, no. 3 (2002).

Fourquet, Jérôme and Marie Gariazzo, 'FN et UMP: électorats en fusion?', Fondation Jean Jaurès, 2013.

Greenwald, Glen, 'Donald Trump's Policies Are Not Anathema to U.S. Mainstream, but an Uncomfortable Reflection of It', *The Intercept*, 4 March 2016, https://theintercept.com/2016/03/04/trumps-policies-are-not-anathema-to-the-u-s-mainstream-but-an-uncomfortably-vivid-reflection-of-it/, last accessed 27 July 2017.

Héricourt, Jérôme and Gilles Spielvogel, 'Perception publique de l'immigration et discours médiatique', *La Vie des idées*, 18 December 2012, http://www.laviedesidees.fr/Perception-publique-de-l.html, last accessed 12 January 2016.

Jolly, Seth K. and Gerald M.DiGiusto, 'Xenophobia and immigrant contact: French public attitudes toward immigration', *The Social Science Journal*, vol. 51, no. 3 (September 2014), pp. 464–73, http://www.sciencedirect.com/science/article/pii/S0362331913001468, last accessed 20 September 2017.

Le Cour Grandmaison, Olivier, 'Après les attentats: la Réaction qui vient', *Mediapart*, 26 November 2015, https://blogs.mediapart.fr/olivier-le-cour-grandmaison/blog/261115/apres-les-attentats-la-reactionqui-vient, last accessed 19 March 2016.

Mayer, Nonna, 'Le mythe de la dédiabolisation du FN', *La Vie des idées*, 4 December 2015, http://www.laviedesidees.fr/Le-mythe-de-ladediabolisation-du-FN.html, last accessed 22 June 2016.

Mélenchon, Jean-Luc, 'Je parle du voile intégral', *Le Blog de Jean-Luc Mélenchon*, 7 January 2010, http://www.jean-luc-melenchon.fr/2010/01/07/je-parle-du-voile-integral/, last accessed 19 March 2016.

Mohammed, Jahangir and Dr Adnan Siddiqui, 'The Prevent Strategy: A Cradle to Grave Police State', CAGE, 2013, https://cage.ngo/wpcontent/uploads/report.pdf, last accessed 19 July 2017.

Observatoire des inégalités, 'Un million de pauvres de plus en dix ans', 20 December 2016, http://www.inegalites.fr/spip.php?article270, last accessed 11 January 2017.

Papin, Marie and Thomas Voltzenlogel, 'Féminisme et anti-racisme: savoir d'où l'on part, pour savoir où aller', *Contretemps*, 9 December 2011, https://www.contretemps.eu/feminisme-et-anti-racisme-savoir-dou-lon-part-pour-savoir-ou-aller/, last accessed 27 July 2017.

Rancière, Jacques, 'Racism, a Top-Down Passion', *Mediapart*, 22 October 2010, https://blogs.mediapart.fr/edition/english-club/article/221010/racism-top-down-passion, last accessed 16 August 2017.

Raynal, Guillaume Weill, 'Raciste, Finkielkraut? Mais oui...' *Mediapart*, 18 April 2016, https://blogs.mediapart.fr/guillaume-weill-raynal/blog/180416/raciste-finkielkraut-mais-oui, last accessed 22 June 2016.

Shariatmadari, David, 'How war on Islam became central to the Trump doctrine', *The Guardian*, 30 January 2017, https://www.theguardian.com/us-news/2017/jan/30/war-on-islam-central-trump-doctrine-terrorism-immigration, last accessed 19 July 2017.

Sayad, Abdelmalek, 'Qu'est-ce que l'intégration?', *Hommes et migrations*, vol. 182, no. 1 (1994), pp. 8–14.

Silverstein, Paul A., 'The context of antisemitism and Islamophobia in France', *Patterns of Prejudice*, vol. 42, no. 1 (2008).

Tevanian, Pierre, 'Pour 100 pour cent des musulmans les sondages sont plutôt une menace', *Les mots sont importants*, 24 October 2012, http://lmsi.net/Pour-100-des-musulmans-les, last accessed 19 March 2016.

Tevanian, Pierre, 'L'Exception au pluriel—et au quotidian', *Les mots sont importants*, 4 March 2013, http://lmsi.net/L-exception-au-plurielet-au, last accessed 19 March 2016.

Tissot, Sylvie, 'Le Repli communautaire: un concept policier. Analyse d'un rapport des Renseignements Généraux sur les "quartiers sensibles"', *Les mots sont importants*, 29 October 2004, http://lmsi.net/Le-repli-communautaire-un-concept, last accessed 22 June 2016.

Valls, Manuel, 'En France, les femmes sont libres', *Huffington Post*, 5 September 2016, http://www.huffingtonpost.fr/manuel-valls/manuel-valls-interdiction-burkini-islam-laicite_b_11865808.html, last accessed 27 July 2017.

Books

Ahearne, Jeremy, *Government through Culture and the Contemporary French Right*, Basingstoke: Palgrave Macmillan, 2014.

Amable, Bruno and Stefano Palombarini, *L'illusion du bloc bourgeois. Alliances sociales et avenir du modèle français*, Paris: Raisons d'agir, 2017.

Bancel, Nicolas, Pascal Blanchard and Sandrine Lemaire (eds), *La Fracture colonial. La société française au prisme de l'héritage colonial*, Paris: La Découverte, 2006.

Baubérot, Jean, *Les 7 laïcités françaises*, Paris: Maison des sciences de l'homme, 2015.

——— *La laïcité falsifiée*, Paris: La Découverte, 2012.

Beauchemin, Cris, Christelle Hamel and Patrick Simon (eds), *Trajectoires et origines. Enquête sur la diversité des populations en France*, Paris: Ined, 2015.

Bouamama, Saïd, *La France. Autopsie d'un mythe national*, Paris: Larousse, 2008.

——— *L'affaire du foulard islamique—La production d'un racisme respectable*, Lille: Geai Bleu, 2004.

——— *Les classes et quartiers populaires. Paupérisation, ethnicisation et discrimination*, Paris: Editions du Cygne, 2009.

Bowen, John R., *Why the French Don't Like Headscarves*, Princeton, New Jersey: Princeton University Press, 2007.

Brustier, Gaël and Jean-Philippe Huelin, *Voyage au bout de la droite. Des paniques morales à la contestation droitière*, Paris: Fayard, 2011.

Cette France-là, *Xénophobie d'en haut. Le choix d'une droite éhontée*, Paris: La Découverte, 2012.

Chabal, Emile, *A Divided Republic: Nation, State and Citizenship in Contemporary France*, Cambridge: Cambridge University Press, 2015.

Chauvel, Louis, *Les classes moyennes à la dérive*, Paris: Le Seuil, 2006.

Chouder, Ismahane, Malika Latrèche and Pierre Tevanian, *Les filles voilées parlent*, Paris: La Fabrique, 2008.

Culpepper, Pepper D., Peter A. Hall and Bruno Palier, *Changing France: The Politics that Markets Make*, Basingstoke: Palgrave Macmillan, 2006.

Delphy, Christine, *Separate and Dominate: Feminism and Racism after the War on Terror*, New York: Verso, 2015.

Deltombe, Thomas, *L'Islam Imaginaire. La construction médiatique de l'islamophobie en France*, 1975–2005, Paris: La Découverte, 2007.

Fanon, Frantz, *A Dying Colonialism*, New York: Grove Press, 1967.

Fekete, Liz, *A Suitable Enemy: Racism, Migration and Islamophobia in Europe*, London: Pluto, 2009.

Fernando, Mayanthi L., *The Republic Unsettled: Muslim French and the Contradictions of Secularism*, Durham, NC: Duke University Press, 2014.

Fysh, Peter and Jim Wolfreys, *The Politics of Racism in France*, Basingstoke: Palgrave Macmillan, 2003.

Guénif-Souilamas, Nacira, *La République mise à nu par son immigration*, Paris: La Fabrique, 2006.

Göle, Nilüfer, *The Daily Lives of Muslims: Islam and Public Confrontation in Contemporary Europe*, London: Zed Books, 2017.

Guilluy, Christophe, *Fractures francaises*, Paris: Flammarion, 2013.

Haegel, Florence, *Les Droites en fusion. Transformations de l'UMP*, Paris: Presses Sciences Po, 2012.

Hajjat, Abdellali and Marwan Mohammed, *Islamophobie. Comment les élites françaises fabriquent le problème musulman*, Paris: La Découverte, 2013.

Hargreaves, Alec, *Multi-Ethnic France: Immigration, Politics, Culture and Society*, Abingdon: Routledge, 2007.

Hennette-Vauchez, Stéphanie, and Vincent Valentin, *L'Affaire Baby Loup ou la Nouvelle Laïcité*, Paris: LGDJ, L'extenso éditions, 2014.

Igounet, Valérie, *Le Front national de 1972 à nos jours. Le parti, les hommes, les idées*, Paris: Seuil, 2014.

Kumar, Deepa, *Islamophobia and the Politics of Empire*, New York: Haymarket, 2012.

Kundnani, Arun, *The Muslims are Coming! Islamophobia, Extremism and the Domestic War on Terror*, London: Verso, 2014.

Lévy, Laurent, *'La Gauche', les Noirs et les Arabes*, Paris: La Fabrique, 2010.

Mabilon-Bonfils, Béatrice and Geneviève Zaïa, *La laïcité au risque de l'Autre*, Paris: Editions de l'Aube, 2014.

Mair, Peter, *Ruling the Void: The Hollowing of Western Democracy*, London: Verso, 2013.

Masclet, Olivier, *La gauche et les cités. Enquête sur un rendez-vous manqué*, Paris: La Dispute, 2003.

Massoumi, Narzanin, Tom Mills and David Miller (eds), *What is Islamophobia? Racism, Social Movements, and the State*, Chicago: University of Chicago Press, 2017.

Maurin, Eric, *La peur du déclassement. Une sociologie des recessions*, Paris: Seuil 2009.

——— *Le Ghetto Français. Enquête sur le Séparatisme Social*, Paris: Seuil, 2004.

Mirowski, Philip, *Never Let a Serious Crisis Go to Waste: How Neoliberalism Survived the Financial Meltdown*, London: Verso, 2013.

Peace, Timothy, *European Social Movements and Muslim Activism*. London: Palgrave Macmillan, 2015.

Pena-Ruiz, Henri, *Qu'est-ce que la laïcité?*, Paris: Gallimard, 2003.

Plenel, Edwy, *For the Muslims: Islamophobia in France*, London: Verso, 2016.

Poinsot, Marie and Serge Weber, *Migrations et mutations de la société française, l'état des savoirs*, Paris: La Découverte, 2014.

Rivera, Annamaria, *Les dérives de l'universalisme. Ethnocentrisme et islamophobie en France et en Italie*, Paris: La Découverte, 2010.

Savidan, Patrick, *Voulons-nous vraiment l'égalité?*, Paris: Albin Michel, 2015.

Sayad, Abdelmalek, *L'immigration ou Les paradoxes de l'alterité: L'illusion du provisoire*, Paris: Raisons d'agir, 2006.

Scott, Joan Wallach, *The Politics of the Veil*, New Jersey: Princeton University Press, 2007.

Talpin, Julien, Julien O'Miel and Frank Frégosi (eds), *L'islam et la cité*, Lille: Presses Universitaires du Septentrion.

Tevanian, Pierre, *Le voile médiatique. Un faux débat: 'l'affaire du foulard islamique'*, Paris: Raisons d'agir, 2005.

——— *La haine de la religion*, Paris: La Découverte, 2013.

——— *La République du mépris. Les métamorphoses du racisme dans la France des années Sarkozy*, Paris: La Découverte, 2007.

Todd, Emmanuel, *Qui est Charlie? Sociologie d'une crise religieuse*, Paris: Seuil, 2015.

INDEX